W. Robert Beavers, M.D., is clinical professor of psychiatry, University of Texas Southwestern Medical School, and founder and research director of the Southwest Family Institute, Dallas. He is the author of *Successful Marriage: A Family Systems Approach to Couples Therapy* and *Psychotherapy and Growth: A Family Systems Perspective* and coauthor (with Jerry M. Lewis, John Gossett, and Virginia A. Phillips) of *No Single Thread: Psychological Health in Family Systems*.

Robert B. Hampson, Ph.D., is associate professor of psychology, Southern Methodist University, Dallas, and research faculty at Southwest Family Institute.

Successful Families

Assessment and Intervention

Successful Families

Assessment and Intervention

W. Robert Beavers, M.D.

Research Director, Southwest Family Institute
Clinical Professor of Psychiatry
University of Texas Health Science Center at Dallas

Robert B. Hampson, Ph.D.

Associate Professor of Psychology
Southern Methodist University
Research Faculty, Southwest Family Institute

W. W. NORTON & COMPANY NEW YORK • LONDON

First Edition

Library of Congress Cataloging-in-Publication Data

Beavers, W. Robert, 1929–
    Successful families : assessment and intervention / W. Robert
Beavers, Robert B. Hampson.
        p.   cm.
    Includes bibliographical references.
    ISBN 0-393-70091-7
    1. Family psychotherapy. 2. Family assessment. I. Hampson,
Robert B. II. Title.
    [DNLM: 1. Family Therapy—methods. 2. Models, Psychological.
430.5.F2 B385s]
RC488.5.B3798 1990   616.89′156—dc20   90-6902

W. W. Norton & Company, Inc., 500 Fifth Avenue, New York, N.Y. 10110
W. W. Norton & Company, Ltd., 37 Great Russell Street, London WC1B 3NU

1 2 3 4 5 6 7 8 9 0

To those clinicians and researchers who embrace science—broadly defined—as a cornerstone of their work, and to the families who may benefit from that work.

CONTENTS

ACKNOWLEDGMENTS

The ideas and words that follow stem from years of experience, careful study, and respectful dialogue among therapists and patients, researchers and subjects, and the authors and colleagues. We would like to recognize and thank several people who contributed significantly.

At Norton, the invaluable suggestions and editorial comments from Susan Barrows led to a more coherent and readable book. We continue to be in awe of Susan's knowledge of her field (publishing) as well as ours!

Jan Thomas and Ruth Hunt contributed clinical case material to the discussion of interventions with families, for which we are most appreciative. The students, staff, and faculty at Southwest Family Institute in Dallas continue to provide clinical and empirical materials for our ongoing studies.

We would also like to acknowledge the major contributions of Ann Wassel and Diane Rotolo, who processed the manuscript through its several drafts. You were most patient and helpful!

We are also grateful to the families and individuals who allowed us to observe them, treat them, and study them. Perhaps most of all, we acknowledge our own families, across several generations, who provided the context, impetus, and support for the whole endeavor.

INTRODUCTION

Family therapy as a generic enterprise has enjoyed rapid growth in techniques, training, professional affiliations, research, and professional writings over the past 30 years. The American Association for Marriage and Family Therapy (AAMFT) has increased 500% in membership in just the past 10 years[118]; the number of journal articles and books has increased dramatically in that same period. We have even seen more television coverage of family function/dysfunction. When one surveys the major textbooks, sourcebooks, and professional guides in the field, one is impressed by proliferation of different approaches to treating families. In Piercy and Sprenkle's sourcebook,[118] there are 10 different chapters covering as many different approaches to family therapy; in Becvar and Becvar's textbook,[24] seven chapters differentiating forms and models of family therapy; in Levant's text,[96] nine chapters covering different forms of therapy; and in Hansen and L'Abate's text,[79] 13 chapters on different approaches to and models of family therapy.

The impressive aspect of this wide array of therapeutic models is that different therapists, with different personal styles and working with different patient groupings, have evolved workable models through which they have come to understand and treat families. There is also a discouraging aspect to this diversity, harkening back to the question all of us as therapists raised following our first graduate-level models of therapy course: "But what do I do with this particular case?" Many of us search for patterned solutions to the treatment of families. We find it particularly curious that no one, to date, has attempted to produce a guide that integrates family assessment and intervention strategies, producing a useful integration of family therapy procedures. In fact, in AAMFT conference bulletins, "Assessment and Research" presentations are separated from the various "Intervention" and "Clinical" presentations. In addition, there has been no systematic attempt, to date, to guide the therapist in choosing what procedures are useful with what kind of family.

This book addresses these issues and at least partially fills that need—providing family therapists with an organized way of thinking systemically and relating family functioning to intervention techniques and strategies.

SYSTEMS THINKING AND SYSTEM ASSESSMENT

In the early days of therapy outcome research, the question of most concern was, "Which school of therapy is *right*?" Now, as Watzlawick[157] appropriately points out, the more appropriate question is, "Which *assumptions* produce better concrete results?" and, we would add, "results that patients and families are more satisfied with and that contribute to functional adaptation in the longer term?"

Hence, we start with assumptions regarding families and behavior rather than a "how to" approach to therapy, since all family therapists are guided by many of their own operating frameworks. These assumptions are built into a practical and clinically useful model of family functioning, with resultant family assessment procedures to facilitate one's clinical assumptions regarding the family.

Some of these global assumptions are stated as follows (and will be elaborated in the text to follow):

1. Family functioning, in terms of systemic qualities of relationships, communication, and exchanges, takes precedence over *form* or typology. Attempting to identify or label clinical typologies of symptomatic families (such as "the schizophrenogenic family") yields little useful information. Instead, functional and behavioral qualities of the unique *system* must be assessed.
2. Family competence, ranging from healthy family functioning to severely dysfunctional, is viewed along a progressive continuum, rather than in categorical typologies. This helps us to assume a potential for growth and adaptation in all families.
3. Families at similar competence levels may show different functional styles of relating and interacting. Further, most competent families are able to balance and shift their functioning styles as developmental changes occur.
4. The successful therapist achieves an understanding of the presenting family and subtly alters such factors as therapeutic orientation, power differential, and operating style to join the family and catalyze its growth.

5. The successful therapist also appreciates the hierarchical structure of interacting systems within and surrounding the family, ranging from the biological/cellular through the individual to higher-order systems, including extended family and larger social networks. While direct intervention with any one specific level or all levels may not be necessary in any given case, ignoring potentially important biochemical, neurological, or larger systems influences may lead to failure.

6. Individual treatment for relationship difficulties, including but not limited to marital or parent-child relationships, is often an ineffective and complicating procedure.

The framework built around these major assumptions becomes the central theme for this book, which is designed for family therapists adhering to many different specific theories and orientations. Our premise is that we must understand family system operation, competence, and style in order to test our explicit assumptions, choose a therapeutic stance, perhaps alter that stance as the family gains competence, and then extricate ourselves from the family.

The material presented in this volume stems from years of clinical, observational, and empirical work by us and our colleagues. We have chosen not to emphasize the presentation of numerical and statistical data. Instead, we concentrate on the descriptive and the useful. Our more empirical/statistical treatises appear in a series of articles either published or to be published in appropriate professional journals.

THE SCIENCE OF THE ART:
FAMILY ASSESSMENT AND THERAPY

"I hate science," pouted the fifth-grade girl after seeing her test grade. "Why do we have to memorize these different kinds of rocks?" For her, "science" was defined by the bounds of a book and the time of day of instruction. For others, "science" represents a process, a methodology of acquiring information, hypothesizing, and testing inferences. For still others, "science" represents technology—the development of tools to explore, to use, to make our lives easier to live. However, in its essence, "science" means knowing. The incorporation of knowledge can lead us to new discoveries, reasonable hypothesizing, growth, and gain. It can also lead us to the *belief* we know all, to compartmentalized knowledge, and to dogma. Science is a product of the human desire to understand our world and to gain a sense of power and control over our (physical, social, and material) lives, which makes it simultaneously powerful and fallible.

What, then, should we tell our fifth-grader about "science"? We have a similar dilemma in dealing with the science of family assessment and family intervention: What is the purpose of such study? What practical results are to be gained from it? Can we escape theoretical dogmatism? Are we bound by the limits of our own book and instruction? Koch accuses social scientists of "a meaningless thinking" couched in "method-fetishism"; Bertrand Russell states that "almost all the questions of most interest to speculative minds are such as science cannot answer.[90]

One of us—Buck Hampson—works in a fairly traditional academic psychology department, where numerical data, statistical significance, and reliability and validity of measurement devices represent the cornerstones of acceptable research and necessary precursors to almost anything to be published. It is in these halls of academia that some of the most esoteric and minimally useful research is conducted, though it is conducted with reliable measures and tight controls. Practitioners are often viewed as unscientific, soft "users" of the good academic research.

The other—Bob Beavers—works primarily in a clinical and clinical training setting, where clinical utility, effectiveness of intervention, and practicality of assessment are principal concerns. Much of the clinical work that is presented to other practitioners is done through direct means (supervision, workshops), with some case studies and treatment outcome studies being published in journals and books. Many of these treatises suffer from a lack of precision, generalizability, and reliability, although they are of great potential utility. Academic researchers are often viewed as heartless number-crunchers with no feel for anything practical.

In the domain of assessing families for research and treatment purposes, which is the better approach? Obviously and optimally, a combination of the two represents an optimum; moreover, it is an operational definition of a good scientist—a humanistic, questioner/scholar, well anchored in the practical and empirical worlds and thoroughly open-minded. The two of us continue to learn from each other and from the body of empirical and clinical materials around us. Most importantly, we continue to learn with our subjects and patients.

We think we have something here (belief). We have a model, based on years of observation and clinical work (forming and testing hypotheses). We have a great deal of observational and statistical data (methodology) and several family assessment devices (technology) to foster understanding and treatment planning for family therapists.

Successful Families

Assessment
and Intervention

Section One
ASSESSMENT

1 THEORY GUIDES RESEARCH

When consistent patterns emerge from repeated phenomena under observation, as in clinical observations of families, they form the basis for theoretical hypotheses. In essence, this process—initiated by a statement of some problem—is the cornerstone of the general scientific method. We start with the problem statement, "There is some emotional/relational/ behavioral disturbance in this (these) individual(s)"; then we seek theoretical and clinical hypotheses on the basis of our initial observations.

Some hypotheses in our field are formulated from limited, if any, direct observations of human behavior. Others take conceptual leaps from association (double-binding occurs in conjunction with schizophrenic offspring) to causal relations (double-binding causes schizophrenia). Still others are based in linear applications of existing theories or hypotheses to currently observed patterns of interaction. It is our belief that the most useful hypotheses aim not merely at answering "why" questions, but tackle "what" questions as well. Such hypotheses result from years of experience and careful observations and fit the consensual realities of other observers of the human condition.

As stated in the Introduction, we believe that most therapists operate from their own hypothetical assumptions, some of which become more ingrained and even inflexible as the therapists gain in experience. There is no doubt that the experience level of a therapist is a major determinant in psychotherapy outcome: More experienced therapists tend to have greater change potential—for better *or* for worse. Those whose assumptions and concomitant actions foster growth tend to promote growth; if they foster dependency and learned helplessness, regression occurs.

This leads to the next step in the scientific process—the testing and refining of the assumptions gained from experience or observation. If the hypothesis or set of assumptions does not fit reality—if therapy is not working, if the assumption does not fit others' observations, or if the patients continue to get worse—then we must rethink our assumptions. This process only occurs through observations of effects and products.

3

Those assumptions which are untestable, for whatever reason (intra-psychic mechanism, belief systems, etc.) become doctrine if widely accepted. Those assumptions which attain some degree of validation in research or practice become theories, which many academicians spend lifetimes building or destroying. Those assumptions which blend theory with current observation-based hypotheses become models, which are attempts to provide useful maps of reality (in this case, for the family clinician). These models can be useful guides in directing one through the actual terrain. In family work, the model builders include the observers, researchers, clinicians, and family members. Hence, clinical experience (broadly defined), research experience (broadly defined), and shared observational experience combine to form a workable model.

The Beavers Systems Model has evolved over a 25-year period. The early system-based observations were conducted in studies of families with adolescent schizophrenic offspring[19] influenced by the work of Bateson, Jackson, Bowen and Wynne.[18] Beavers and coworkers[76,97] isolated the essential differences between dysfunctional and better-functioning families in later studies of healthy and nonlabeled families.

THE ROLE OF ASSESSMENT

Early in training, one of us (RBH) had the privilege of presenting a case at chairman's rounds, a formal diagnostic conference held weekly on Thursday mornings. As a newly arrived undergraduate summer extern in psychiatry, I had to interview the patient and then present historical and observational data to the house staff, faculty, and chair of the department (primarily since the medical students were on a three-week break at that point).

I met the patient, a 25-year-old man who had been hospitalized for the third time in so many years for a psychotic episode, currently stabilized on Thorazine. I spent several hours a day talking with him, inquiring about school and family history and social relations, which seemed important to one so untutored in classical psychiatry. On Wednesday afternoon, a psychiatric resident who was a veteran of diagnostic conferences advised me to spend more time getting "current symptomatology" to present the next morning. As I inquired about this young man's mental confusion, persecutory delusions, and visual hallucinations, he became more sullen and withdrawn and actually retreated into a visual hallucination in which rainbow-colored rays of light emanated from his groin. I was interested—and a bit scared—but I had it: some good clinical symptomatology.

The conference was scheduled for two hours. The resident introduced the case. Then the psychologist presented the MMPI and Rorschach test protocols. Next the social worker was called upon to present the family information. She had never met the father, described as a distant and rather ineffectual man; the mother was described as having a "very close" relationship with the patient and as guaranteeing all the necessary "love and support" that she could offer. With these and other historical elements of family life deemed unremarkable, it was my turn to present the history and clinical observations.

Seated at the far end of the conference table from the chairman of psychiatry, I went through about 30 minutes of history. Group members started to nod off. However, as I described the patient's delusions and visual hallucinations, they leaned slightly forward; eyes widened and posture oriented even more at the mention of the rainbow hallucination. At that point, as my presentation ended, the chairman left to interview the patient (fed back to the conference room by closed-circuit TV).

Immediately following the interview, the chairman rejoined the group, and a short discussion followed. He announced that the diagnosis was "chronic paranoid schizophrenia," and the group adjourned. I asked the resident who had helped me, "What happens next?" and she answered, "The usual—he stays here for a few more weeks, on medication, and then social work places him in another facility, maybe even a group home."

After 20 years, I still remember the sinking feeling in my stomach: "But what about the real world? The family?"

The role of assessment for diagnostic purposes has focused on the identified patient, with differential diagnosis (*dia* = apart; *gnosis* = to know) representing ideally a professional shorthand form of communicating etiology, symptomatology, prognosis, and treatment. However, diagnosis in its own right, exclusive of any specific treatment planning that considers context, becomes a futile mental exercise.

The current language of diagnosis is individual-based, as it has been since the writings of Hippocrates. In fact, for some of the best clinical descriptors of individuals we can turn to literature; the best authors are also keen observers of the human condition. Take Dickens' description of the tight-fisted Scrooge: "a squeezing, wrenching, grasping, scraping, clutching old sinner! Hard and sharp as a flint . . . secret, and self-contained and solitary as an oyster. The cold within him froze his old features, nipped his pointed nose, shriveled his cheek, stiffened his gait, made his eyes red, his thin lips blue . . . he carried his own low temperature always about with him."

Those characters who have touched us through literature and through living are those we have gotten to know through keen observations; the ones we carry with us are those we have gotten to know through their interpersonal worlds, as well as through individual descriptions. The best authors share a common talent: They expose us to the patterns of interpersonal connections of the character. The most tragic individuals are those who show a deficiency of satisfying, coherent, self-defining experiences with meaningful others, including family members, throughout life. Hence, describing the patterns of interaction that define a personality leads to the most cogent understanding of the unique person. In the case of Scrooge, the whole rest of the novel builds on the assessment of the interpersonal, a task less easily done.

Once pathology is defined as existing within and outside the skin of the individual, as literary works have been proclaiming for centuries and psychiatry has been acknowledging for perhaps decades, the complexity and content of mental health and mental "illness" change. Unfortunately, our current and most widely used diagnostic system assesses and diagnoses only individual pathology; marital or family therapies are not covered by our third-party insurance payments. Though these are efforts to change this state of affairs,[66] the current situation clearly ignores context.

Our research literature is filled with statistical and empirical support for the effectiveness of family therapy for most child, adolescent, and member-specific disturbances, and of marital therapy for a variety of psychological and physiological/psychosomatic disorders. While seemingly effective, the field of systems-based therapy is still fairly new, and a comfortable methodology of diagnosis, assessment, and treatment planning is still being developed (see any recent volume of *Family Process* for spirited debates over which models or methods are "right").

At the outset the role of family assessment is not radically different from that of individual assessment; however, assessing *systems* of individuals demands more complex methodology. While the initial task is still to understand patterns and build hypotheses, family assessment differs in several key ways from individual assessment:

1. Assessment is an ongoing process, as opposed to a procedure conducted only at the beginning of therapy. As Haley[68] has observed, the assessment of the individual and the family unit does not stop with a diagnosis, but must be altered and updated continuously as the family moves. It is also necessary for clinical work that at least one member

of the assessing/observing team and the therapist be the same person, since that person must react in therapy to changes as they occur.

2. Assessment is based on multiple levels of systems hierarchy. In family assessment, we are observing/testing the identified patient and all other family members (the individual level). We are also observing, coding, or testing how they all behave, act, and react as an operating system (system level) and how they behave with therapist(s) present (system/therapist level). If necessary, we also assess the patient's biological/biochemical status (tissue/organ system level), although most family therapists will have this done by others.

3. Assessment often involves integrating reports and materials from family "insiders" and observing "outsiders."

4. Assessment occurs simultaneously with treatment. In our clinical practice, no separate "testing" or "assessment" sessions are scheduled; the family assessment procedure is incorporated into the first and subsequent therapy sessions.

5. Assessment can be microscopic (looking at small pieces of family behavior or exchanges) or macroscopic (larger elements of family interaction coded or rated). In general, the smaller and better-defined the behavior being rated, the higher the inter-rater reliabilities; the larger the inferential leap to a more global rating, the better the cross-situational (test-retest) reliabilities and clinical validity.

6. Interactional assessment is ahistorical and focused on current functioning, rather than historical and problem-focused. Usually, observations, ratings, or family members' codings are centered upon descriptions of communication, behavior, roles, and feelings, rather than details regarding the current problem statement. It is also quite apparent in our clinical work that the initially stated problem is usually not the *problem* as treatment and assessment progress.

7. Assessment must be clinically relevant. Unfortunately, some of the best-scaled family assessment instruments and extrapolated scientific theories regarding family functioning do not offer useful clinical information to clinicians. Good assessment devices must show good reliability and, just as importantly, useful clinical validity.

8. Assessment of families must be based on a clear concept of what is normal and healthy, what is dysfunctional, and the gray areas in between. Many family dysfunction theories stem from clinical observations of symptomatic families of schizophrenic patients, with no reference point for nonsymptomatic functioning. We must be able to recognize competence or at least adequacy in families; the family

assessor/therapist must also be able to live by the adage of the scrupulous auto mechanic: "If it ain't broke, don't fix it."

9. Assessment guides intervention: The information gathered from the assessment exercise helps the therapist enter the system appropriately and plan a therapeutic stance toward the family.

A CLINICALLY USEFUL MODEL
OF FAMILY ASSESSMENT

The Beavers Systems Model of family functioning reflects 25 years of research and clinical work, merging a clinical psychiatric orientation with general systems theory. It was the framework for a study of families, especially healthy ones, that was reported by Lewis, Beavers, Gossett, and Phillips[97] and was subsequently elaborated in a family systems approach to psychotherapy.[10] Since then, several descriptions of the model have been published.[11,12,22]

Utilizing this family model as the basis, we have continued to study interactions and outcomes with clinical families and with nonlabeled families with developmentally disabled children. We strongly believe that clinicians markedly increase their therapeutic skills as they embrace a systems approach to illness and health. This family assessment schema can be a valuable heuristic device in learning to "think systems"—i.e., to think of patients and illness as contextual phenomena.

It is regrettable that such an important systemic integrative orientation must be an incidental rather than an intrinsic part of the education of psychotherapists and physicians. There are, however, some graduate schools (of social work and of marriage and family therapy) that teach solid systems concepts; in addition, some basic processes encompassed in a family systems orientation are already being taught in medical schools. Medical physiology, for example, provides such a foundation. If the physician extrapolates physiologic principles (such as homeostasis, circularity, the whole being more than the sum of parts) to the environment beyond the skin, family systems concepts can take root.

Engel[41] contrasts the multilevel systems view of illness with what he terms the "biomedical" model. The latter has molecular biology as its basic scientific discipline and "assumes disease to be fully accounted for by deviations from the norm of measurable biological (somatic) variables." It demands that disease be dealt with independently of social behavior and further requires that behavioral aberrations be explained as disordered somatic processes. The biomedical model could be characterized as reductionistic, perpetuating a false mind/body dualism.

Obsessive focus on one system level to explain illness is not, unfortunately, limited to biology. Recently a colleague visited a family therapy institute and observed the institute director and a trainee jeering at the mother of a 20-year-old manic patient for allowing the medical establishment to "give her son poison." These therapists coerced the mother into reading the warning material from the lithium container, with the apparent goal of enlightening her and abolishing the young man's "irrelevant and dangerous" lithium treatment. Such a procedure is as antithetical to a systems paradigm, which emphasizes the interaction of many levels, as is the previously described biomedical model. Accurate, humane assessment requires appreciation of the many system levels in which we exist.

Several underlying principles contributed to the characteristics of this model. These include:

1. Family functioning is best described on a *continuum* rather than as discrete "types." Most of the dangers inherent in psychiatric labeling result from trying to put our varied universe into small boxes and then forcing some sort of fit. Indeed, such a concept as family types encourages noncontextual, nonsystems thinking. Visualizing qualities, patterns, and functioning abilities as existing on various continua promotes the conception of health and disease *in relation to* other people other processes.
2. The model provides for measurement of *competence* in whole families engaged in current task performance. When family members are asked to discuss something, such as, "What you would like to see changed in your family?" the resulting behavior is valuable in determining the current negotiating capacity of that family. Some of our previous research has shown that competence in small tasks is closely correlated with competence in the larger family responsibilities, such as raising children.[97]
3. Families also have various *styles* of functioning, which may be unrelated to adaptation or competence. Family assessment must take these stylistic differences into account.
4. The model should be compatible with major clinical concepts of family functioning, which have been derived from family therapy. For example, Minuchin's[104] structural concepts and Bowen's emphasis on differentiation of self[30] fit easily with this model; they are consistent with an assessment approach generated out of clinical material and guided by systems concepts.

The data for evaluating clinical families are usually developed as follows: The interviewer or therapist asks the family members to perform a task (usually, to discuss what they would like to see changed in their family); then the interviewer leaves the room. The family is observed with a video camera or through a one-way mirror, or both, for approximately 10 minutes. In the home or in clinical settings without such technical advantages, the interviewer can remain silent and inactive during this interval. It is important for the interviewer not to interact with family members while they are fulfilling this task, since the interviewer's participation makes for another system with significantly different characteristics. The resulting interactions would reveal a great deal about the interviewer/family system but relatively little about the family itself.

Health Related Studies in Which the Model Has Been Used

This model was developed during a study of family health, with the goal of identifying those family qualities associated with success in important family functions, such as the raising of competent children. There was necessarily a contrasting study of families under stress, with an identified psychiatric patient, in which the extremes of the dimensions of competence and style were glimpsed and reported.[97] A research team at the Southwest Family Institute is currently concluding a study of nonlabeled families with developmentally disabled children in an effort to explore further the qualities found in healthy, coping families.

In our treatment facility, we use the assessment model daily while working with families who present all kinds of difficulties, including behavior problems, psychosomatic illnesses, psychoses, and drug abuse. Research in progress using the assessment methodology correlates the different family groups with the therapist's relationship style and strategies, and then connects both of these with the outcome of intervention. A great many family treatment and training facilities have requested our research packets of measuring instruments and are gathering similar data. Assessment based on how differentiated, adaptive, and capable of negotiation a family is, as well as on the family's stylistic differences, assists our clinicians in planning strategies and selecting from the many intervention approaches that are available.

A slightly modified version of the competence scale has been used by Steidl and coworkers[137] in studying the family qualities associated with several aspects of a family member's behavior and experience as a renal dialysis patient. Steidl has also used the instrument in evaluating family dynamics where one member has bronchogenic cancer.[138] In other studies, families with a retarded child were evaluated,[76] as well as families that have a member with a chronic physical illness.[51] There is at least one research group using the instrument with young adult criminal offenders.[59]

The strengths of this model are derived in part from its conceptual aspects and its good track record. Grounded as it is in a clinical family systems approach to illness and health, it offers a clinically sound approach to assessment. The concepts are immediately applicable to clinical problems, and the instruments help trainees begin to think systematically.

We have added a self-report scale to the observational tools, and this instrument adds to our assessment capabilities. Further, when used by the therapist as a 10-minute portion of a traditional initial family interview, the process is neither time-consuming nor expensive (assuming a video camera is available). We know of no better model for planning family treatment strategies and methods of intervention. Assessment and intervention are then considered simply as different aspects of a systemic comprehension of the family.

Finally, the assessment language is simple enough to be learned easily and comprehensive enough to allow researchers and clinicians to communicate valuable information about families to each other. Thus, the model facilitates the design and completion of vitally needed outcome studies of family intervention methods.

2 THE ASSESSMENT OF FAMILY COMPETENCE

Assessment devices that stem from a history of clinical observation and clearly refer to family competence vs. dysfunction are more useful for treatment planning and therapy outcome research than those which have little or no clinical roots.[111] (These more clinical models include the Beavers Systems Model and the McMaster Model of Family Functioning.[42]) The Beavers Model incorporates clinical observations of healthy/competent vs. dysfunctional families in treatment and research settings across a 25-year period with clinically relevant interpretations of systems theories. Three family assessment instruments have been developed; two are observational rating instruments and one is a family member self-report scale.

OBSERVATIONAL RATINGS

As the initial session begins, the therapist introduces a discussion task for the family to perform for 10 minutes while the therapist is *out of the room*. The 10-minute exchange is observed and videotaped. The discussion task is: "Discuss together what you would like to see changed in your family."

This exchange provides a sample of the family's interactional and goal-directed behavior. We have found that competence in such small tasks is highly correlated with family competence in larger tasks of family life; these repetitive interactional patterns can be captured through observational assessments of such negotiating capacity.[97]

Some system purists may contest the assessment of the family with the therapist out of the room, since the family and therapist(s) system becomes the arena for therapeutic change.[68,148] While this assertion cannot be refuted, it is rarely relevant to change in families. Presumably, the family goes on after interacting with the therapist; its improved functioning is the goal. Further, our choice is based on experience in assessing with and without the therapist present. With the therapist present, a

12

sample of presenting family difficulty is harder to obtain. Some families adopt a "reporting" style of verbal exchange, with one spokesperson or mediator reporting to the therapist. Others search for a judge or mediator and attempt to draw the therapist/interviewer into a triadic struggle[166] or blame-placing maneuver. We have found that observing the family without the therapist gives us an initial understanding of the family and furthers our goal of promoting family competence.

Based on the 10-minute observation (or videotape), the therapist (in the treatment setting) or teams of trained raters (for research purposes) rate and code the interactional family scales.

BEAVERS INTERACTIONAL SCALES:
I. FAMILY COMPETENCE

Before some modification, this instrument was titled the Beavers-Timberlawn Family Evaluation Scales. It was initially developed in 1972 and was used in the Timberlawn Research Foundation's study of healthy families.[97] The original 13-item scale has been shortened to 12 items, with subtle changes in the ratings of invasiveness now included in the closeness/autonomy subscale. The scale is presented in Appendix A, along with current descriptive scale data (Table 1) and interrater reliabilities (Table 2). The subscales are:

I. Structure of the family
   A. Overt Power: chaotic to egalitarian
   B. Parental Coalition: parent-child coalitions to strong parental coalition
   C. Closeness: indistinct boundaries to close, distinct boundaries
II. Mythology: reality perception of the family, from congruent to incongruent
III. Goal-Directed Negotiation: efficient to inefficient problem-solving
IV. Autonomy
   A. Clarity of Expression: directness of expression of thoughts and feelings
   B. Responsibility: voicing of responsibility for personal actions
   C. Permeability: open vs. unreceptive to statements of others
V. Family Affect
   A. Range of Feelings: broad range to limited range of feelings
   B. Mood and Tone: open and optimistic to cynical and pessimistic
   C. Unresolvable Conflict: chronic underlying conflict vs. ability to resolve conflict

    D. Empathy: empathic vs. inappropriate responses to individual
       feelings
VI. Global Health Pathology Scale: optimal/adaptive (1) to severely dys-
      functional (10)

    The major construct assessed through the competence scale is a glob-
ally defined quality of health/competence, which captures how well the
family performs its necessary tasks: providing support and nurturance,
establishing effective generational boundaries and leadership, promoting the developmental separation and autonomy of its offspring, negotiating conflict, and communicating effectively. While we have found
that some families perform certain tasks better than others, we have also
found that it is unlikely that a family will be extremely efficient or competent in a certain domain and extremely dysfunctional in others. Hence,
the concept of a global competence rating to capture the common denominator of combined qualities of the system takes on important clinical relevance.

I. Structure of the Family

A. OVERT POWER

1	2	3	4	5
chaos	marked dominance	moderate dominance	led	egalitarian

    This scale is an important starting point for family ratings, since it
provides an indication of the degree of entropy (system decline) versus
negentropy (increasing structural and functional complexity). The rating
is based upon *overt* power observed in present interactions, such as who
addresses whom, and who directs the exchanges among the family
members.

    At the lowest level of power relationships (*1*), *chaos* represents a high
degree of entropy and low levels of effective leadership related to task
performance. Attempts at direction are covert, and the fact that no one
seems to be in charge contributes to a lack of clarity in generational
boundaries. Such chaotic power presentation need not be synonymous
with the "three-ring circus" behavior of leadership groups; in many
cases, chaotic structure is actually very rigid and stereotyped, allowing
for little change and an eerie sense of timelessness: These families show
little capacity for adaptation as their children mature or attempt to leave.

At the next higher level of competence (2), marked dominance, typically by one adult member, is seen. This rigid and authoritarian leadership signals an attempt to organize the chaotic nature of the system (or to prevent an entropic slide into chaos). There are attempts at absolute control by one member, along with a corresponding dominant-submissive pattern in the marital couple. Interpersonal boundaries are clearly and rigidly marked. Families in this lower level of functioning (1 or 2 on this scale) may vacillate between chaos and attempts at rigid control, as parents shift back and forth between tyrannical control and abandonment of all limit-setting. Olson[88] has termed families such as these "chaotic flippers."

While these different levels of structure are viewed as closely related on the system competence hierarchy in the Beavers Model, they are postulated as polar opposites in Olson's Circumplex Model,[111] as extremes of adaptability: Chaos is "too adaptable," while rigid control is "too rigid" and lacking adaptability. We shall present support for the Beavers Model over the Circumplex Model in Chapter 4.

This movement from chaos to marked dominance may be seen in many different system levels. For example, in emerging third-world nations, attempts to unite diverse tribes or villages into a "country" are often facilitated by a dictatorship or tyrannical monarchy; the shift from chaos to marked leadership is actually a progression toward increased competence and flexibility when the "country" is viewed as a system. Each tribe or village gains general operating rules for the larger system, and all can *begin* to coordinate actions and reactions within the whole. Clinically, the progression towards family competence requires a similar shift when families are in chaos; attempts to govern start with definition of relationships, even if just vis-à-vis a dictatorial leader.

We saw the close relationship between these levels of power and leadership during a recent marriage and family therapy delegation trip to China, the purpose of which was to unite professionals from many diverse fields, descriptions, and agencies in common discussions of the need for and practice of family counseling in that country. The Chinese system is based on a relatively high degree of formality (rigidity) in its seating assignments and meeting protocol; we as leaders were always seated at the head table and the "presentations" were arranged so that the leader of the particular hosting group lectured the assembled guests. This format did not allow an egalitarian exchange among professionals, so we used the induction of chaos (politely asking for a break or requesting a cessation of business for a visit to the bathroom) to negotiate breaking into small groups, which facilitated more open exchange.

As a given system moves up this scale (3), adaptability and flexibility increase; midrange power orientation allows for more lateral exchange and development of relationships, as we noted with the Chinese delegates. As the benevolent dictator moves toward acknowledged leader, some negotiation skills emerge, even though a more traditional dominant-submissive stance is still evident. At the led (4) level, these dominance patterns are tempered more, allowing increasingly direct, open, and respectful negotiation and movement toward shared leadership. Respectful challenge and comfort are noticeable currencies of exchange.

At the egalitarian (5) level, shared leadership between parents is characteristic, with the flexibility and adaptability to handle different situations variously in different domains. This does not imply *equal* power status in *every* domain, but rather the capacity for flexible negotiation and competent management. It is also not inherent in this description that the parents make equal numbers of important decisions or that they are interchangeable in their attitudes toward discipline or values (Dad may still be more predictably the "softie"). The key is respectful and flexible co-leadership, important qualities of any joint enterprise.

B. PARENTAL COALITIONS

1	2	3	4	5
parent-child coalition		weak parental coalition		strong parental coalition

All of the various theories of family health or competence versus family dysfunction give paramount importance to the strength and quality of the parental dyad. Likewise, a vast majority of the treatises on clinical families, including those with schizophrenic,[163] anorexic,[107] and borderline[20] patients, points to a breakdown in generational boundaries, often with a parent-child coalition predominant over parent-parent coalitions.

This scale is clearly used for two-parent families. It is the only scale that needs to be modified to some extent in assessing nontraditional families. It can be eliminated in such families (single-parent, multigenerational), with appropriate reduction in the arithmetic of competence computation. We prefer to relabel the descriptors, however, in assessing nontraditional families, such that the strength of the working relationship in the caretaking role(s) is assessed. This can refer to a parent-oldest child coalition, parent-other adult coalition, or parent-grandparent(s) coalition. Once key caretaking relationships are identified, the scale is interpreted as such, and so rated and coded.

At the dysfunctional end of the scale, one or more parents have entered a reciprocal coalition with one child, from whom support, advice, and often nurturance are solicited. This crossing of generational boundaries may take the form of overt side-taking or pawn-gathering struggles between spouses, or it may take a more covert form of substituted love-seeking, depending on the style of the family. Regardless of the form, the result is usually an undermining of combined or individual parental authority in deference to a child.

At the midpoint of the scale more neutral parental coalitions are observed, in which neither parent-parent nor parent-child coalitions are predominant. Parents may undermine each other's authority at times, and even solicit some support from children, but the consistent parent-child coalition is not evident, nor is there evidence of unresolved love relationships between parents and children. This midpoint rating connotes a family not consistently joined in strong coalition patterns, but rather a group of individuals in which "each person for himself or herself" seems to be the operating rule structure.

The higher-functioning rating point (5) represents a strong and firm parental coalition, whether the nature of that relationship is symmetrical or complementary. Parents are seen as working together and engaging in minimal undermining tactics, although they may not always agree (and may disagree openly). The generational boundaries are clear and consistent, and those parents respect each other and usually present a unified stance of support; disagreements are typically kept within the couple, without soliciting support or allegiances with the children.

C. CLOSENESS

1	2	3	4	5
amorphous, vague and indistinct boundaries among family members		isolation, distancing		closeness, with distinct boundaries among members

Invasiveness (whether or not members speak for one another without invitation, or make "mind-reading" statements

_____observed
_____not observed

The chief assumptions of the closeness ratings, particularly on the "boundaries" scale, involve the development of intimacy in the Erikson-ian[43] sense: In order to be close, or intimate, one first has to be an autonomous, separated individual. Hence, in order for family members to experience emotional closeness, each needs to have a clear sense of his/her personal identity and to feel that such individuality is a desired feature. In those families bound by role relationships ("children," "housewife," "breadwinner") rather than individuality, there is diminished capacity for emotional connection. Conversely, we have seen families (often with many children), in which names may be confused in spontaneous verbal exchanges, but the emotional closeness and individuality are noted in the behavioral exchanges and spontaneity of the members.

The closeness scales, then, represent ratings of the clarity of interpersonal boundaries, as well as the related distribution of power, which affects the potential for and the manner in which families *express* closeness, understanding, and respect.

At the low end of the scale (*1*), the family shows vague interpersonal boundaries and apparent lack of intimacy; no strong sense of individuality is observable, reminiscent of what Bowen[30] has described as an undifferentiated family ego mass. Family members may violate each other's boundaries, often in age- or generation-inappropriate manners, for if no boundaries exist between individuals no higher-order generational boundaries can exist. Parents competing with children for nurturing and parent-child sexual contact are blatant examples.

One potential sign of boundary invasion in some (but not all) families at this lower end of functioning is verbal invasion ("invasiveness" subscale) or speaking for another person as if mind-reading. If present, verbal invasions signal boundary violations; however, the absence of observed invasiveness does not necessarily connote higher-level closeness in and of itself. A rating of invasiveness does not stem from interrupting, clarifying, disagreeing, or reporting of past events, but from speaking for another in the present in the context of interpreting or talking for another's feelings or individual world view. While a mother's statement to her son, "I don't care whether your sister hits you or not, you still should love her," is annoying, it is not invasive. In contrast, "You don't hate your sister, you really mean you love her," represents a speaking for the child's inner self and is invasive.

At the midpoint of the closeness scale (*3*), individual boundaries are clearer and more distinct; the rigid defense of these individual boundaries creates an atmosphere of some individuality but with great effort and little spontaneity or enjoyment. Because of an unspoken fear of being swallowed in the mass, individuals may vacillate between attempts at closeness and distancing or maintain a rigid posture of deliberately keeping apart. To the beginning observer, this position may appear less "close" than the lower-functioning mass, but one must remember that individuation is central to the concept of closeness. Those who have worked with dysfunctional families note that, as the families improve in their functioning, authoritarian control replaces the chaos, and individuals in the family begin testing limits, seemingly pulling apart and becoming more "distant." The family often appears as if it is getting "worse" before it gets better.

At the highest level of functioning (5), boundaries become more distinct, with greater ease in spontaneous expression of individual feelings and world views. Family members spend less time overtly defending their positions and are more spontaneous; each member is accepted as unique and whole. While certain behaviors may be prohibited and even punished, the person is accepted and understood. This forms the basis for intimacy.

II. Mythology

1	2	3	4	5
very congruent	mostly congruent		somewhat incongruent	very incongruent

Every family has a conception of how it functions and how it appears to the outside world. This scale asks the rater to ascertain the degree to which the family's concept of itself appears congruent with that of the rater. Beyond, "We are a happy family," this concept has to do with verbal and behavioral presentation of relationships, closeness, power structure, and affective tone of the family.

The rating focuses on the degree of difference between the observer's perception of family qualities and how the family actually regards itself descriptively. This rating requires attention to subtleties of family action and reaction throughout the observed segment. For instance, if the family presents itself as loving and caring, yet throughout the segment one observes ignoring, distancing, and stereotyped discounting behavior, the rating would be (4) or (5), depending on the degree of disparity.

One subtle yet important way to assess congruence is to observe the reactions of the recipients (often children) to any given parental maneuver. If the family attempts to be egalitarian in discussion but typically operates in a rigid authoritarian way, the children may appear uneasy, confused, or uncharacteristically silly. These reactions are also typical when chaotic families mimic leadership or distant marital couples try to simulate openness.

(Congruence of mythology also surfaces in other types of systemic assessments. One of us [RBH] is frequently called upon to perform peer teaching evaluations of academic colleagues in the classroom. Those settings in which the teacher is good [or bad] and the students appear congruent [the message that this is familiar ground] contrast with those where the students seem to be wondering "What the hell is going on?" On one visit, the professor began the class with a brief review of what was covered during the previous class period, which apparently all of the students had missed as they all leafed through the past several weeks of notes. As he called for the continuing Socratic discussion of comparisons and contrasts of several different counseling methods, the students' eyes widened. They played the evaluation game, but with considerable confusion.)

III. Goal-Directed Negotiation

1	2	3	4	5
extremely efficient	good		poor	extremely inefficient

This subscale describes the family's interactional ability to negotiate problem situations, whether concerning discussion tasks or more profound differences in perspective. Negotiation does not equal compromise; the former implies active participation, the latter more "giving in" or "meeting in the middle," regardless of process.

This process of negotiation is based upon several related observational features. First, does the family identify and orient towards the task at hand? In the 10-minute discussion task, this involves identifying and responding to the nature of the question. In larger tasks of life (money, discipline, etc.), the family must identify and then respond to the issue at hand.

Next, who participates in the problem-solving process? In the observational assessment, the negotiation process is in part assessed by how many of the family members are heard from. This variable is based on several considerations: Are all members' views solicited? Is participation random or voluntary? Is there a primary spokesperson? Is participation itself negotiated? ("Nobody asked me; I have something to say about that.")

Next, do all members actually participate? Many verbal "contributions" may be attention-seeking, tension-defusing, or tangential considerations of some minor points. Finally, does the family use its time efficiently in attempting to reach some closure in the allotted time? It is important to note that a final product is not essential for an extremely efficient (1) rating; what counts is that the family utilizes its resources, personnel, and time efficiently in negotiation of problem solutions.

Inefficient negotiators are those who cannot focus on the task or problem and/or cannot discuss openly and directly the differences which may have led to the problem. The husband who accedes to his wife about a marital issue but then passively grumbles or sabotages, the sullen adolescent who refuses to discuss disciplinary problems with parents, and the dictator-like spokesperson who assumes all responsibility for family negotiation—all produce or contribute to ineffective negotiation processes.

IV. Autonomy

A. CLARITY OF EXPRESSION

1	2	3	4	5
very clear		somewhat vague and hidden		hardly anyone is ever clear

As should be apparent by now, each of these family competence elements is intimately related to the others, so that it is impossible for a family to be rated as optimal in some areas and dysfunctional in others. The clarify of expression scale, a rating of the clarify of disclosure of individual feelings and thoughts, obviously is related to many of the other rating points. Several observable qualities form the basis of this rating.

First, the degree to which family members are allowed and encouraged to speak clearly and directly in expressing their own thoughts and feelings is closely related to boundary issues. Competent families encourage separate individual members to honestly express feelings and thoughts, whether different from or similar to group consensus. In contrast, as clarity diminishes (lower ratings), there is less clarity of individual expression, more verbal/nonverbal discordance in expression, and some degree of "safe groupthink" in which bland acceptance of the "proper" authority is observed.

Next, clarity of expression is also based on the family's ability to allow safe disclosure of thoughts and feelings, for members to assume personal responsibility for expressed thoughts and feelings, and for others to be respectfully responsive and permeable to the member(s) speaking. We have seen many families in which certain members have felt that they have presented their positions clearly—only to be misheard, misunderstood, or ignored in the discussion or negotiation process.

Third, the manner in which the family deals with ambivalent feelings is also attended to in this subscale. A clear disclosure of mixed feelings, acknowledgment of shifting from pole to pole, and family members' helping an individual resolve ambivalent feelings are signs of greater competence in expressed clarity of expression. Some of the futility experienced in families with schizophrenic members, for example, is based in the indirect, ambivalent (unresolved), and "flip-flopping" messages passed around in the family.

At the least competent level (5), hardly anyone in the family is clear and direct in expression of thoughts and feelings; assumptions, "groupthink," and unresolved ambivalence predominate. There may also be a high degree of individual shifting of perspective, not through negotiation but through switching of allegiances. In many dysfunctional families, members (usually parents) appear afraid of setting definite limits or making self-statements, reminiscent of the "rubber fence" relationships described by Wynne[163] in his early work on schizophrenic families.

At the midpoint of the clarify of expression scale (3), individual expression is somewhat vague and hidden; expression is possible in certain contexts but appears moderately suppressed in the here and now. The observer can envision most members of these families being clear and direct in other extrafamilial contexts, but authority, attempts at control, or prescribed role relationships may inhibit clarity in the family context. Ambivalent feelings may be addressed but not resolved in these families.

At the most competent end of the rating (1), family members are clear and direct in their expression; a sense of spontaneity and encouragement of such feelings promote contextual clarify of individual members and throughout the family. In addition to minimal coercion or active suppression of feelings, there is a degree of respect and active solicitation of more depth of expression. There is usually less monopolizing[164] and more active exchange between family members. Finally, the observer can note family members' attempts to help resolve one another's ambivalent feelings through clarifying (empathic) statements and questions, rather than the blaming, authoritarian, hurtful, or bland ignoring seen in lower ranges of competence.

B. RESPONSIBILITY

1	2	3	4	5
members regularly are able to voice responsibility for individual actions		members sometimes voice responsibility for individual actions, but tactics also include sometimes blaming others, speaking in third person or plural		members hardly, if ever, voice responsibility for individual actions

Responsibility refers to the degree to which family members acknowledge and take personal responsibility for their own past, present, and future actions, both in and outside of the bounds of the family relationship. Obviously, a high degree of truth and trust accompanies this concept. The family that fosters personal responsibility acknowledges that people do make mistakes but contends that they should not be punished for acknowledging personal responsibility for those mistakes.* In the context of family living, these mistakes range from the trivial (spilling milk at the dinner table) to the monumental (having an affair). The rating is based upon the degree to which individuals take (or are allowed to take) personal responsibility for their behavior. Blaming another person ("you shouldn't have put the glass so near my elbow"; "you weren't interested in having sex with me") and bland discounting are mechanisms to disown such responsibility.

At the lower end of the scale (5), accompanying lower clarity of expression and muddier boundaries between members, there is little voicing of personal responsibility and a great deal of avoidance. At the lowest levels of competence, there may also be bland denial, forgetting, or confusion about whether a problem even existed on one or more members' parts. The most prominent avoidance tactics in these less competent families include blaming another (or the rest of the family), attacking (physically or verbally; the attacks are usually leveled at the accuser,

---

*Note that the mistakes, as behaviors, may meet with some consequences, but the "owning" of responsibility does not.

often the spouse), and scapegoating (consensual blame placed on a single member of the family). Other verbal signs of avoidance include speaking in the third person or in plurals ("everyone else does . . . "; "all husbands . . . ").

At middle ranges (3), characterized by more rigid attempts at control and a prescription of "proper" behavior, there may be more fear or anxiety related to personal acknowledgment of responsibility, where punishment, love withdrawal, or severe "disappointment" may result from ownership of the responsibility. In these families, one hears statements such as, "I can't believe we have a son (daughter) who would even think about doing _____; where did we go wrong?" Avoidance tactics involve many of those mentioned above, although with less scapegoating, as well as lying and secret-building. In many families, secrets regarding transgressions of one person are stored as arsenals by the knowing party (or parties)—often siblings or a parent-child duo—in the event that the other's sins are exposed.

At the far end of the continuum (1), family members express a higher degree of personal responsibility and less blaming, avoidance, or distorting. It is obvious that clarity, openness, trust, and egalitarian, respectful relationships must accompany personal responsibility as systemic qualities; personal voicing of responsibility stems from each spouse's family of origin and is based firmly in the operating rules of the current family system.

C. PERMEABILITY

1	2	3	4	5
very open	moderately open		members frequently unreceptive	members unreceptive

Permeability refers to the degree to which family members are open and *receptive* to the statements and self-statements of each other. Much like the question, "If a tree falls deep in the forest, and no one is there to hear it, does it make a sound?" so goes the family system circular question, "If one communicates clearly and acknowledges responsibility, but no one will hear him, is it clear?" Hence, permeability both accompanies and fosters clarity. Observational clues to permeable receptiveness include whether family members acknowledge each other when talking and listening, whether there is active listening to the person talking (orientation, posturing, nodding), whether there is simultaneous speech and "running over" each other, and/or whether one member "drones on" unheard and ignored.

At the lower levels of competence (5), family members are frequently unreceptive to personal statements of individuals, allowing for little "connection" in terms of boundary-related verbal behavior. In some cases, the lack of permeability is manifested in bland non-reception of others' statements; in others, manifest contradictions, distortions, or confusion of meaning result.

With moderate ratings of permeability (3), communicational boundaries are more rigid, with some individuals' expressions being closed down, placed in more predetermined role relationships. In the most competent families (1), members both listen to and acknowledge each other's messages, verbally and nonverbally.

V. Family Affect

A. RANGE OF FEELINGS

1	2	3	4	5
direct expression of a wide range of feelings	direct expression of many feelings despite some difficulty	obvious restriction in the expression of *some* feelings	although some feelings are expressed, there is a masking of most feelings	little or no expression of feelings

On this subscale, the observer is directed to attend to the range ("band width") of expressed emotions in the family, rather than the intensity of those affective expressions. Much like the disturbed individual who experiences and expresses a truncated affective world (depression, anxiety, hostility), the more disturbed family expresses a limited *range* of affect. Disturbed families allow relatively few types of feelings to be expressed, while competent families usually show a variety of feeling states, even in our 10-minute interview segments, as the discussion moves across several themes. It is important to note that the particular *type* of expressed emotion (despair, hostile distance) in disturbed families depends on the stylistic qualities of the family (Chapter 3); what is important here is that there is a limited *range* of feelings.

Whatever the length of the interview, it is unlikely that all possible feelings will be expressed; competent families will not progress from raucous laughter to depressive weeping within a given interview. However, there are subtle qualities that signal the relative ease of transition and *allowance/acceptance* of individuals' expression of a variety of feelings.

At the least competent level (5), family members express little animated emotionality; a sense of sadness or despair permeates all family members. One gets the impression that there is a sense of futility in expressing emotions that would promote clarity and individual boundaries. This may even take the form of monotonic, superficial, bland "cheerfulness" in families that allow little expression of any potentially negative or status-challenging feelings.

At middle levels of rated range of feelings (3), there is obvious restriction in the expression of *some* feelings. In this range, one sees acknowledged leadership and attempts at some rigid control; such control carries with it a covert mandate that certain feelings—those that could threaten the structure or attempts at leadership—must be prohibited. (In poorly functioning centripetal families, these prohibited feelings are angry, hostile ones—breeding grounds for passive-aggressive tendencies; in poorly functioning centrifugal families, the prohibited, threatening feelings are typically warm, tender, and loving ones.)

At the more competent levels (1,2), the family members are able to be clear and direct in expressing personal feelings overtly and directly; hence, as the issues under discussion change, so will individuals' emotional tones. One will see some humor, along with some anger or sadness around emotionally sensitive issues, as the situation warrants. The sense of overcontrolled or "bottled up" feelings is diminished.

B. MOOD AND TONE

1	2	3	4	5
usually warm, affectionate, humorous, and optimistic	polite, without impressive warmth or affection; or frequently hostile with times of pleasure	overtly hostile	depressed	cynical, hopeless, and pessimistic

Just as one may characterize the general emotional tone of an individual, representing a general average of emotions expressed over time and situation, one may characterize the overall mood and emotional tone of observed family interaction. The rating is based on the combination of expressions ("optimism" and "pessimism" are cognitive attributions, but contribute to the type and nature of affective expressions) and general emotional tone of the family. In general, better functioning families are more energized; their interactions are catalyzed and charged with emotional energy and spontaneity. In contrast, dysfunctional families appear "stuck," less spontaneous, and less energized; the depressed or hopeless tone that permeates the interaction is reflected in diminished intensity and expression.

At the lowest levels of competence (5), family interaction and tone are characteristically hopeless and pessimistic; there is a pervasive cynicism regarding the status of family and, often, people in general. Hope, future, and "fun" are not part of the vocabulary and tone of these families. These families are often frustrating to work with therapeutically, since the engendering of hope and a vision of a future that *could* be brighter is difficult. One gets the sense that Dame Fate has cast them a bad lot, and there is no way out.

At higher levels, the passive hopelessness is replaced by more consistent expressed feelings, although these are often "negative." A depressive tone is characteristic of families at the next higher level (4), whereas more energy and potential hostility are characteristic of midrange families (3). It is important to note that overtly hostile tones may be more characteristic in centrifugal families; this midpoint rating also signals a midpoint on the expressed positivity pole, with ambivalent feeling tones frequently present.

At the more competent levels, evidence of a predominantly positive or optimistic feeling tone, along with the energy or charge that accompanies such feelings, is observed in family interactions. At a moderately competent level (2), family members are likely to behave in ways that signal that they expect the next encounter or exchange to be fun and positive; there may be some anger/hostility or a sense of polite positivity without spontaneous warmth. At the highest level (1), there is a sense of fun, humor, optimism, and spontaneity that creates an atmosphere in which people like each other and enjoy their time together. Even in the face of disagreements or acknowledged difficulties, these families maintain a sense of optimism that effort or luck will see them through.

Several years ago we were struck with some of the profound differences we found in this rating of overall mood and tone in a group of families with retarded children we studied.[9,76] Consistent with the themes presented here, but in contrast to previous clinical literature, those families whose members were more vocal with their feelings of frustration and ambivalence (including "chronic sorrow") were actually more competent, with a more optimistic overall "gestalt" feeling tone than those who were less clear and direct in personal feelings or promoted a sense of taboo about speaking of such feelings.

C. UNRESOLVABLE CONFLICT

1	2	3	4	5
severe conflict with severe impairment of group functioning	definite conflict, with moderate impairment in group functioning	definite conflict, with slight impairment of group functioning	some evidence of unresolved conflict, without impairment of group functioning	little, or no, unresolvable conflict

All groups of people encounter issues on which members do not all agree. In fact, general systems theory posits that growth and adaptation derive from the necessary resolution of conflict; Hegel and Marx hold that a new thesis stems from the synthesis of a preceding thesis and its antithesis (conflict). This synthesis marks a resolution by some means, whether through coercion, war, compromise, or negotiation. In families, there is conflict, and there are usually attempts to resolve the conflict. The issue for the observer is to rate the effectiveness of the family in negotiating conflict and the resultant degree to which group functioning may have been impaired by unresolved issues, hurts, or cold wars that have existed over time. Exchanges which stop dead in their tracks— which appear to be repeated themes of unresolved disagreements or disarmed truces—signal unresolved conflicts.

At the lowest levels of competence (1), there is severe impairment in group negotiation and clarity; there appear to be some grudges held by individuals or factions and stored hurts and disagreements throughout the system. Family members may be quite vocal and confrontational about old unresolved issues (more in CF families), or quietly seething in a tense silence (more characteristic of CP families, where conflicts are "masked" in pseudomutuality).

At more moderate levels of competence (2,3), there is definite conflict, with some impairment in group functioning. In most instances, unresolved conflict is hinted at or alluded to; members may start blaming or criticizing one person (CP) or defensively blaming one another for current or past family troubles. However, the process of resolution through understanding and negotiation stops short of a satisfying outcome. The process is begun, ended, and repeated over time, as in Albee's play "Who's Afraid of Virginia Woolf?" (probably a 1 on this scale). Differences tend to be "gunny-sacked" for the next encounter.

At higher levels of competence, with correspondingly more competent levels of clarity, closeness, and permeability, family members are clearer and more direct in expressing and understanding their differences, which occur more in the form of differences than of personal attacks and continual blaming. Even when differences are incompatible or irreconcilable, they are usually viewed as individual *perspectives* rather than as evidence of evil, chronic discontent, or mutiny.

D. EMPATHY

1	2	3	4	5
consistent empathic responsiveness	generally empathic responsiveness with one another, despite obvious resistance	attempted empathic responsiveness, but failed to maintain it	absence of any empathic responsiveness	grossly inappropriate with regard to feelings

Empathy pertains to one person's accurate reception, understanding, and response congruent to another's emotional overture, and a resultant joining and sharing of those feelings. The literature on counselor and therapist effectiveness[35,123] indicates that empathic tendencies of therapists are necessary (but not sufficient) qualities related to therapeutic facilitation. The empathy subscale refers to the same phenomena at the family system level—the degree of affiliative, understanding, and empathic responses versus oppositional, inappropriate, or resistant responses to expressed emotion.

At the least competent levels (5), dramatic or passively inappropriate responses to expressed emotions are often seen, with individual family members dramatically "out of tune" with one another in emotional tone. This may take the form of overt oppositional attitude (daughter: "Mother, I can't even tell you how I feel without getting criticized"; mother: "You'll never grow up if you can't take any constructive criticism") or inappropriate fitting of response to plea (laughter in response to a member's tears or anger). At the next level (4), there is a masked absence of any consistent attempt at empathic relating. Often members will sit in stony or wide-eyed silence to another's expression, or roll their eyes ("here we go again") in passive allowance of the plaintiff.

At middle levels (3), there is evidence of members' beginning to respond empathically to, and being moderately permeable to, the emotional statements of others. At this level, there is acknowledgment without exploration or further facilitation, occasional sparks of affective affiliation without current.

At higher levels of competence, there is more consistent cross-member empathic responsiveness and affiliative tendency. In some families, some members may prefer to remain less involved with the feelings of others or some resistance of all members to acknowledge certain feelings in others (anger, disappointment) is evident (rating of 2). The most competent rating (1) connotes accurate, open, and facilitative responses throughout the system to individuals' expressed emotions.

VI. Global Health-Pathology Scale

10	9	8	7	6	5	4	3	2	1
most pathological									healthiest

The global rating is an attempt to capture the overall level of competence of the family, based on the summary and integration of the aforementioned considerations. This subjective summary represents the global impression of the structural, communicative, affective, and effective qualities of the system. Obviously, we do not have frequencies for the cross-section of all American families and across all subcultures; however, certain guidelines can be useful:

1. In general, families with clinical members typically score at low-midrange, borderline, or dysfunctional levels.
2. Extreme-scoring families (1, 10) are less frequent than those encountered in the middle ranges. Hence, the optimal, highly competent family, while representing a psychological ideal, is by no means the norm.
3. The global rating should be close to the overall mean of the subscales, with appropriate reversals and multiplied by two.
4. Each family will show relative strengths and weaknesses—areas of greater and lesser competence—which will be helpful in planning therapy strategies (see Section Two of this book).

Optimal families: Ratings of 1 or 2. These families show consistently high degrees of capable negotiation, clarity of individual expression, respect for individual choices and ambivalence, and affiliative attitudes towards one another. Each member appears competent, acknowledged, and assured; the resultant product is a group of individuals who are spontaneous, enjoy each other, and are allowed clear and direct expression of feelings, attitudes, and beliefs. There is a consistent theme that individuals are unique and respected, rather than the role stereotyping that occurs at lower levels. The parents in these families are clear leaders, support and care for each other, and provide appropriate models of respect and intimacy for the children. Centripetal or centrifugal forces may be predominant at any given time in these families, but not to the extreme and inflexible degree encountered at less competent levels.

Adequate families: Ratings of 3 or 4.   Adequate families are also relatively healthy, competent systems; they also encourage and respect individuality, clarity of expression, and responsibility of individuals. We have found, however, that there is usually less efficient and competent negotiation of differences, a weaker parental coalition, and less spontaneity in emotional exchanges. Also, in contrast to the optimal families, and more like midrange families, there is more role stereotyping, even to the extent of the family's having a spokesperson, referee of conflict, or mediator. Autonomy and individuation are less easily accomplished—often successfully only by progressive distancing—yet warmth and support are possible at times. Some, if not most or all, of the members are competent individuals, although it appears to have taken more effort and struggle to attain such a status.

Midrange families: Ratings of 5 or 6.   As the rating of family competence moves toward lower levels, the family style (CP, CF) becomes more salient and differentiating; less competent families show more extreme and relatively inflexible style differences (these will be elucidated further after we discuss style ratings). In general, however, midrange families have considerable difficulty in smooth, efficient functioning, some degree of emotional pain, and at least one member who has had, at some point, a diagnosis of mild to moderate emotional disorder. These families produce "sane but limited"[10] offspring, typically diagnosed as neurotic or behavior disordered.

Within the family, reasonably clear boundaries exist between members, and generational boundaries are present. The relationship between parents is shaky and unequal in power status; hence, negotiation and clarity are difficult, while affiliation and spontaneity are at minimal levels. As clarity and respectful negotiation decline, attempts at control increase; there are more absolutes in terms of types of feelings allowed expression and of strict "shoulds" that family members must feel and demonstrate. Blame and defensiveness replace clear and direct statements of feelings and responsibility. Feeling tone of the family as a whole is usually anxious, on edge, or depressed (hidden conflicts, CP) or outwardly angry (CF).

Borderline families: Ratings of 7 or 8.   As competence and negentropy decline, the structure and interactional functioning in all areas decline as well. A major theme in these families is sporadic, ineffective, and chaotic power struggles as the system vacillates between chaos and attempts at dominant control. Parental coalitions are loose and vacillate in dominance/submission struggles, and interpersonal relations are continually in flux, as these families are not as effective as midrange families in establishing rigid and stable control-oriented relationships. Family members are unable to attend to each others' (or their own) emotional needs, and what looks like suspicious and tenuous distancing occurs. The overall tone is typically a system afraid of itself, in some cases markedly depressed (CP families, in which overt rage and rebellion are not allowed) to hostile and enraged (CF, in which control struggles and hostile battles are overt). These families tend to produce more disturbed offspring who mimic the chaos and attempts at overcontrol, including borderline personality disorders and severely obsessional and anorectic patients.

Severely disturbed families: Ratings of 9 or 10.   The severely disturbed family's greatest need/deficiency is coherence, reflected in patterns of communication and relational boundary structure. As a result, family members have little ability to resolve ambivalence, negotiate conflict, and move ahead individually in pursuit of autonomous initiatives. In their observed interactions, these families are uniformly poor at focusing attention on task; instead, members maintain an uncomfortable distance from each other. Our clinical observations of these families reveal what Wynne has described as pseudomutuality, the lack of satisfying and predictable interpersonal encounters; these families behave as if they expect that human encounters and individual disclosures will have uncomfortable (at best) or destructive consequences. Hence, the tone is oppositional, the mood is cynical and desperate, and the emotional dealing is covert and under the table.

The functioning of these families is hampered further by a lack of clear leadership and a dysfunctional or emotionally divorced parental coalition. Depending upon the inflexible style of the system, the parental relationships are either rigidly complementary or markedly schismatic, often with parent-child coalitions supplanting the illusory marital coalition. Also, dependent on the style of the system—which becomes more extreme and rigid with greater dysfunction—is the relative permeability of the system itself to outside influence. Centripetal families have a nearly impermeable outer boundary, and children are quite disabled in their progression through normal autonomous development. These systems are also extremely time-bound, denying the necessity and eventuality of change and growth. These centripetal families adopt denial of the future and cynicism of the present (conservative reactionary), while centrifugal families adopt a disavowal of past in some desperate struggle for a different future; these latter families have an insufficient outer shell, with much leave-taking and lack of clarity as to who actually "belongs" in the family.

Assessing and understanding family competence are necessary steps in recognizing a family's strengths, structure, and relationships. However, the assessment of an intimately related dimension, family style, is essential in planning for effective therapeutic intervention. The assessment of family style is covered in the next chapter.

3 THE ASSESSMENT OF FAMILY STYLE AND CLINICAL FAMILY GROUPINGS

The Beavers Model has incorporated systems theory, clinical family observations, and various treatises on family dysfunction into the concept of family competence. However, continuing work with families having different types of emotional and behavioral disturbances in members (acting-in vs. acting-out, internalizing/externalizing,[121] for example) and clinical observations of binding vs. expelling patterns of interaction[87] have led to the related, inseparable style dimension central to our family assessment model. The terms chosen—centripetal and centrifugal—are systemic/relational concepts, as opposed to clinical descriptors such as enmeshment/disengagement and internalizing/externalizing, which may be used to describe individuals, dyads, or subsystems. The concepts and terms were influenced by the works of Erikson[43] and Stierlin.[140]

FAMILY STYLE

Centripetal Systems

Erikson[43] described the Yurok tribe of the Pacific Northwest, who, in contrast to nomadic hunters, lived in a narrow river valley: "They considered a disk of about 150 miles in diameter . . . to include all there was to this world." Outside their horizons were those of "crazy" tendencies or "ignoble birth." "There was no centrifugal east and west, south and north. There was an 'upstream' and a 'downstream,' a 'toward the river' and an 'away from the river,' and then, at the borders of the world, an elliptical 'in back and around': as centripetal a world as could be designed."

Likewise, Stierlin[140] described the centripetal pattern of families dealing with adolescent separation progression as "binding" occurring at several levels. First, affective binding involves exploitation of dependency needs and "regressive gratification," a time-binding process. Second, cognitive binding involves parental interference with the offspring's "differentiated self-awareness and self-determination" (p. 41), as reflected in intrusiveness and "ego binding." Third, binding through the exploitation of loyalty involves parents' instilling excessive "breakaway guilt," with the message that "they can live only through him" (p. 49).

The concept of the centripetal (CP) system, then, involves both the issues of world view boundaries and the internal maneuvers to maintain the tenuous balance of the internalizing system. Members of CP families look to the family as a source of pleasure, joy, and satisfaction, whether they find it there or not. In the science of astrophysics, the centripetal force of orbital trajectory is the gravitational pull to the center of mass.

Centrifugal Systems

In contrast, Erikson[43] described the functional world of the Sioux tribes (*Hunters Across the Prairie*) as centrifugal: "The Sioux roamed the plains and cultivated spatial concepts of centrifugal mobility; their horizons were the roaming herds of buffalo and the shifting enemy bands" (p. 166). The boundaries of these nomadic tribes were different nearly every day; the concept of storage over any prolonged period was foreign to them. These tribes, therefore, placed a high degree of emphasis on the "give-away," providing hosts and others with items other than the bare necessities for traveling on; they hoped, in return, to get some essentials from outsiders at the next stop.

Stierlin's[140] description of the centrifugal family system responding to the adolescent separation drama (associated more with casual runaways) involved an "expelling" pattern. These families typically show ongoing neglect or rejection of the children, who are "pushed into premature and foreclosing autonomy" (p. 37). Stierlin uses the German word *verwahrlost* to describe children who are "unduly left to themselves and constantly get the message: 'You are expendable; the earlier you leave home, the better'" (p. 67).

The concept of the centrifugal (CF) system also involves the integration of boundary issues and internal mechanisms to describe the family that has tenuous external boundaries, releases its offspring too early, and has little of the internal "glue" or balance seen in well-functioning systems. CF families look outside the family for pleasure, satisfaction, and joy, whether they find it there or not. In astrophysics, the centrifugal force of orbital trajectory is the tangential propulsion out and away from mother earth. The balance or harmonic mixing of both forces creates a stable orbit and a balanced system.

It is important to recognize that relatively competent families are able to accomplish subtle shifts in style during the course of normal family development. In the early years of marriage and child-rearing, a more centripetal style is adaptive, since it promotes the necessary caretaking—and satisfaction derived from within the family—to nurture dependent individuals. As the children reach adolescence, a shift toward a more mixed or centrifugal style is adaptive, as the offspring are released progressively to the outside world. Any system that maintains a rigid style becomes stuck and inflexible, signals of diminished family competence.

BEAVERS INTERACTIONAL SCALES:
II. FAMILY STYLE

This scale attempts to rate observable qualities related to family style from an ahistorical interactional basis. While knowledge of a detailed history of parental qualities may provide the therapist with a temporal frame in which to map stylistic adaptation and change (better functioning families move from moderate CP toward moderate CF style as their children mature), the present style rating is based on *current* observations. It is also important that the rater (therapist) is aware of his/her own family style and style scale rating as a point of reference. This scale is presented in Appendix B, with descriptive scale data presented in Table 3 and interrater reliabilities in Table 4.

I. Dependency Needs

1	2	3	4	5
discouraged, ignored		sometimes discouraged, sometimes attended		encouraged, alertly attended

All families must deal with the dependency needs of members. This subscale deals with the manner in which family members respond to one another's overt and covert requests for affiliation, nurturance, aid, or attention. The principal issue being rated is the degree to which family members encourage and attend to nurturance and dependency requests, either verbally or nonverbally. To make this assessment, the rater must keep in mind the age-appropriate behavior of the children in the family being observed; dependent overtures such as climbing onto mother's lap or clinging are more appropriate for a two-year-old than for a six-year-old. Likewise, the attention granted to such behavior is in part determined by age-appropriateness: A mother's allowing or encouraging a seven-year-old to cling is less appropriate than it would be with a much younger child. The converse—ignoring or discouraging the two-year-old's overtures—would also represent a less appropriate age-related response.

At the most centrifugal level (1), such dependency needs tend to be discouraged and ignored by all members, regardless of the children's ages. These families tend to keep supportive distance, disparaging all behavior that seems clinging and ensnaring. At the next level (2), there may be some attempts to provide for some dependency needs; often one will see an older child assigned as the caretaker for a toddler to free the parents of such emotional burden.

At middle levels (3), responses to dependency and nurturant needs are sometimes attended to and sometimes ignored or discouraged across the system. Family members are more attuned to age-appropriate differences in nurturance/dependency solicitations and may also provide differential limitations on degrees of dependent or attention-seeking behavior. For example, a mother may allow her four-year-old to sit on her lap but prohibit the child's attempt to further monopolize her attention through continual talking. The midpoint rating is chosen to represent an "in-between" rating, intermediate between the extremes.

At more centripetal levels (4,5), dependency needs are more consistently and alertly encouraged and attended to. At the extreme (5), family members tend to be clinging and interdependent, solicitous of such signs of dependency. One or both parents appear to derive special meaning from having one or more children "needing" their emotional fuel for survival. A typical exchange might be:

Interviewer: "What TV shows do you enjoy watching?"
Twelve-year-old son: "We like watching football games."
Interviewer: "What teams do you root for?"
Son: "What teams do we like, mother?"

II. Adult Conflict

1	2	3	4	5
quite open	usually open		sometimes hidden, covert	indirect, covert hidden

This subscale is not a rating of the presence or absence of conflict (all systems have some conflict) or *degree* of conflict, but whether such conflict is handled *overtly* or *covertly*. Centripetal families tend to hide and minimize their conflicts, glossing over problem areas and emphasizing harmony and mutuality. Centrifugal families, in contrast, are overt and direct in expressing conflicts, often being highly vocal in that regard; instead, expressions of love and mutuality are suppressed.

At more centrifugal levels (1,2), the adult family members appear openly confrontational in handling their conflicts. There is no attempt to hide disagreements, and all family members know when the parents are fighting. This rating is independent of how the conflict is resolved; instead, it reflects the overt quality of that conflict.

At more centripetal levels (4,5), adults are more indirect and covert in their handling of conflict. The greater this tendency, the less likely one is to witness any angry expressions of conflict between adult family members. At the higher levels of family competence, these adults may be able to resolve conflicts efficiently without such expression or be able to wait for less public situations in order to negotiate. At less competent levels, the conflict is usually suppressed completely; a distant marital skew[98] is often the result.

III. Proximity

1	2	3	4	5
all members give and expect lots of room between members		some members touch, others stay apart		all members stay physically close, and there is much touching

This rating addresses how family members physically space and position themselves in the interview situation. The rating is based on the whole system rather than specific dyadic spacing. For example, if a mother and young child sit close to each other and also touch, but all other members keep a physical distance, a rating of 2 or 3 on this scale is appropriate.

Centrifugal families (1,2) tend to space themselves with tolerable distance across the board. If the interview setting does not allow for a great deal of free space between members, centrifugal families appear nervous and uncomfortable, posturing and orienting in order to establish as much personal space as possible. It is not unlike a gathering of ex-spouses, each with a new partner, brought together to discuss issues regarding one of the children.

Centripetal families are prone to place themselves close together in the room; extreme ratings (5) signify families in which members huddle and maintain a high level of physical contact. These families appear comfortable and relaxed with physical closeness; they may even show signs of discomfort or distress if the seating arrangement requires that a family member sit away from the center of gravity. (Some families "make room" for another, sometimes squeezing four people on a couch to include him/her proximally.)

IV. Social Presentation

1	2	3	4	5
try hard to appear well-behaved and to make a good impression on others		sometimes appear concerned with making a good impression		seem unconcerned with appearances and social approval

The rating on this subscale is based on the degree to which the family needs to present itself in a socially appropriate and desirable manner, in terms of manners, dress, emotional expression, and behaving in a "proper" demeanor. All family members may not be equally concerned about social presentation or behave in the same manner. The rating concerns the family as a whole and is based on the judgment of preponderance of social presentation and concern. The full range is from none of the family members showing concern and resultant demeanor to all members being concerned with making favorable impressions on others.

Centrifugal families (4,5) show little concern for socially appropriate demeanor. They may indicate this in numerous ways: overt lack of interest, diminished eye contact, lack of concern with the issues being presented, overt resistance or defiance. These families are typically more overt in disagreements; they may exhibit name-calling or adopt negative references to their members and to outsiders.

Centripetal families (1,2) are generally more concerned with "appropriate" behaviors, respect, cooperation, and appearing polite and well-intentioned; these trends become more stereotyped and limiting of individuality at the extreme (1). The family also appears to be concerned about its appearance: grooming, dress, manners. These factors are also associated to a great degree with social class/socioeconomic status, in that social presentations and properness are characteristic of middle to upper classes and lack of concern for such social "niceties" more characteristic of lower classes. In fact, we have found in our research[74] a high degree of association between style and socioeconomic level in *clinic* families.

V. Expression of Closeness

1	2	3	4	5
consistently emphasize that they are close		don't make an issue of closeness		deny being close

This scale rates the extent to which family members express verbally that they are and feel close to each other. This is a rating *not* of emotional closeness per se (which is part of the competence dimension) but of the verbal proclamation of closeness.

Centrifugal families (4,5) usually do not refer to "closeness" in discussing themselves; they may actually deny feeling close to one another. At more competent levels these families may refer to how independent and self-sufficient they are. At lower levels independence is translated into pained distance, and overt denials of caring and loving are more frequent.

Centripetal families (1,2) make a strong point of stating (often repeatedly) how close and loving they are. This "loving" is the predominant theme, with little dissent or display of individual differences. The more extreme the style (1), the lower the tolerance for differences in individual views of family ties. At lower levels of competence, as the verbal expressions of closeness contrast with the rigid relational roles and boundaries, the family appears to be presenting a façade of happy and close relationships.

A related quality observed in CP families is internal scapegoating, which refers to one member's bearing the burden of blame for family problems. The prerequisite for this scapegoating is an unambiguous and unchanging agreement among family members as to who is responsible and to be blamed for family difficulties. In contrast to CF families, in which coalitions fluctuate too greatly to allow consistent scapegoating, centripetal families may label one person as the cause of the family problems. Hence, while the absence of scapegoating does not signify a particular style, the presence of observed scapegoating suggests a CP style. With regard to scapegoating, the checklist on the style scale calls for a present vs. absent determination (observed/not observed), rather than any dimensional rating.

VI. Assertive/Aggressive Qualities

1	2	3	4	5
discourage aggressive or disruptive behavior and expression				solicit or encourage assertive, even aggressive behavior and expression

At times, family members behave in assertive (direct expression) and aggressive (angry, hostile) ways. This scale rates the degree to which parents, in particular, may encourage such behavior in members by word or deed; it also notes whether they tend to discourage anything that even looks like assertive and/or aggressive behavior. The rater must attend to (1) whether such exchanges and expressions occur; and (2) how the family members respond to assertive and aggressive behavior.

Centrifugal families (4,5) do not discourage assertive/aggressive types of behaviors and may even encourage such expressions. A covert rule in these families is that angry and even hostile expressions are allowed, whereas the expression of closeness and tender feelings is risky. Independent assertiveness, challenges to authority, occasional defiance, and disruptiveness are seen in CF families. CF families also encourage independent assertiveness, including direct disagreement and challenging.

In contrast, centripetal families (1,2) tend to discourage assertive and aggressive behaviors. They tend to be quiet, to control active children quickly, and to show displeasure at independent assertiveness. Angry, hostile, or challenging expressions are disallowed; in the extreme CP family (1), people are not allowed to be angry at all, especially in the close, loving family unit.

VII. Expression of Positive and Negative Feelings

1	2	3	4	5
positive feelings are easier to express than negative		about the same		negative feelings are easier to express than positive

While the most competent families allow and express a wide range of feelings, most families have some restrictions on the range and types of emotional expressions. This subscale assesses the comfort with which family members express positive vs. negative feelings during the observed interview. Positive feelings are those which are nonconflictual, including love, support, loyalty, pride, closeness at more competent levels, and disappointment (not anger!), neediness, covered sadness, and even pseudomutual "loving" at less competent levels. Negative feelings are less "safe" and more confrontational; anger, hostility, and resultant attacks on other members are most common.

One connotation of "negative" feelings is a subjectively uncomfortable affective state ("negative is whatever makes me feel uncomfortable"). If we adopt this larger subjective view, it is true that members from both centripetal and centrifugal families experience emotional distress. The differences between CP and CF families lie in the observable manifestations and expression of emotional pressure. Centripetal family members tend to internalize discomfort, anger, and most emotional distress; anxiety and depression are often the concomitant expressions. Members from centrifugal families tend to express their discomfort by acting-out; the anger, attack, or defiance is often a mask for internal depression.

The specific expression of types of feelings, then, differs between CP and CF families. Centripetal families (1,2) find it harder to express negative (acting-out expression) feelings, and prefer to express and allow less challenging ones. At more extreme levels (1), there is actual prohibition of direct expression of anger, which is viewed as not merely impolite but downright evil. Members under duress tend to suffer alone, experiencing internal states of anxiety or depression.

Centrifugal families (4,5) express feelings more directly, especially if they are negative/angry. Conflict and attacks are open and intense in extreme CF families (5). In many CF families, members have a hard time expressing warm, tender, supportive feelings; they may become suspicious or wary if such expressions are aired. Members in these families tend to share their suffering by involving others in their pain through provocation and acting-out.

The balance of affective expression in more competent systems usually shifts as families develop and evolve from taking care of young children—when love, support, and nurturance are expressed—to releasing young adults into their own worlds. Part of the adolescent breakaway phenomenon is to foster independence, reduce time-binding, and introduce centrifugality to a system which may be highly centripetal. The second child "always has it easier" implies that a centrifugal element has been added to the family balance.

Adolescents may use anger at their restrictions, clothes, parents, etc., to mobilize movement toward separation. Many CP families view anger as attack and try to suppress this mutinous behavior. One mother of a midrange CP family said she was taken aback when her oldest child—a 14-year-old boy—yelled, "Jesus Christ, I need to pick out my own clothes one morning." "All he needed to do was ask me politely," said she; the boy insisted that he had done so on a nearly daily basis.

VIII. Global Centripetal/Centrifugal Style

1	2	3	4	5
CP				CF

Rating of 1: Centripetal family style.   This extreme CP rating indicates a rather inflexible and inner-directed family system, which places a high degree of emphasis on looking to family members as the main source of gratification of emotional needs. A common theme in centripetal families is peaceful, nonconflictual relating, more easily accomplished when children are young than during adolescence. These families emphasize "proper" behavior, prescribe somewhat inflexible role-related status, and typically present themselves well to the outside world. Children from centripetal families separate from the family unit later than expected, and dependency needs are continued at later-than-expected ages of children.

The "golden years" for highly centripetal families are the young child-bearing and child-rearing years. Husbands are "husbands" and wives are "wives." The family stopwatch is set at about the time of birth of the second child. The centripetal family is set more in the context of middle and upper classes.[74] In the extreme, control is maintained by dependency, guilt manipulation, and looking to authority; the father's (midrange competence) authority is unchallenged overtly, and overt defiance is minimal. Instead, members internalize their feelings such that disappointment is seldom expressed; depression and anxiety are the predominant negative feelings. Hence, the extreme CP style does not connote "closeness" per se, in the positive sense; nor does it represent "enmeshment" in the extreme. These connotations can be ascribed only when CP-CF style and level of family competence are considered interactively. Further, we make every effort to have language appropriate for and related to each hierarchical level. The CP/CF continuum is used for family (group) interaction and the disengagement/enmeshment continuum is used to describe dyads within the family.

Rating of 2: Moderate centripetal style. In these families, there is a tendency to look inward for much gratification, but there is simultaneous movement toward allowing individuals to evolve and separate. If one were to observe these families over time, one would see increased potential for differentiation and emergence of the individual, especially in the more competent families. The "best of times" are often those of the elementary-school years of children, when the family is dealing with the unfolding of its members into the larger world. There are still strong emotional pulls toward the center, but these are less powerful than in the extreme CP family. Feelings—especially anger—are more internalized than expressed overtly, allowing for some challenges to the structure of authority.

Rating of 3: Mixed family style. Like the stable satellite orbit, the mixed family style blends centripetal and centrifugal forces, allowing a blending of need gratification within and outside the family, permitting and encouraging (in more competent families) age- and development-appropriate demeanor and extrafamilial pursuits. Second-borns have fewer internalizing pressures and developmental restrictions than first-borns, as the system adjusts its balance of stylistic tendencies with human development. Direct and autonomy-related challenges and pushes are allowed, balanced by supportive and internalizing pulls from within the system. This mixed stylistic pattern is prevalent in competent families; we did not observe it in the most dysfunctional families, which present more rigid extremes of CP or CF style. The balance (yin-yang, love-hate, near-far) allows for movement without rigidity, for developmental unfolding of offspring, and for some equilibrium during adolescent struggles.[149]

Rating of 4: Moderate centrifugal style. As the style rating moves from the midpoint toward a moderate centrifugal style, the balance in the family tips toward an externalizing and acting-out pattern. The tendency to express more defiance and anger, with overt and shifting blaming patterns, abrupt exits, and rule-breaking, replaces the internalizing and repression of the CP family. The parental dyad shows signs of overt conflict, which may take the form of competitiveness and put-downs under pressure. Anger and futility are experienced and expressed directly, with diminished tendency to suppress or "talk things out." In fact, the more centrifugal the family, the more such talking is distrusted; behavioral responses such as failing, acting-out, distancing, and drug-taking replace the magical power of words and guilt-driven repressive mechanisms of the centripetal family style. Authority and attempts at control are absolute but generally ineffective; inconsistency and seemingly more random attempts at behavioral control of family members become increasingly apparent. Members of such families derive proportionately more satisfaction from people and activities outside the nucleus of the family; hence, the system membrane is more diffuse and permeable than in CP families.

Rating of 5: Centrifugal family style. The extreme patterns of centrifugal family style represent an "ungluing" of the nonconfrontational and mutual (or pseudomutual) patterns characterizing the centripetal family. There are no illusions presented regarding family closeness, unity, or solidarity. Somewhat like the nomadic warriors described by Erikson, family members come and go freely, distance and stay away in periods of distress, and exchange with the outside world sexual, emotional, and behavioral allegiances. Children from centrifugal families are released to the outside world too early, with minimal supervision and accelerated status with respect to social, sexual, substance-related, and at times, reckless behavior. (These are the children who represent the counterpoint to our children's arguments about having "too much" parental supervision.)

Centrifugal families lack an effective parental coalition; in fact, the parents are habitually bucking for control of the children, blaming each other for family problems, and attempting to line up allies (sometimes through illicit alliances) in their offspring. The children receive minimal nurturance; discipline is sporadic criticism, attack, and ridicule (interspersed with ignoring for more appropriate behaviors). Hence, children develop a sense of cynicism about themselves, about relationships (playing one parent off the other), and about consistency and depth of trust in other people.

In contrast to CP families, who wish to appear well to the outside world, CF family members tend to spill out into the community with their crises: drunkenness, recklessness, running away. There are no attempts to present a picture of utopia; instead, the family may actually tout the individual's behavior as evidence of how rotten the *current* scapegoat makes life for the rest of the family. However, while in CP families there is a stable scapegoating pattern (one member takes the blame), in CF families members share and trade off the hot-seat position.

These families are more often found in the lower-middle and lower social classes, regardless of ethnic grouping of the family.[74] Dependency needs, loving and tender feelings, and requests for emotional support are generally lacking. Instead of the family watch being stopped at any one point (as when the children are young), the extreme CF family watch is stopped at no point: Time passes slowly and painfully, with little satisfaction at any point in the life span of the family.

Some observers[10] have speculated that some CF families deal with this slow and painful passage of time by attempting to accelerate the temporal process: Their members become sexually active at 13, parents at 16, and grandparents at 35. Many lower-class CF families, headed by single, deserted mothers, seem to have an unspoken rule that a daughter's emancipation is marked by presenting her mother with a baby to occupy her time and parental interests. These speculations serve to highlight the diffuse boundaries in definition of family; CF families include more never-married single-parent, multigenerational, and diffuse family types.

THE RELATIONSHIP OF COMPETENCE AND STYLE

Our clinical and empirical work with families over the past 20 years indicates that competence and style are useful constructs through which to understand family and individual functioning. Each construct may be observed and assessed separately; however, as we have been noting throughout, competence and style dimensions are not independent but are somewhat related. As in the world of living systems, there is no such thing as pure orthogonality in describing the personality of a system (orthogonality exists primarily in the computers of test-makers and the eyes of those reductionists who choose to view only one system level at any time).

Competence and style, when considered simultaneously and interactively, provide a useful map for locating essential system characteristics associated with family and individual psychological and behavioral functioning. As Figure 1 illustrates, the combination of competence (horizontal dimension) and style (vertical dimension) produces a conceptual map of family functioning, analogous to the combination of latitude and longitude that provides geographical location. While the orthogonal elements of latitude and longitude produce combinations of loci that could have land forms all over the world, the actual land forms are only in certain combinations (one-quarter to one-third of the earth's surface). Likewise, competence and style, were they considered orthogonal elements, could produce a range of possible combinations, only some of which are actually observed in families.[73] Consequently, Figure 1 presents a map of family functioning based on theoretical, empirical, and clinical work with families.

Figure 1

DIAGRAM OF FAMILY ASSESSMENT SCHEMA

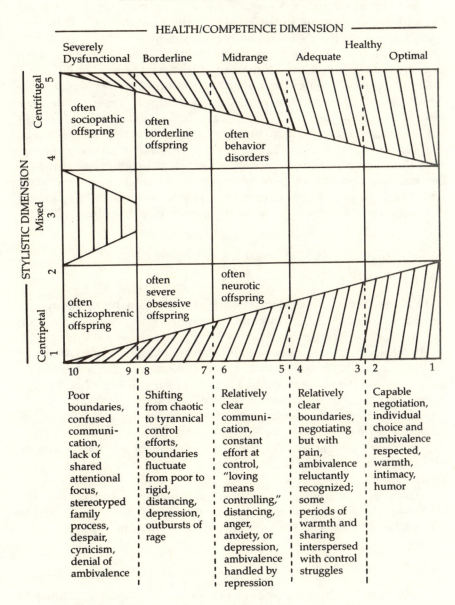

In terms of the "actual terrain," the possible family patterns are presented in the shape of an arrow. The most obvious omissions on the possible terrain map are the extreme styles in the most competent families and the mixed style in the most dysfunctional families. This illustrates the concept that "systems sickness is system rigidity":[153] The more competent the family, the more balanced and flexible the current style, since the family can change if needed. The extreme forms of CP or CF styles are seen only in rigid and poorly functioning families; their stereotyped and inflexible patterns of behavior produce a simple, unalterable stylistic extreme.

Our studies, which have involved hundreds of assessments of clinical and nonclinical families, indicate that this schema is an accurate portrayal of the pattern of competence/style ratings gathered on each family. Our clinical work also suggests that it is possible to talk about important and meaningful groupings of clinical or symptomatic families following this assessment scheme.[24] These family patterns are described below.

NINE CLINICALLY USEFUL GROUPINGS OF FAMILIES

Group 1: Optimal Families

These well-functioning families are seldom seen by clinicians yet serve as our model for effective and adaptive functioning. In these families, as described earlier, intimacy is sought and usually found, a high level of respect for individuality and the individual perspective is the norm, and capable negotiation and communicational clarity are the results. There is a strong sense of individuation with clear boundaries; hence, conflict and ambivalence (at the individual level) are handled directly, overtly, and (usually) negotiated efficiently. The hierarchical structure of the family is well-defined and acknowledged by family members. Yet there is also flexibility—a high level of adaptation to individual development, stress, and individuation, which reflects morphogenetic forces balancing the system. In fact, in the later years of the evolution of the family—a process acknowledged throughout the course—the family becomes a "loosely connected, lovingly respectful group of equal adults with another generation emerging."[18]

Group 2: Adequate Families

These families show some characteristics of the optimal families in terms of the importance of family life, caring for members, and relatively low incidence of individuals' psychiatric disturbance. In contrast, they show diminished negotiation skills, are more control-oriented, and often resolve conflict by intimidation and/or direct force. The parental coalition is usually effective, though less emotionally rewarding; sex-role stereotyping and some dominance patterns are more characteristic throughout the family (including the marital couple): Males are typically prescribed to be powerful, unemotive, and conventional, while females are relatively less powerful, highly emotive (sometimes depressed), and more traditional in providing or seeking nurturance. Hence, compared to those in optimal families, interactions produce less intimacy and trust, less respect for personal individuality, and less spontaneity in minute-to-minute exchanges. While there is some pain, some loneliness, and some feeling of being misunderstood, these families can function quite well, although with less flexibility and adaptation than in optimal families. Previous study showed these families able to produce children with competence equal to that of optimal families. These parents care about parenting and work hard on it.

Group 3, 4 and 5: Midrange Families

While optimal and adequate families are rarely seen in clinical practice, midrange families usually rear "sane but limited" offspring, and both parents and children are susceptible to emotional or behavioral disorders. These control-oriented and rigid systems revolve around power, status, and the (assumed) belief that people are basically evil, untrustworthy, and in need of discipline. Although there are few flagrant boundary violations or invasions, there are frequent projections. Beavers[18] has noted that ambivalence is frequently handled by denying one strong emotion and using repression or projection for the other, as in statements such as, "You never have a good time when we go out." Even so, there is room for some rebuttal and clarification, often taking the form of mutually accusatory statements. The parental relationship offers little emotional support and is generally conflicted and distant; parenting varies with family style. It is not uncommon for each parent to have a "favorite" child, often following oedipal (father-daughter, mother-son) patterns.

Group 3: Midrange Centripetal Families

These families manifest great concern for rules and authority; they expect overt, authoritarian control to be successful in controlling the base impulses of family members. Since the expressions of hostility and overt anger are disapproved and expressions of "love" and "caring" approved, raised and vented feelings of frustration and conflict are infrequent. Therefore, conflict resolution, clarity of expression, and competent negotiation are compromised. One sees only modest spontaneity shining through the web of concern for rules, order, and authority. Sex stereotyping is very strong in these families: Dependent, emotional women and strong, silent, authority-based men are predominant. Hence, the marital relationship takes on a flavor of a male-led unit, often with depressed females carrying out the vast majority of household and child-rearing duties.

These families promote internalizing and repression as means of dealing with distress and upset. Anxiety disorders, mild depression, and somatizing disorders are usually seen. The patients' concern for properness and authority make them "good" psychiatric patients who pay their bills, work hard, and keep their problems well hidden until next week's session.[18]

Group 4: Midrange Centrifugal Families

Like midrange centripetal families, midrange centrifugal families attempt to control by authority and intimidation; however, they find over time that such control is ineffective, and so come to expect that their control efforts will not be successful. Hence, it is inevitable that people will find out about their base nature. These family members deal with this inevitable lack of control through frontal assaults and blame, usually spread across members from time to time, and manipulation. Anger and derogatory blame are more frequent than the anxiety-provoking expressions of warmth and tenderness. The parental dyad is openly conflictual and competitively hostile; the mother and father spend little time in the home; the coalition is tenuous and unresolved power and control struggles are commonplace. Children observe that one survives through maneuvering and blaming others; they move out into the streets earlier than the norm, have difficulty with authority figures, and typically manifest acting-out behavior disorders, such as sexual precocity, substance abuse, vandalism, and conduct disorders.

Group 5: Midrange Mixed Families

This group of families has competing (rather than balancing) and alternating centripetal and centrifugal behavior, which reduces the rigidity of more extreme style but concomitantly increases inconsistency and uncertainty of position in the family. The attempts at control are consistent, but the effects vary at different times or with different children, depending on internal scapegoating patterns. Couples in this group experience role tension and struggles; they can present well socially but engage in blaming and hostile attacks on other occasions or in private. Distancing is handled through more "appropriate" channels: work, going to "the club." Internal blaming and scapegoating work differently with different members; it is not uncommon for one child to manifest internalizing symptoms while another is openly defiant and hostile.

Group 6 and 7: Borderline Families

These families are characterized by chaotic overt power struggles, with persistent (though ineffective) efforts to build and maintain stable patterns of dominance and submission. It appears to outside observers that the members have lost sight of any satisfaction to be had in family life. Individual family members have little ability to attend to and accept emotional needs in themselves or others. There is little spontaneity or warmth catalyzing these families' interactions; pain, amorphous personal boundaries, and seemingly random attempts to establish rigid control are more characteristic of these groups.

Group 6: Borderline Centripetal Families

In these families the chaos and discomfort are more verbal than behavioral, and control battles are usually covert, internalized, or somaticized by members. The parental coalition is dramatically skewed, often with one parent the verbally controlling member and the other passive. Generational boundaries become diffuse, with increasing tendency for covert parent-child coalitions or triangular patterns of dominance with one (scapegoated) child. Open rebellion and overt rage are discouraged, so family members must retreat and protect themselves through patterned rituals and attempts at individuation or attention-seeking. Severely obsessional and anorectic patients are frequently found in these families.

Group 7: Borderline Centrifugal Families

These families are much more open than borderline centripetal families in the expression of anger, with ample leave-taking and frequent direct assaults. The parental coalition is loosely connected, and stormy battles occur with high regularity. These systems produce a sense of "no-man's land," with children left with little or no nurturance and support. Each individual is on his/her own to try to derive whatever goodies can be gained by manipulation or reckless attention-seeking. Ambivalence is felt strongly, but is expressed in terms of manipulating and testing others. Since the desired nurturance is never gained, depression is masked by assault and defiance. Children learn to manipulate within the unstable but oscillating system; many receive a psychiatric label of "borderline personality disorder" as they carry these tendencies into the outside world.

Groups 8 and 9: Severely Dysfunctional Families

These families are the most limited in negotiating conflicts, adapting to developmental and current crises, and resolving ambivalence and choosing goals. The main lack—and greatest need—is for communicational coherence. There is a lack of shared focus of attention and contribution to discussion, accompanied by a peculiar distancing that prevents satisfying or clarifying encounters. Hence, boundaries are diffuse and relational clarity is minimal. There is also no effective leadership (although there is frequent maternal domination), so family functioning appears chaotic, disjointed, random. However, since control is attempted through a variety of covert and indirect methods, there may actually be some repetitive themes in these families. Hence, what appears chaotic to the outsider may be viewed by insiders as "more of the same" attempts at maintaining rigid balance. Nevertheless, there is virtually no spontaneity or satisfying personal exchange.

Group 8: Severely Dysfunctional Centripetal Families

These families have a tough, nearly impermeable outer boundary, allowing little independent or autonomous growth; time is an unwanted stranger. Hence, children are handicapped in their progression through normal sequences of emotional and personal development. The parental coalition as a functional unit is nonexistent; its appearance is maintained awkwardly through polite role playing, although the spouses' inability to relate to and define each other is obvious upon direct observation. In those families in which relationships do exist, the parental coalition is often supplanted by a significant parent-child coalition, often mother-son or father-daughter pairs. This family group is often associated with a schizophrenic member, history of many losses poorly mourned, occasional dramatic rule-breaking during an outburst of rage on the part of one member, dissociation, emotional blunting, and alcoholism.

Group 9: Severely Dysfunctional Centrifugal Families

These families, as locked into their stylistic pattern as the CP families are, show a loose and tenuous outer membrane; one sees frequent absence, desertion or running away, and even some lack of clarity as to who actually belongs in the "family." Members express hostility and deride each other for their faults; since the principal medium of exchange is action rather than words, there is frequent abuse, neglect, and assault. As in the CP family, however, relational and communicational clarity is never achieved. Since expressions of tenderness, vulnerability, and dependency are met with contempt and derision, no one addresses these needs or has them satisfied. People frequently hurt each other and are usually insensitive to others' pain. Since the necessary nurturing provisions are minimal in these families, character development is severely limited and is often antisocial in nature. Guilt is pervasive and therefore has no controlling effectiveness. Members feel bad but do not know how to behave in order to feel good.

CLINICAL APPLICATIONS

Grouping families in this way makes clinical family systems thinking easier, but there is a clinical reality that makes the task even simpler. After one learns the qualities of optimal, adequate, and midrange centrifugal families, these can be ignored for all practical purposes in assessment. This is due to the fact that they are rarely seen in treatment! Families whose functioning is currently optimal or adequate generally do not seek out mental health professionals, and midrange CF families do not trust words or authority enough voluntarily to come for treatment. Their offspring rarely come to the attention of mental health clinics or law enforcement institutions, since their misbehavior is not that severe. Hence, we can focus on methods of intervention for midrange CP, mixed, borderline CP and CF, and severely dysfunctional CP and CF families.

This identification of clinical groupings of families is useful in guiding intervention and is intuitively and clinically relevant to experienced therapists who have encountered a wide range of families. However, this classification may conflict with many of the concepts and "buzz-words" circulating in the mental health field. For example, the concept of "co-dependency" in the "alcoholic family" may pertain to centripetal families in the midrange or borderline levels of competence, but it carries little value in describing CF families with an alcoholic member(s). Likewise, incestuous relations may exist within CP or CF families but the pattern and level of aggressiveness related to sexual abuse vary dramatically. Families with "eating disordered" patients may be borderline centripetal (more often characteristic of anorexic-restrictive patients) or midrange mixed to centrifugal (more often characteristic of bulimic patients). Consequently, describing the family's functioning qualities, rather than its form or the diagnostic grouping of the identified patient paves the way for more effective intervention.

Before focusing on intervention we need to cover several other elements related to assessment of families. Chapter 4 will deal with several different types of family assessment devices, including observation and self-report questionnaires, and how they relate to each other. Chapter 5 deals with issues in assessment, including comparability of this and other models, timing of assessment, and inclusion/exclusion of the therapist in the systemic evaluation.

4 "INSIDER" VIEWS OF THE FAMILY

The American drive for quick and efficient means of cooking, telephoning, computing, and dieting has also been felt in the mental health fields. When Binet's concepts of intellectual assessment were imported from France in the early 1900s, they were quickly translated and transformed from observational, individual performance-based measures to booklet/questionnaire formats. These were "quick and easy" assessments, not requiring one-to-one time with an assessor, and could be mass-administered (in fact, these "IQ" tests became the primary means of determining personnel and officer-candidate assignments of draftees in World War I). In addition to changing the format of testing, the use of these self-report scales also requires a shift in the philosophy of assessment: from the perspective of the expert as observer to that of the individual as respondent; from the domain of the subjective and interpretable to the "objective" questionnaire; from the individualized assessment view of a client to scoring against sampling norms.

With the development of objective personality tests, led by the MMPI in the 1940s, researchers demonstrated that there was some degree of consistency in individual symptomatology across assessment methods (for the individual) and that there was reasonable diagnostic validity for the MMPI and related instruments (although it was, and is, easier to recognize pathology than health).

Machine and computing technology, coupled with mechanistic thinking of some behaviorists, introduced the concept of self-assessment and self-teaching by computers or machine, thereby eliminating *completely* the role of the other human being in the assessment or learning process.

Hence, self-report assessment usually involves an individual's responding to a set of standardized questions, with a delimited range of answers (yes or no; Likert scale 1–9, etc.). These are scored in a patterned way, producing the individual's scores, which are referenced against a set of norms. Sadly, though, there is no feeling, no interpersonal contact, no sense of how individuals relate. The content becomes the meat of the self-report assessment, while process/relational themes are often unattainable.

Nevertheless, self-report assessment of the individual, dealing with that person's thoughts, feelings, perceptions, and self-view, has shown reasonable success in the area of personality assessment. Typically, self-report instruments are less successful in measuring physiological (anxiety, fear) or behavioral responses ("altruism" and actual prosocial behavior).

When the focus of the assessment is the *family*, that unique *collection* of individuals, there is a further strain on the self-report method. Not only are we asking a member of the group to rate the group itself, but we are also asking content questions in an attempt to access important relational themes, not all of which may be shared consensually by all family members.

Self-report ratings of family functioning—by a single subject or by all members of a family—assume that systems concepts can be measured from within the family, using structured responses from individuals. Essentially, an "insider" views the style, behaviors, and feelings from his/her individual perspective,[110] much as an individual patient is asked to report his own symptomatology on a self-report personality scale.

Obviously, self-report scales, tapping individual family members' ratings, rely heavily on individual perspective and subjective appraisal of a number of emotional, communicational, and structural aspects of family life. It may be very difficult to measure certain family constructs from within the family. Specifically, we have discovered that family "style" is a difficult construct for family "inside" raters to assess. The problem is not unlike the proverbial forest and trees: a rater within the forest can offer certain perspectives on that plot that an observer flying over could not gain; likewise, the overhead observer can gain perspectives on the scope and size of the forest that the "insider" may not have. From this difference in rating perspective, Olson[110] asserts that "we can assume to find greater congruence across theoretical models if they use a similar methodology, i.e., self-report methods or behavioral tasks. Conversely, we can assume little congruence across models using different methodological approaches." While Olson's assertion came in response to studies finding little convergence between the Circumplex Model and other assessment models, it is generally accepted that opinions and beliefs expressed through self-report are not paralleled by observed behavior.[83]

Sigafoos and Reiss[130] have suggested a reframing of this issue, proposing that the critical dimension is a "system level" one rather than an "inside-outside" one. From a systems perspective, the family member responding to a questionnaire is reacting to the constraints of the particular questionnaire items, cards, games, or oral questions that are set by outsiders—the researchers or clinicians—rather than the family members. The difference between self-report (investigator + individual context) and family card-sort or family interaction or discussion (investigator + family group context), then, can be seen as one of system levels and reactivity to context, rather than one of insider versus outsider perspective. In fact, when a single family member is asked to rate his/her family system, forming an investigator + individual family member system, that person becomes a functional "outsider" for that purpose.

A related issue involves the genesis of the particular stimuli that researchers present to family members. The construction of tasks or questions based on observations and clinical work with families[18] may be subtly or grossly different from materials generated from nonclinical theory. The material presented to families must approximate family realities if researchers are to find commonalities between observations and self-reported family ratings. Hence, higher correlations between insider and outsider ratings may provide an operational definition of convergent validity and clinical utility of family measures.

With all these constraints in mind, we have developed a self-report scale based on the critical dimensions of competence and style presented in Chapters 2 and 3. The Self-Report Family Inventory (SFI) is a 36-item questionnaire which (like other self-report scales) can be used as a reasonable screening device to identify potential dysfunction; it is less accurate as a measure to identify equivocally healthy or competent family functioning.

The reasons for developing a clinically and empirically useful self-report are several. First, since the vast majority of research studies of family functioning and family therapy use self-report methodology, contributing a useful self-report measure of competence and style as conceptualized in the Beavers Model is one way to join in more empirical dialogue among researchers. Second, the use of a questionnaire format in assessing families represents a move toward increased efficiency in collecting information about families, since observational assessment requires videotape equipment, time, and teams of trained raters. Third, the self-report device allows us to examine patterns of relationships between insiders and outsiders and to see how individuals in different family groupings agree or diverge in their family assessments. Finally, and perhaps most importantly, we can listen to what family members say and report about their perceived qualities of competence, as they attempt to join us as collaborators in the investigation.

Note that the development of the SFI *followed* careful observational study of healthy and dysfunctional families, rather than preceding or

substituting for such observation. Hence, the self-report measure is analogous to a "reader's digest" version of a great novel, attempting to condense rich observational material into understandable lay statements
about feelings, relationships, and people. It is our view that it is easier
and perhaps more valid to condense the plot from the full novel than to
attempt to create the rich interpersonal material from the condensed
version. Hence, models that have been built upon self-report assessments solely, or initially, may be subject to more "sketching in" than
those, like ours and Epstein et al.'s McMaster Model,[42] which start with
the rich clinical material.

In a sense, an individual "sketches in" his or her own family novel as
he/she responds to self-report items, regardless of the model. An important part of our scale development and of our ongoing research in evaluating different instruments involves talking to and watching respondents
who are reading and completing these questionnaires. For instance, one
of us (RBH) was administering several family scales to an undergraduate
class, asking students to paraphrase what they felt or interpreted from
each question, when he noticed a female student who was laughing
heartily while taking the SFI. She reported that many of the items trig-
gered memories of funny or happy occasions as she sat in that classroom
of more than 100 students, 1500 miles away from home. Her "sketches"
in response to these items were quite different from those of many others
in that large, impersonal setting.

We have found that individuals' perceptions of the family vary across
levels of family competence, across sexes, across generational boundaries, and across individuals in the same family. We have published several articles dealing with these individual perceptions of the system[21,72,73]
and are in the process of completing and analyzing several other sets of
data. Our window to the individual's view of family is chiefly our own
Self-Report Family Inventory (SFI), although we routinely use self-report
measures from other models of family assessment, including Epstein et
al.'s Family Assessment Device (FAD: McMaster Model), Moos and
Moos' Family Environment Scale (FES), Olson et al.'s FACES II and
FACES III (Circumplex Model), and Bloom's Family Functioning Scale[27] a
cross-model scale.

THE SELF-REPORT FAMILY INVENTORY

Our self-report questionnaire (Appendix C; scoring profile in Appendix D) is a 36-item rating scale designed to tap individuals' perceptions of
competence and style, as described in the observational scales in Chapters 2 and 3. (Table 5 in Appendix C provides test-retest reliability data

for the SFI.) Through serial analyses with observational and other self-report scales and comparisons of respondents from clinical and nonclinical families, we have developed confidence in knowing what this scale can and cannot do in terms of assessing families.

First, factor analyses of the SFI tell us that the scale measures some consistent themes of family life across many different samples. These subscales are derived using the scoring key and profile provided in Appendix D. These factors are:

1. *Health/Competence* (19 items), the largest and principal scale, corresponds with the global competence ratings from the observational scales. The themes addressed in this scale are those of happiness, optimism, problem-solving and negotiation skills, family love, strength of parental (or adult) coalitions without supplanting parent-child coalitions, autonomy/individuality emphasis, and minimal blaming/increased responsibility patterns.
2. *Conflict* (12 items) is related to competence, in that "healthy" scores indicate low levels of overt unresolved conflict, fighting, blaming, and arguing, with higher levels of negotiation and acceptance of personal responsibility in solving conflict situations.
3. *Cohesion* (5 items) is also related to competence and includes items originally designed to measure self-ratings of family style (centripetal-centrifugal). The items on this scale involve satisfaction and happiness through togetherness and emphasis on family closeness. (We have found relatively little correspondence between this scale and observationally rated style, emphasizing our finding that family raters view "closeness" in self-report scales as a positive, healthy, more-is-better characteristic. Hence, we are in the process of pilot-testing a separate "family style" self-report scale [Appendix E] which creates a forced-choice bipolar rating of perceived elements of family style [parental overcontrol, dependency, overt anger, etc.].)
4. *Leadership* (3 items) involves ratings of strong and consistent patterns of adult leadership in the family (whether shared or single); this scale also corresponds well with overall competence, in that healthier families show higher leadership scores.
5. *Emotional Expressiveness* (5 items) is also related to overall family competence ratings and involves perceptions of feelings of closeness, physical and verbal expressions of positive feelings, and the ease with which warmth and caring are expressed by family members.

As we mentioned, it appears that the SFI is a reasonable *screening* device to assess a family member's view of overall family competence. In fact, our research has shown a fairly high degree of consistency in the ability of the competence scale of the SFI to discriminate clinical from nonclinical families (R = .62). We have also found promising results in studying SFI ratings by family members accompanying patients into a public psychiatric emergency room. Forty-six consecutive cases entering the public psychiatric emergency room accompanied by family members were diagnosed independently by house staff while the accompanying family member completed the SFI. When the identified patients were grouped by diagnosis, and their corresponding SFI competence and cohesion scores plotted on the diagram of the Beavers model, there was a good fit for schizophrenic, depressed, borderline, and substance-abusing patients. This pilot study suggested that self-reported family competence levels corresponded well with hypothesized patient/family groupings from the Beavers Systems Model (Figure 2).

Second, it appears that neither the SFI nor any of the self-report scales we have incorporated in our studies measures family style particularly well. This has led us to search for reasons why.

One potential explanation lies in a "levels of perception" issue, in that interactional bonding patterns, locus of emotional satisfaction (within or outside), and different developmental patterns of bonding/expelling forces are difficult to see from the vantage point of the "insider" rater. This is evident in a couple one of us (RBH) saw, in which the husband was having an affair, the wife was alternately depressed and hostile, and profound distance was evident in their interaction. In an attempt to have them see their pattern (the husband's agenda was to have his wife seduce him back into the relationship; hers was to keep a safe distance until he decided which way to go), we played for them a videotape of one of their failed and distant attempts to communicate feelings. Lacking a higher, more empathic standard by which to compare their current interaction, both partners acknowledged that this was fairly "normal" and "typical."

An alternative or additional explanation of the scales' failure to measure style stems from the terms used in self-report measures to address aspects of cohesion, centripetal vs. centrifugal forces, enmeshment vs. disengagement, and the like. Since these terms are incomprehensible to the general public, we use simple terms such as "closeness," "independence," "going one's own way," "it's okay to fight and yell." In asking people what they are thinking and feeling as they encounter such items, we find that what family members are perceiving may not be the same as what the scale developers hoped to access. For the vast majority of our respondents, "closeness" implies a unidimensionally "good" quality—

Figure 2

PILOT STUDY (Π= 46) FROM GENERAL PSYCHIATRIC EMERGENCY ROOM. PLOTTED POINTS REPRESENT MEAN HEALTH AND STYLE/COHESION SCORES FROM PATIENT FAMILY MEMBERS' SELF-RATINGS ON THE SFI.

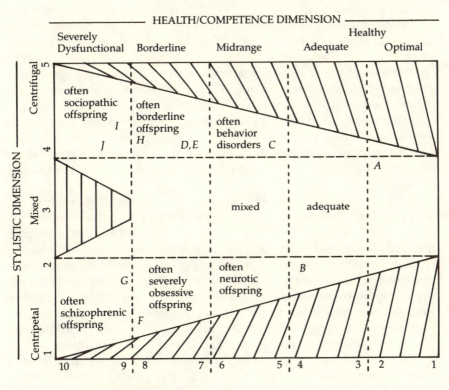

A = Atypical Anxiety Disorder (n = 1)
B = Organic Disability (n = 1)
C = Adjustment Disorder (n = 3)
D = Substance Abuse (n = 7)
E = Bipolar Manic (n = 8)
F = Unipolar Depression (n = 6)
G = Schizophrenia (n = 10)
H = Borderline Personality Disorder (n = 4)
I = Alcoholism (n = 5)
J = Atypical Psychosis (n = 1)

the more the better. In fact, cohesion ratings on most of the scales we have studied (SFI, FES, FACES) correlate very highly with family idealization,[72] involving a sense of "prizing" one's family. "Independence" is viewed as positive by some raters (adolescents, primarily) and as potentially negative by others (some parents, some younger children). "Coming out and saying what's on one's mind" is also viewed by most raters as related to competence; some raters view such behavior as expected and good, while others view such directness as threatening or conflict-producing.

With this in mind, it is not surprising that we find very strong and positive correlations between our SFI Competence scale and some of the different scales labeled "cohesion" (FACES II, FACES III, FES, Bloom). Correlations between the SFI and these other scales are provided in Tables 6, 7, 8, and 9 in Appendix C. Warmth, closeness, and enjoying time together are perceived as healthy family qualities; however, ratings on these may tell us little about relational and affective style of family behavior.

Third, we have considerable evidence that insiders (self-report) and outsiders (observer-raters) do share similar views of family competence, in contrast to Olson's[110] statements that comparability across levels is minimal. This is especially so in less competent and clinical families.

We have found significant and high correlations between related concepts of health and style in a clinical sample (n=44 families); in fact, these families showed significantly higher inside-outside correlations than did nonclinical families. Specifically, the correlation between our observational competence scale and SFI Health for clinical families was +.77; for nonclinical families (n=62), it was +.38. Relationships between CP/CF style and SFI cohesion were +.61 for clinical families and +.35 for nonclincal families. Table 10 in Appendix C presents these insider-outsider correlations. Further analyses indicated that there was less cross-member within-family variance in the clinical families, suggesting greater consensual insider views in the less healthy families.[75]

However, comparisons of the self-report and observational measures of the Circumplex Model[112,113] suggest only low to moderate correlations between these instruments. In the Friedman et al.[55] study, which assessed families of adolescent drug abusers, clinical ratings and family self-report differed on both cohesion and adaptability scales. Clinicians rated these families as chaotic and enmeshed, while the families rated themselves as rigid and disengaged. The highest correlations obtained were for fathers and clinicians on adaptability ($r=.40$) and for adolescents and clinicians on cohesion ($r=.31$). One potential explanation for the discrepancy between observers and family members, other than that of perspective, is a problem with the theory behind the scales. In the Circumplex Model, rigidity and chaos are polar opposites, while in the Beavers Model these characteristics are proximal on a systems organization level; rigid control is the next higher step above chaos in the developmental progression of structure. It is possible that both family members and observers were seeing something fairly close in organization, instead of the polar opposites interpreted through the Circumplex Model.

These findings suggest the usefulness of the SFI as a rough screening device for assessing family competence and identifying families in trouble. In general, less competent SFI scores ($X \geq 3$, raw score 57 or above) can be viewed as suggestive of a less competent family, especially if that view is shared across individual raters. "Healthy" scores are less meaningful for diagnostic purposes but potentially useful in examining the *pattern* of self-ratings *within* the family.

The patterning or variability of several members' self-ratings within a family has been the subject of some of our more recent work, which addresses the issue of what to do with a set of family ratings. Some researchers average the scores[85]; some analyze different members' scores separately by family role (mothers, fathers, adolescents, etc.). Our research treats each respondent as "nested" within the family, neither independent nor totally dependent (as people or variables!).

In one large sample of nonclinical families, we found lower variability and higher pairwise correlations in families observed and rated as *more* competent; conversely, we found higher variability and *lower* pairwise correlation in less competent (nonclinical) families. The better functioning families show slightly less variability than other families, but in fairly predictable patterns: Mother and father tend to rate the family as most competent and in the healthier direction on the SFI subscales. Adolescents typically take a dimmer view of the family's competence; their scores are significantly different from the parents' on most or all of the scales. These patterns are also evident on other self-report scales that we have studied. Younger children (down to about nine or ten years of age, which is about the youngest possible age for independent responding) tend to rate the family intermediately, choosing ratings between their siblings' and their parents' perspectives.

We have also looked at the response patterns of male and female offspring in nonclinical families, in terms of consistent similarities and differences in family perspectives. Across samples, we find no differences in overall competence ratings between males and females; however, we do find important pattern differences on subscales of leadership, cohesion, and emotional expressiveness. Males rate leadership qualities as having higher association with competence, while females rate the cohesive, warm, positive emotional qualities as more highly associated with competence.[72] One has only to saunter around an athletic field, where boys' teams and girls' teams are playing whatever sport, to recognize that leadership and performance carry more weight on the boys' field and emotional expression (including warmth, tears, or touching) more valence on the girls' field. One of us (RBH), who has been a soccer, basketball, and softball coach for both daughters' teams for a number of years, has been impressed by differences in "coach behavior" related to the tone, felt and expressed level of competitiveness, and the "foghorn factor"—vocal decibel level. One of our team's competitors had a coach who demonstrated all of the qualities that a high school boys' baseball coach should show, but he was a mismatch for a third-grade girls' softball team. "Poor John," said his wife, "he should have had boys."

In contrast to the healthier, nonclinical families, where differences and varying perspectives are typical, particularly in the middle range of competence, the less competent *clinical* families show more stereotyping in their family ratings. There are fewer differences between parents and offspring, higher pairwise correlations among family members' ratings, and closer correspondence with observational ratings. Often, it is the adolescent rater's view of family that is closest to that of our clinical raters in these less competent families, while in midrange and adequate families it is more frequently one of the parents whose view most closely tracks the outside raters' view. These differences in perspective allow for some speculation and preliminary interpretation.

For a family member to gain a view of the family that corresponds well with the views of outside raters, he or she must be able to obtain a vantage point based on some external frame of reference. In our studies of families with handicapped children,[9,21,76] it was the breadwinner (most often father, and in some families a working mother) who had the highest shared view of family with our observers. In nonclinical families, the pattern is less clear: In some cases mother, in some cases father, and in some cases offspring share the strongest association with raters. In more disturbed families, it is often an adolescent (the identified patient or sibling) who shares the view of the family held by the outside raters. The adolescent, by developing symptoms, acting out against a rigid system, or defying the parents, steps outside the chaotic or rigid structure. Even rats sense when a ship is not seaworthy, knowing perhaps better than the captain that something is wrong.

Consequently, the overall level of competence (gained either by observational rating or by averaging all family members' competence scale scores), the pattern of individual ratings within the family, and the degree of variability within the family are all important considerations in using the self-report instrument in screening families. For example, an adolescent rater's perspective can tell us relatively little in and of itself; the rater may be a typical adolescent (scoring the family lower) from an adequate or midrange family, or a "clear" perceiver of family dysfunction in a borderline family. Clearly, we need several people's perspectives to examine the pattern and profile of family competence, cohesion, and an empirically-derived "style" factor from the SFI.

The necessity of examining the patterns of scores within the family is demonstrated graphically in Figure 3. If we had only the SFI ratings from the two adolescent sons (14-year-old in Family A and the 16-year-old in Family B), we might conclude that these boys came from families of quite similar competence levels. However, the pattern of scores from the different members and the overall "grand mean" of these competence ratings are much more useful in terms of screening for family dysfunction. The patterns depicted in Figure 3 are representative of family ratings at

Figure 3

EXAMPLE OF PATTERN DIFFERENCES IN SELF-REPORT

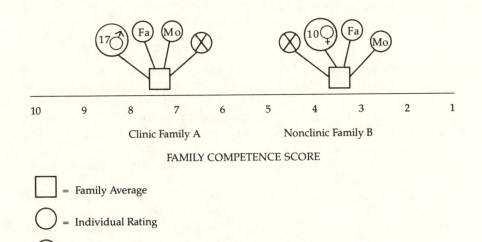

Clinic Family A   Nonclinic Family B

FAMILY COMPETENCE SCORE

◻ = Family Average

○ = Individual Rating

⊗ = Adolescent Ratings being Compared

these different levels of competence. When all of the SFI subscales are used, a profile of perceived family strengths and weaknesses can evolve for each member, assisting the therapist in assessing perceived needs and family strengths.

SELF-REPORT OF FAMILIES: CONCLUSIONS

Clinicians and researchers can gain valuable information regarding perceived qualities of family life from members of the families themselves. The self-report method is generally reliable, cheap, quick, and relatively unobtrusive (in contrast with observational measures).

In the domain of personality assessment, the MMPI provides a high degree of clinical and empirical utility and has assumed the role of a "gold standard" in measuring personality. In family assessment there is currently no single "gold standard"; there is too much uncertainty about whether a self-report questionnaire can measure system functioning. There are self-report scales that have been used for face-valid reasons (they appear to measure what they claim to measure); among the more popular, Olson's FACES, FACES II and FACES III provide concise and theoretically based means of obtaining self-report family information. There are also a handful of self-report scales derived from clinical observations and clinical studies of families, most notably the Family Assessment Device (FAD) of the McMaster Model of Family Functioning[42] and our Self-Report Family Inventory.

Still, a self-report is one member's view of the system; it may be that a self-report format that attempts to measure some collective view of the family will generate a more systemic product. This collective insiders' view may be best measured by some group interaction task resulting in a product that is minimally influenced by the observer or researcher, such as family games (SIMFAM[143]), or family Rorschach procedures.[99] We are investigating the relationship between family-produced drawings and observational ratings of family competence; preliminary findings suggest moderate correlations between family health and affective and structural elements of family drawings.

However, the most important issue regarding the commonality of insiders' and outsiders' views has to do with the nature of the theory and scales. Studies using inside and outside ratings on conceptually and clinically valid measurement scales (FAD, SFI, Paradigm Model, etc.) show higher degrees of relationships than do studies using less clinically valid scales. Conversely, it appears that measurement scales derived from theory but not based in clinically relevant data correlate poorly across rating levels. Kuhn[93] proposes that scientific explanation is a give-and-take process by which we construct models of reality while interpreting reality by those paradigms. When the latter becomes the predominant mode, the balance is tipped toward skewing the difference between observing and knowing and increasing the difference (in this specific case) between insider and outsider perspectives. When clinical material is emphasized in theory and empirical work, the balance is tipped toward more consensus across levels.

Given these constraints, a few cautionary guidelines regarding the use of self-report scales for research or clinical planning are in order:

1. It is advisable to use more than a self-report scale in assessing a family, whether for research or clinical purposes. If the unit of interest is overall/total family competence, the self-report combined with observational measurement provides a larger system perspective.
2. Unless you are interested just in how one particular member of a family views his/her family (mothers, fathers, anorexic daughters, etc.), more than one member of the family must be assessed via self-report. The pattern and overall averages of the scores are as meaningful as individual scores themselves. It is hard to grasp the fullness of a symphony by studying only the percussionist's sheet music.
3. Different self-report scales have different levels of clinical relevance and statistical properties. The McMaster Model and the Beavers Systems Model, both with relatively high inside-outside correlations, hew closer to clinical realities and appear to have greater clinical value than models, such as Olson's, that show lower inside-outside correlations.
4. Self-report scales are also subject to bias, faking, and distortions from the respondent. While many of the individual personality scales have "validity" scales to detect such faking, none of the family scales has such response checks. Our studies using a social desirability scale[37] in conjunction with family self-report scales indicates more tendency to "fake good" in midrange or better-functioning families and among those more centripetal (CP) in style.

The self-report procedure offers great convenience and a reasonable degree of clinical utility, depending upon who (and how many) answer(s) what (the choice of the scale), when (before, during, after therapy), and under what conditions (hospitalization, research study).

5 ISSUES FOR CLINICIANS IN USING FAMILY ASSESSMENT INSTRUMENTS

As a systems approach to illness and health becomes increasingly accepted and utilized, and the practice of psychotherapy involves more and more family-systems-oriented therapists, there is an increasing need for standards of assessment and terms describing family functioning. As we have already stated, there is currently no "gold standard" in the field that is widely used, theoretically sound, and representative of pan-theoretical views of family functioning.

In the following pages we address some of the issues facing the clinician with regard to using some types of assessment procedures in planning for therapy, determining effectiveness, conducting research, and training others.

CHOOSING AN ASSESSMENT TOOL OR PROCEDURE

The type of assessment device or procedure you choose will depend on the primary needs to be served. In the family clinic or practitioner's office, clinical utility and case planning are of paramount importance. For a research thesis in psychology, efficiency and numerical properties (reliability and validity) are often most important. We contend that both settings benefit from both sets of requirements. For the clinician, an instrument that is useful in case planning must also be reliable—that is, consistent in measurement—and valid—that is, measuring what it is supposed to measure. These same qualities are necessary for meaningful research. The scales of the Beavers Model offer these qualities, as well as providing clear guidelines for the therapist in terms of intervention strategies and style based on the assessment results.

Utility

As we have indicated, there is no sense going through a family assessment exercise if little useful information can be gained on how to intervene with the family.

Akin to the experienced organizational consultant, who recognizes that he has to assess the structure and function of the company he is entering in order to decide how to proceed effectively, the family therapist must make decisions regarding initial style and strategy. We are (it is hoped) past the belief that the therapist is an unvarying dispenser of techniques and paradoxes; different patients—and families—require and respond to different levels of power differential, disclosing, talking vs. behaving, activity level, pace, and general style of the therapist. Those family therapists who see themselves doing the same thing with all families are either largely unsuccessful or poor perceivers of systems-therapist interaction. Conversely, those therapists who are conscious of altering stimulus conditions, pace, type of intervention(s), level of joining vs. distancing, etc., are usually more successful with a wide variety of family types.

The clinical/theoretical model comprising the Beavers Model identifies nine useful family groupings, based on level of competence and predominant style (see Chapters 2, 3). The identification of a family as sharing characteristics common to one *clinical* grouping offers useful information on the family strengths and weaknesses, the needs of the family (and the therapy), and the tasks and relational requirements of the therapist. Other major assessment devices are less useful in guiding therapeutic intervention.

Ease of Administration

Our field has become enamored with "quick and easy" measurement, compared to microwave gourmet meals and dial-a-prayers. One of us (RBH) was asked recently to participate in an adult education panel at our church, dealing with the not-too-simple topic of the healthy family. The panel chair, a bright, energetic counselor, had found a 10-item questionnaire, self-rated, self-scored, and self-interpreted. For each of the items, one rated a "0" for "not like us" to "3" for "very much." At the bottom, your score total was magically interpreted for you: 26–30: "You have a healthy family"; 21–25: "Your family has some strengths, and some areas for improvement," etc. "But-but-but, said the academic/

empiricist in me, "this deals with *form*, not *functioning*; it is too simple; it neglects process; it is misleading; it. . . . "

"Oh, come on, it's just a fun exercise," she counsels warmly, and my scientist persona retreats. But the message is meant seriously: Short, easy questionnaires or scales, often based on someone's ideas about family *traits*,[38] do not capture functional qualities of family life. Just as a short-form, self-administered "IQ" test has limited utility in determining one's strengths and weaknesses or in planning one's academic future, a short and easy Rate Your Family questionnaire provides limited information on family functioning.

It should be noted that shortness/length is not necessarily the most important dimension of utility, although shorter instruments are usually easier and take less time to administer. For example, Olson's FACES III,[112] which has only 20 items, has been shown to be reliable and empirically valid in measuring dimensions of the Circumplex Model—adaptability and cohesion. Unfortunately, the model itself has difficulties in theoretical domains related to clinical utility (as detailed in Chapter 4).

In general, questionnaires are easy and cost-efficient to use and administer. The cost is measured in terms of utility, accuracy, and treatment planning ability of the instrument. Videotaped observational ratings (Beavers Interactional Scales) or detailed clinical assessment interviews (McMaster Clinical Interview) require time, trained raters, and recording equipment. If one is unable to obtain such observational ratings, the choice of a questionnaire obviously must be guided by utility, a high ability to separate clinical from nonclinical families, and a high correlation with external interactional assessment. The SFI does well in both these areas and is a valuable complement to the interactional scales.

TIMING OF ASSESSMENT:
ASSESSMENT GUIDES INTERVENTION

Most therapists want to perform their most detailed assessment of a family at the initial meeting, for the purposes of classification and treatment planning. As an initial procedure, observational (and questionnaire) assessment orients the family and the therapist/rater to the nature of the problem(s) and the needs of the family. At this juncture, it is important to point out the further advantages of observational assessment over self-report. First, it is often assumed[156] that a family's initial problem statement reflects one content area in which its members are currently "stuck" but not the complex interpersonal processes that underlie and predispose them to these (and other) difficulties. In this regard, self-report/questionnaire instruments access conscious content domains but not interactional qualities of the system. Second, the self-report is one individual's view of the family or the problem, while the family "problem" is most likely an interpersonal, interactional difficulty.

At our Southwest Family Institute in Dallas, all families are observed and videotaped for rating on the Beavers Interactional Scales, and members age 10 or older complete several self-report instruments (including the SFI). These initial assessments are used by therapists to guide their interventions (Section Two) and by the research team to study therapeutic efficacy, therapy outcome, and appropriate therapist/family "match" factors.

Historically, diagnosis and treatment have been separate and sequential processes in the mental health field, but in family work both must occur simultaneously and continuously. As the family evolves and changes, tactics, relational qualities (of therapist to family members), and therapist power differential will have to shift. Hence, the therapist must be able to assess changes in interactional qualities of the family on an ongoing basis. An initial observational rating sets the frame for continuous assessment of interactional qualities throughout treatment. If "assessment" is based on questionnaire data only, this ongoing assessment cannot occur.

We also require periodic self and systemic observations from therapists. In addition to their process notes, therapists complete a therapist self-rating following their third session with a family; this self-rating requires the therapist to rate the degree of: (a) disclosure of strategy; (b) degree of maintained power differential; and (c) degree of openness and personal joining; these qualities are theoretically important in working with CP families, which need disclosure, joining, and openness, or CF families, which need structuring and low levels of openness and disclosure of strategy. Therapists are also rated on the Family Therapist Rating Scale[117] and describe the general therapeutic orientation they are using with the family (e.g., structural, psychoeducational, family of origin).

At the final session, families (without therapist present, again) are videotaped as they discuss the question, "What would you still like to see changed in your family?" In addition, family members complete self-report measures, including an evaluation of their therapist and the treatment. In purely clinical settings, this final "assessment" is less important than the initial (formal) and ongoing (embedded in therapy) assessments; in our clinical research, such closing assessments provide operational and multilevel perspectives on change, therapy, and therapist-

family system. In addition, families are called six to twelve months following treatment for a brief follow-up assessment.

WHO RATES THE FAMILY?

Self-Report/Questionnaire Format

When family members encounter a questionnaire item such as "We
pay attention to each others' feelings," there may be widely discrepant
responses based on one's perspective. A 16-year-old son would conceiv-
ably rate such an item (or many items) quite differently from a parent or a
younger child. In fact, our studies of clinical and nonclinical families
indicate that parents tend to rate family competence, cohesion, emotional expressiveness, and conflict differently from adolescents, who, in
turn, are different in their perspective from their younger siblings. In
clinical families, there is actually slightly lower correspondence across
raters; better functioning and nonclinical groups of families show slightly less variability across raters, with parents rating the family as better
functioning than offspring.

Consequently, a family rating by a single "insider" rater does not
connote an "objective" assessment of the whole system. A parent's rating may reflect a "healthier" view of family than that shared by adolescent offspring; this does not mean that the parent is willfully distorting
in a "good" direction any more than the adolescent may be distorting in
a "bad" direction. Quite simply, different individuals have different vantage points. Knowing this, one must keep in mind the position of the eye
of the beholder in interpreting self-ratings of family.

Observers: Raters or Therapist?

If one is to gain an accurate assessment of family functioning as part of
treatment planning or for research purposes, on which observers should
one rely? Obviously, in an individual clinical setting, the observer/rater
and therapist are one and the same. In team therapy settings, live supervision, or training/research settings such as our Southwest Family Institute, there is room for two or more individuals to observe and rate family
interaction.

In this latter instance, who are the most reliable and accurate raters?
An interesting study by Michael Kolevzon and his associates[91] compared
observational ratings by therapists and by independent coders with family self-ratings before and at termination of family therapy. They used

earlier versions of the Beavers Competence Scale (then titled the Beavers-Timberlawn Family Evaluation Scales) for the observational ("outsider") ratings, and their own self-report version of competence scale items (not our SFI) for family members' ratings.

At the outset, therapists differed from the ratings of coders and family members, who showed higher rates of agreement. Therapists rated the family as less functional overall than did coders or family members at the outset, and as better functioning at the end of therapy when compared with the independent coders. There was also a greater tendency for insiders' (family members') self-ratings to agree at the end of therapy than before.

This study suggests that therapists' ratings are not necessarily objective measures of family functioning, supporting Gurman's[64] contention that those of us who treat families may see more problems at the outset and view our therapeutic encounter with the family as having greater positive impact than would a neutral observer.

Several important suggestions follow from these conclusions. First, the potential importance of a team approach or live supervision is underscored. Multiple viewpoints can foster increased perspective-checking in the clinical setting. For example, one of us (RBH) was supervising a student who was having significant difficulty with the husband in a couple he had in therapy; the man was described as powerful, tyrannical, and quite hostile. In viewing the videotape, what became clear was a recursive pattern of the wife's expression of hurt and anger at her husband's lack of caring, his flaring back at her, and the therapist's becoming afraid of this man's anger. When the therapist saw frustration accompanying the anger, he could abandon the label of "hostile and tyrannical" (recognizing that these were perceptions of his own father) and join the couple with less self-protective distancing and more appropriate exercise of power.

Second, it is important for the therapist to assess and recognize both competence and style levels in families, since both factors are important in tailoring one's approach to the family initially. Most traditional therapists and a good number of family therapists come from centripetal families of origin and may be uncomfortable with the direct expression of anger and behavioral defiance in centrifugal families. This degree of discomfort can add to the therapist's perception of deviance or dysfunction in the family. In the specific case of Kolevzon's study, the families were court-referred for adolescent offenders and probably included a large proportion of CF families (family style was not measured formally). If the result of discomfort is to increase one's power differential and structuring, this is appropriate for CF families initially but less so with CP families. (Note that an acting-out adolescent can emerge from a rigid CP structure, rebelling against the rigid tyranny of guilt or obsessionalism. Therefore, it is important to assess whether the sinner is part of a like pack [CF] or is a fallen saint [CP] as one begins work with the family.)

THE ROLE OF THE THERAPIST
FOLLOWING ASSESSMENT

The study of "therapist-offered conditions"—empathy, warmth, and genuineness—has provided important guidelines for the selection, training, and refinement of counselors and therapists for many years. In general, experience, expertise, and the above personal qualities have been associated with client improvements in individual therapy,[26] especially when the client is from the traditional YAVIS (young, attractive, verbal, intelligent, successful) category.

In family therapy, it is entirely possible that a warm, supportive, self-disclosing person will fail miserably with certain families that require more structuring, power differential, or even manipulation. Hence, several writers[5,117] have emphasized a multiplicity of skills and qualities important for the family therapist. In Alexander and Parsons'[5] model, structuring skills (directiveness, clarity, confidence) and relationship skills (warmth, nonblaming, humor, self-disclosure) are central themes of therapist behavior and effectiveness. The supposition is that therapists who show high levels on both dimensions are "superstars" who produce "rapid change in families and rarely have dropouts."

It is our view, based on the data and clinical observations, that good therapists are those with the capacity to use structuring and joining skills, but know when, with whom, and with what balance. It appears, for example, that CF and more disturbed families require structuring and power differential initially. Conversely, CP families look for warmth and relationship-building initially, with the establishment of structure and pragmatic rule-building following.

We have employed Piercy's Family Therapist Rating Scale[117] in our training and research work, and find the structuring and relationship dimensions to be highly reliable discriminators in terms of who does best with, and prefers, what types of families. While relationship skills are important across the board, our trainees with greater structuring skills prefer a wider variety of client types in their family therapy caseloads.

We also require our trainees to complete a fairly simple self-assessment at the third session with each family, addressing the degree of openness, the degree to which they disclose or share strategy with the family, and the degree of power differential they are attempting to maintain with the family. Not surprisingly, we see greater gains in CP families with more openness, more disclosure, and less power differential. The pattern is reversed for CF families.

SOME PRACTICAL GUIDELINES

We have studied families of different ethnic groups and social classes, families with different levels of "enlightenment" in terms of sex-role equality, and some with significant handicaps or other medical conditions. As is the case with the larger perspective, there is no single theme or thread that characterizes any of these groupings of families; there is as wide a range of competence as we find across the larger samples we have studied.

Ethnic Variations

In our studies of white, black, and Mexican-American families,[74] we have found that there are some patterned differences in observed family interaction patterns, but *no* overall differences in competence or style. Specifically, black families were rated as less direct in individual verbal expression of thoughts and feelings (in the observation room); they are also rated as less attentive to and solicitous of dependency needs in offspring. Black families showed a more truncated *range* of feelings in direct observation, and these were geared more toward a balance of positive and negative feelings stylistically.

Hispanic families were more comfortable fostering and attending to dependency needs of their offspring; they also tended to discourage intrafamilial aggressive and assertive behaviors (at least in the presence of outside observers). They described themselves as close-knit and scored as more centripetal overall than black or white families.

These differences are potentially useful for the therapist dealing with families of various ethnic backgrounds. Specifically, therapists working with black families may be frustrated in attempts to foster high levels of verbal expression in the therapy room or to acknowledge verbal overtures regarding dependency needs of their children. Blacks who appear mute in the therapy room may talk extensively with extended kin or trusted friends about personal issues; trust and familiarity are key concepts in fostering this expression.[81] However, our research indicates that lower levels of overt verbal behaviors exist in competent black families; the adage "if it's not broken, don't try to fix it" can well apply to these circumstances.

Similarly, in working with Mexican-American families, therapists must attend to subtle variations in the expressions of family competence. Since many of these families show a more centripetal style, including controlling of aggressive and angry feelings (especially in the presence of an "outsider"), expressing closeness and harmony, and encouraging dependency needs of offspring, therapists may be frustrated in attempts to join with such families emotionally. In addition, fostering clarity in potential conflict situations and encouraging family members to "break away" from the nucleus may be difficult and even counterproductive.

These data encourage the view that for families of all backgrounds subtle ethnic and social class differences exist. Imposing one's own ethnically influenced standards regarding clarity of expression, autonomy, egalitarianism, and even sex-role standards may limit therapeutic efficacy. Appreciation of a variety of manifestations of family competence and style is necessary for effective intervention, as opposed to relying on a single concept of family health and family therapy.

Social Class Differences

The chief differences noted in lower-class samples have been on the style dimension, with lower-class families showing a more centrifugal (CF) style overall, characterized by more leave-taking, overt parental conflicts, and some early emancipation of offspring. These tendencies are reflected in slightly (insignificantly) lower competence ratings in comparison to white middle- and upper-class groups. The stylistic difference, with lower classes showing more centrifugal qualities and upper classes more centripetal qualities (at midrange or lower levels of competence), helps account for the decreased likelihood of lower-class families entering and remaining in therapy, which, traditionally, has relied heavily on words, not actions and feelings. Hence, the challenges to the family therapy field are to develop approaches that cater to those families with centrifugal style, rather than accusing the lower classes of being incapable of benefiting from our heady forms of talk therapy. Innovative approaches can include activity-oriented problem-solving, competitive games, and composite picture-drawing, all coordinated by an active, directive therapist.

Gender Issues

We have emphasized the nature of the egalitarian adult relationships in competent family systems, meaning a balance in terms of sharing duties and responsibility and of showing respect, negotiation capabilities, mutual love, and shared agreements. When a couple negotiates its "typical" role allocation, this egalitarianism shows in the degree of mutuality in arriving at role allocation, respect for one another's world view, and a degree of flexibility in negotiating new roles. Less functional couples are unable to negotiate and often "stuck" in roles. They do not feel respected or appreciated and do not work well as a team. At lower levels, there are signs of overt competitiveness, undermining of power, and attempts at authoritarian control.

It is sometimes difficult for a therapist to be respectful of choices made by family members when those choices differ from the values of the therapist. In this way, therapists are in a similar situation as parents—wishing to pass on those beliefs that they consider valuable, even sacred, yet wanting also to assist people to grow, develop, and learn to make their own choices.

Healthy families are very much alike in functioning, very different in form. This is a natural result of individuals' in the group being rather more autonomous than the average—unconventional roles, interests, and patterns of handling chores and problems are more evident in the most competent families.

A traditional family, with woman as housewife/mother and man as breadwinner, may be quite effective or terribly maladaptive. Competence depends not on the role definition but on the negotiation that goes into the role definition, which allows the expression of choice and an atmosphere of flexibility. Conversely, a two-career couple with children can be extremely effective and nurturing or miserably dysfunctional. Again, the difference lies not in the roles chosen but in the process of negotiating, choosing, and renegotiating from time to time as family members' needs change.

One of us (WRB) has observed that the most conventional sex roles are most rigidly held or idealized by midrange family members. Variations are more common in the optimal and the dysfunctional groups.[10]

Families with Handicapped Children

Much of the literature describing families with handicapped, disabled, and retarded children points to parental reactions such as "chronic sorrow" and "perpetual grief" to characterize such families' adaptation to the birth of a handicapped member. The overall tone, we presume, is negative and pathological throughout the life cycle of the family. Unfortunately, this is another example of clinical tunnel vision, of relying on form rather than function. Our studies of families with retard-

ed and disabled children[9,76] indicate that there is a wide range of competence and style in these families, not unlike families without such offspring. We did find that the expression of a wide variety of feelings
(including sorrow and frustration) is characteristic of the *better* functioning families, while little or no expression of these or any feelings is
characteristic of *less* competent family systems.

With some of these pragmatic issues addressed, the role of assessment of a given family becomes a means of isolating functional strengths
and weaknesses that can guide intervention. The next chapter presents
five different families, using the observational competence and style
scales. Then we shall follow these families into the treatment setting,
where we address the appropriate tailoring of intervention to the family.

6 CLINICAL ASSESSMENT EXAMPLES

Mr. and Mrs. Faraway—Carl, age 44, and Brenda, 38—have been married to each other for nine years, each having been married previously and each bringing one child to this blended family. The most noticeable partnership, in terms of verbal and interactional exchange, lies between Brenda and Michelle, Carl's 15-year-old daughter from his previous marriage. On the flanks are two male offspring. To Brenda's side is Walker, her 14-year-old son, who smiles and nods with some regularity but offers little verbal material. Peter, the eight-year-old product of this marriage, sits to Carl's side, looking lonely and somewhat frightened.

This middle-class family has provided a stable physical home environment but has experienced Carl's walking away for days (sometimes) or weeks (only once). The referral was prompted by some acting-out behaviors in the adolescents; the most dramatic was the couple's discovery of Michelle's sexual activity with a male acquaintance. A major lack/need in this family appears to be closeness and intimacy.

Competence Scale

I. Structure
   A. Overt power: 2.5
      This family demonstrated some attempts to lead and structure the discussion; most of the directing was done by Brenda, in terms of directive questions to the boys and her husband. Michelle at times joined her stepmother in free exchange or acted as a conduit between parents.
   B. Parental coalitions: 2.5
      The parental coalition is rather weak, and there is some strength in the coalition Brenda and Michelle have forged. This relation-

ship, rather than being a complete supplanting of an adult-adult power differential, appears more like one of companionship and verbal efficiency. The males speak little in this family.

C. Closeness: 3

The mechanism of relating comfortably in this family is to maintain distance. While there is acknowledgment that members "wish they could be closer," there is a marked sense of personal isolation. Carl acknowledges that his mechanism for dealing with his own loneliness and pain is to distance himself even further from those around him.

(No "mind reading" invasions were noted.)

II. Mythology: 2

The Faraways are mostly congruent in describing themselves, especially in terms of inefficient leadership and couple coalition, emotional distance, and difficulty in problem-solving situations.

III. Goal-Directed Negotiation: 3.5

This family is quite poor at negotiating and reaching some sort of solution for problems. Nevertheless, family members are able to acknowledge that a problem exists and are generally able to identify areas of family behavior that require improvement. Most of this ability lies between mother and stepdaughter, with little participation from Carl and the boys.

IV. Autonomy

A. Clarity of expression: 3.5

When family members discuss issues on their own (without probing by the therapist), most feelings are vague and hidden; when feelings are followed up or challenged within the family, many are disowned. Anger is usually manifest as sadness, fear as isolation, and guilt as blaming. On occasion, the silent responses of Carl and Walker lead to a "guessing game" of "name that feeling."

B. Responsibility: 4

There is some "owning" of past and present behaviors among the parents evidenced in a discussion related to parental (particularly Carl's) frustration in trying to get "these kids to do their duties" at home. When confronted with past transgressions, ranging from the boys' not taking out the trash to Michelle's having a boy in bed, the children express little personal responsibility; they defend themselves with forgetfulness, assignment of responsibility to another person (a "not really" boyfriend), or blaming another family member.

C. Permeability: 3

For a group with some noticeable emotional distance, most members are actually quite open to the statements and feelings made by others. In essence, members are somewhat reluctant to express and own powerful feelings, but when such feelings are expressed, they are attended to and received.

V. Family Affect

A. Range of feelings: 3.5

There is some restriction on the range of feelings allowed expression in this family. Anger and disappointment are the most common themes; there is an apparent and unspoken fear regarding closeness and the expression of vulnerability, tenderness, and affiliative, loving feelings.

B. Mood and tone: 3.5

While Brenda and Michelle provide some "banter" bordering on the light and funny, the overall tone of the system is somewhat depressed. The "grand mean" of tone generated across the players is one of disengaged sadness.

C. Unresolvable conflict: 2.5

There are lingering and unresolved issues within the marital dyad, which, when raised, bring the discussion to a grinding halt; these overt themes are related to consistency of discipline and "turf" issues with the older children (yours vs. mine). When these themes arise, group functioning is impeded.

D. Empathy: 3.0

On those occasions when vulnerable or sad feelings are expressed overtly, they are usually received appropriately and with empathic acknowledgment. These "connections" (nods, handholding) are typically short-lived, but appropriate for the immediacy of the exchange.

VI. Global Health/Pathology: 6 Midrange.

Style Scale

I. Dependency Needs: 3

While there was some provision of physical contact with the youngest child, Peter (especially during overt conflict) had to take the initiative, reaching out and grabbing his father's hand. While the needs of the children are not ignored, they are expected to fend largely for themselves while their parents deal with their own pain.

II. Adult Conflict: 4

When Brenda and Carl disagree, their conflict is usually quite covert; nothing is resolved. Dealing with conflict by distancing is quite frequent.

III. Physical Spacing: 2

Some members of this family did touch each other. For several minutes, Peter held his father's hand, and the spouses were able to orient and touch.

IV. Social Presentation: 3

Family members did not appear overly concerned with presenting themselves to make a good impression; the chuckling and laughing of Michelle and her stepmother appear to be related more to tension relief than to social presentation. There were no corrective suggestions to have Walker sit up straight from his usual slouch or to instill taboos on any topics.

V. Verbal Expression of Closeness: 3

Closeness is an issue for this family; members do not deny closeness but are aware that they experience little closeness.

VI. Aggressive/Assertive Qualities: 3

There was little direct expression of hostility or overt anger in the family discussion. The tone of this family interaction gives the distinct impression that angry feelings and aggressive themes are not easy to express in this family.

VII. Positive/Negative Feelings: 2.5

Loneliness, anger, frustration, lack of closeness, sadness, and defiance were all discussed and expressed in the observed interaction. Expressions of happiness, love, and joy (positive feelings) were also observed but were more difficult to maintain.

VIII. Global Style: 2.5 Mixed style.

This family experiences some of the classic qualities of midrange mixed families: some isolation and distancing, some acting-out behaviors, and frustrations regarding closeness. Tenderness can be experienced at times, and feelings of disappointment and futility are often expressed directly and overtly.

Discussion

The assessment of this family leads us directly to treatment planning and hypothesis-building, as illustrated in Chapter 7 and detailed in Chapter 9. These clinical examples describe how ratings of family competence and style emerge from observation of an interactional sequence without the therapist present. The result is an identification of strengths and weaknesses in the individual family, and the categorization of the family into one of our clinically useful groupings, which follow from the assessment of competence and style. These groupings, as well as guidelines for intervention, will be presented in detail in Chapters 8, 9, 10, and 11.

THE PROMOM FAMILY

Mrs. Promom is an attractive, assertive, and competent businesswoman who was divorced two years ago from a driven, Type A businessman husband. She moved, with her two sons (now ages 10 and 8) to a different city; the ex-husband has very little to do with her or the boys. Mrs. Promom works in a high-pressure sales situation, which demands long days and emotional intensity. She has employed a maid/caretaker to stay with her sons before and after school, but complains that this woman is not "strict" enough, since many of the boys' duties are incomplete at her evening homecoming or there are lingering conflicts she must settle.

Mrs. Promom feels unappreciated and misunderstood by her sons, who are often antagonistic and attention-seeking (manipulations, feigned incompetence, argumentative encounters) with her at times when "they should know I'm tired and need my space." Acknowledging that such times are necessary and harder to find for single parents, we note that the desire for distance is not in itself problematic; rather, there is very little clarity regarding feelings, expectations, hopes, and wishes. These are replaced by manipulative games, sibling assault (mostly when mother is in the house), and desire for distance. Everyone attempts to gain what he/she wants (time, respect, attention, love) but ends up feeling shortchanged.

In observed interaction, the mother attempts to structure and elicit cooperation. The boys, obviously not used to such tame or boring behavior, either smile and look blank or respond noncompliantly. In this latter instance, Mrs. Promom persists as long as she can in trying to restate or re-ask, then (as she says) "loses it," launching into a tirade; some of this takes the tone of "I was never allowed to . . ." (she, in fact, comes from a fairly dysfunctional, abusive family of origin) or "one of these days, I'll . . ." (ranging from "just leave" to "start really disciplining you both"). There is ample blaming, little acknowledgment of pain, and a rather high degree of "mind-reading," intuiting and ascribing motives to any conflictual behavior.

Competence Scale

I. Structure
   A. Overt power: 1.5
      This family fluctuates between attempts at power-oriented control
      to more chaotic exchanges, with the flavor of the noncomply-
      challenge tirade pattern.
   B. Parental coalitions: 3
      Since this is a single-parent family, we measure this in terms of
      presence/absence of perceived parent-child symbiotic or patho-
      logical coalitions. This form of relationship was not observed in
      this family.
   C. Closeness: 3.0
      While the predominant mode is one of distancing and isolation
      (particularly mother/sons), there is some antagonistic closeness
      between the two sons. By and large, these family members at-
      tempt to maintain autonomy and "space" by keeping distant. On
      the related invasiveness dimension, several invasions were not-
      ed, particularly in the context of Mrs. Promom's interpreting the
      reasons behind certain of her sons' behaviors:

      > Mother: "Sure, you forgot. You just like to tick me off."
      > Son: "No, I really forgot."
      > Mother: "I know you too well. Don't forget that!"

II. Mythology: 2.0
   There is not much idealizing in this family; family myths are most
   congruent with observations regarding frustrations, blaming, and
   emotional distance.

III. Goal-Directed Negotiation: 4.5
   This trio is inefficient in negotiating differences or problem situations. The younger son takes on the role of the ("innocent") provoca-
   teur for the older to assault or disagree with Mrs. Promom's perspective. They appear to play with her until a point of frenzy, after which
   they comply agreeably, as if on cue. In actuality nothing is actually
   negotiated or changed.

IV. Autonomy
   A. Clarity of expression: 4.0
      While members of this family are often clear about *what* (or who)
      has angered or disappointed them, they are universally less clear
      of their *own* thoughts and feelings. In fact, there is relatively little
      evidence of *personal* levels of expression; instead, the relation-
      ships are almost role-defined: sons/mother-worker.

B. Responsibility: 4.5

No one in this family is clear in expressing or owning responsibility for actions or feelings. Instead, there is considerable blaming of sibling, parent, or child (or housekeeper, a person responsible for little but blamed for a great deal, from both sides).

C. Permeability: 4

There is a distant, judging, and put-down quality that tinges much of this family's interaction. Both Mrs. Promom and her sons are frequently unreceptive to each other's statements, particularly those which attempt to explain feelings that are at odds with the negative intentions to which they are attributed.

V. Family Affect

A. Range of feelings: 4

Much of the potential feeling domain in the family is shut down; the primary mode of expression is through disappointment, anger, and distancing. There is little room for spontaneity or tenderness.

B. Mood and tone: 3.5

The pervasive tone of this family is *tension*, which vacillates between anger and hostility at one extreme and a depressive tone at the other. When they are fighting, they are at least energized enough to show strong feelings; much of the time, they appear resigned to feeling blue.

C. Unresolvable conflict: 2

There is chronic and unresolved conflict, both in the nature of expectations and exchanges between mother and sons and in the tone of antagonism that permeates discussions of even neutral topics.

D. Empathy: 3.5

Much of this family's emotional interaction is marked by individuals' often futile attempts to be heard, attended to, and understood. There are occasions where some tenderness is expressed and received, but the predominant tone is one of anger and frustration, which is viewed more as an attack than as a signal to join one another.

VI. Global Health/Pathology: 7 Borderline.

This single-parent family lacks some of the internal supports and structure found in a more competent two-parent family. However, it should be noted that the single-parent status does not automatically connote a borderline or lower competence rating; many single-parent families are capable of functioning in adequate or midrange levels of competence. These family members have great difficulty with adaptation, structure, and attending to one another's emotional needs, issues that were reportedly present even when the Promoms were married.

Style Scale

I. Dependency Needs: 1
Virtually all attempts of the children (and the mother) to solicit attention, help, or nurturance are ignored or punished. The boys are left to their own devices much of the time, with the housekeeper providing physical and safety needs.

II. Adult Conflict: No rating
In the single-parent family there is no arena for the observation of how the adults handle conflicts. A rating would be possible in a single-parent family living with a grandparent (multigenerational family) or in some other context where two or more adults are consistently present.

III. Physical Spacing: 2
The distance between Mrs. Promom and her sons is great; they choose and maintain seats at opposite ends of the room. The two boys are closer, although seated at opposite ends of a couch; there is no physical touching (except for some play-punching between the boys); these family members appear more comfortable at a safe distance from one another.

IV. Social Presentation: 4
There is little concerted effort to "look good" to outsiders; behavioral controls attempted by mother are ineffective and appear atypical to family interaction. The sons appear more invested in giving mother a hard time than in presenting a picture of compliant or appropriate behavior.
   (No internal scapegoating was observed.)

V. Closeness: 4
There is little verbal emphasis on closeness in this family; members tend to say, "We could be close if . . . ," following with more blaming statements about the shortcomings of the others.

VI. Assertive/Aggressive Qualities: 4
The principal token of exchange in this family is the verbal assault; there does not appear to be any likelihood or history of physical aggression (at least in this triad).

VII. Positive/Negative Feelings: 5
The balance and relative ease of expression of feelings are strongly

skewed to the "negative" side, including anger, blaming, frustration, and some hopelessness. Warm, tender, and supportive feelings are potentially desired but absent from the family repertoire.

VIII. Global Style: 4.5 Borderline centrifugal.

This family has a strong outer-focused orientation where gratification of emotional needs is perceived as existing outside the family—in the workplace, in peers' eyes, in school social activities. The greatest threats to one's esteem are viewed as within the family; there are also great burdens and upsets within the family, which makes going "outside" more attractive.

Discussion

The Promoms are classified as a "borderline centrifugal" family, in which the expression of anger is open and children learn to manipulate an unstable but oscillating system of control. The children are at risk for developing some behavior/acting-out problems or unstable patterns of relating to others (manipulations, assaultiveness, dependency conflicts). There is a need to restrain and structure interaction through the therapist's maintaining some power differential. Conflict must be reframed as representing nurturing needs and bad behaviors as needy. Communication will progress from accusing to validating, distancing to joining. Also, for the CF family, activity becomes as important as speaking the words; cooperative games and tasks, as well as "fun" activities, are important therapeutic vehicles.

THE ADAMS FAMILY

This family consisted of Phillip, 52, Agnes, 50, married for 28 years, and John, 25 and Sherry, 20. Sherry was the identified patient, with a five-year history of anorexia nervosa; she restricted her food intake and severely abused laxatives on a regular basis. Outpatient treatment had been unsuccessful and Sherry currently had low plasma potassium, abnormal blood ph, weighing 86 pounds on a 5'4" frame.

The family was interviewed and assessed at hospital admission. Phillip was a highly aggressive industrial psychologist who controlled the family discussion by sermonizing energetically and interrupting frequently; his control over family *behavior* was considerably less than his dominance of the discussion. This man was obviously used to being in charge. He had connections with the executive officers of the company that controlled the family health insurance, successfully arranging full coverage for Sherry's hospitalization even though she was not eligible as a dependent college student. He also had professional connections with the hospital chain that owned the unit in which Sherry was residing and threatened repeatedly to use his influence in various efforts to control her treatment regimen.

Agnes, well-dressed and moderately overweight, carried an air of sullen and subdued anger. Matronly and proper in her demeanor, Agnes spoke sparingly and carefully, taking special precaution not to take issue *directly* with her husband. Her exchanges with Phillip were walking-on-eggshells careful, while her interactions with her children alternated between accusing and inviting.

John was still living at home after graduating from college three years previously. He was working and was viewed by his parents as a model son. This attribution excused his continuing to remain at home and frequent unexplained absences. John presented as smooth, docile, and agreeable, nodding most emphatically whenever his father asserted this or that.

Sherry was disheveled in appearance and loose in verbal interaction, becoming almost incoherent at times. She would alternately ramble on about the idiocy of her going to the hospital and immerse herself in silence, casting her head down or putting her hands over her ears like a four-year-old. She had many of the characteristics of a typical anorectic patient: she was depressed, angry (and vacillated between the two), lacking in a sense of autonomy, fearful of sexuality and closeness, and devoid of peer affiliations. She was, however, the most effective member of the family in dealing with Phillip's monologues by either shutting down or rambling.

Competence Scale

I. Structure
   A. Overt power: 2.0
      There is little doubt that there is a sense of absolute authoritarian control by Phillip, and the others have chosen to respond with varying degrees of distancing (withdrawing, disappearing and alternately complying and regressing). The control is tenuous and not very effective but strongly felt by all members.
   B. Parental coalitions: 2.5
      There appears to be a surface-level parental coalition, in that there is a tacit agreement not to explode into overt disagreement or hostility. However, there is little room for negotiation. There is

also some evidence of relatively weak parent-child coalitions that follow gender lines: Phillip reports admiration for John, and Agnes and Sherry appear to share some common ground in the "victim subsystem."

C. Closeness: 2.0

With the exception of Sherry, the members of this family are quite predictable in their verbal and emotional reactions; their roles are quite patterned. Still, there is a vague quality to the interactions, vacillating between the isolation felt in midrange families and the amorphous blurring in the most dysfunctional families. Closeness is neither solicited directly nor provided.

Phillip and his daughter trade invasions: his regarding her stubbornness and inability to comprehend reason; hers regarding her father's wanting to control her life continually.

II. Mythology: 3

The Adams family members are able to recognize and describe their frustrations, particularly regarding the sense of futility in working with Sherry's disorder. However, they present themselves (particularly from the perspectives of Phillip and John) as more efficient and competent than they appear in the "management" of people in the family.

III. Goal-Directed Negotiation: 4

Accompanying Phillip's organized, businesslike demeanor, there is little room for give-and-take, much less active negotiation. Not more than two minutes into the observational discussion task, as no one was volunteering much, Phillip began, "I'll tell you exactly what is wrong here," and any semblance of negotiation disappeared. Phillip lectured and challenged, Agnes deferred, John acceded and generally agreed, while Sherry engaged in one of her "shut down" modes to end father's ramblings.

IV. Autonomy

A. Clarity of expression: 4.5

The common denominator on this scale is indirect and unclear, rather than vague, communication, since all members of this family talk in generalizations or tangentially. Even though the words are delivered forcefully by Phillip, they reflect little of his personal feelings. His wife and son say little except to placate or buffer. Sherry is perhaps clearest in her expression, although much is nonverbal (looking down, covering ears), and much is lost in the vagaries of loose rambling.

B. Responsibility: 3.5

Since most of the discussion revolved around Sherry's disorder and the ineffectiveness of the medical and mental health professions, there was plenty of room for blaming (Sherry and her doctors) and speaking in the third person. There was very little sense of any of the family members' owning personal responsibility for actions or feelings.

C. Permeability: 4

Family members are quite unreceptive to each others' statements. Phillip's monologues are processed at some automatic level, since there is some "listening"-looking behavior (occasional glances, nods). John's occasional comments are acknowledged by his parents as unusually perceptive and insightful, whether they in fact are or not. Agnes is not attended to actively, except if she offers a terse disagreement; this usually signals the attention of all, but shuts down further verbal exchanges. Sherry's ramblings are usually not heard.

V. Family Affect

A. Range of feelings: 4

There is considerable masking of most feelings in the family interaction. Statements of disappointment or dissatisfaction are quite clear, but tend to be watered down and misdirected. There appears to be a tacit agreement that direct expression of anger is not appropriate. There is little overt display of happiness, much less warm and tender feelings. There is an unstated expectation that family members will try to be respectful when another is speaking; this translates, however, into serial monologues with occasional interruptions.

B. Mood and tone: 3.5

The overall tone of the family is depressed, with occasional spurts of anger and frustration. Agnes harbors anger and resentment, but she has no direct outlet for these feelings; these feelings are internalized and appear more as sullenness. Phillip's attempts at control generally produce withdrawal in the other members.

C. Unresolvable conflict: 2

While overt conflicts and disagreements were not observed in the discussion, there is a definite sense of futility in dealing with the issues of control, Sherry's anorexia, and the marital relationship. Hence, there is considerable evidence of chronically unresolved conflict hampering current negotiating capacity.

D. Empathy: 4

Overall, there is a noticeable lack of empathic responding to each other's feelings. For one, honest feelings are not expressed directly; Phillip's verbal material is more like a lecture, to which others respond with agreement or indifference. When one member does express feelings (usually nonverbally, as with Sherry's putting her hands over her ears), there is little acknowledgment of feeling; the typical response is Phillip's frustration and continued lecturing.

VI. Global Health/Pathology: 8 Borderline.

The classification of the Adams family in the borderline range of family competence signifies some fundamental difficulties in family structure and interaction. The family is in a tenuous limbo state, often shifting from seeming chaos to tyrannical efforts at control. Interpersonal boundaries also fluctuate from rigid to amorphous; the strongest indication is the rather distant relationship between Phillip and Agnes. Communication is masked and obsessively businesslike or regressively childlike, and a generally depressed tone with occasional outbursts of anger predominates.

Style Scale

I. Dependency Needs: 4

Obviously, the family does not have young children whose presence would promote clinging or highly dependent behavior. However, there is tacit encouragement for John to stay close by (living at home), and Sherry's regressive behaviors are often effective in getting attention or her way on an emotional issue.

II. Adult Conflicts: 4

In the observed segment, there was only one open disagreement between Phillip and Agnes, which was brief and shut down communication. While they may have had open conflicts in the past, their current style is significantly more covert than overt in handling differences, and Agnes' style in dealing with Phillip is basically passive-aggressive.

III. Physical Spacing: 4

Despite the emotional distancing, the family members actually placed themselves quite close physically. Phillip and Agnes sat next to one another on a couch, and John sat (quietly) on a chair close by. Sherry maintained more physical distance by sitting to her father's left.

IV. Social Presentation: 1

There is a strong need to look good, competent, businesslike, and orderly that is shared by all except Sherry. There were also several "corrective" statements made by Agnes and, less frequently, by Phillip regarding Sherry's posture and demeanor.

   Internal scapegoating was observed. While no direct blaming statements were directed at Sherry, the other family members indicate quite consistently that all this bother surrounds her stubborn and immature behaviors, and that they would be just fine if Sherry's behavior could be fixed properly.

V. Verbal Expression of Closeness: 3

The issue of closeness received little overt attention or verbalization in the family exchange. The main themes had to do with the organizational and management-oriented deficiencies in the family.

VI. Assertive/Aggressive Qualities: 2

There is a difference between power/control orientation, which is shown consistently by Phillip, and direct expression of feelings related to interpersonal aggressive, angry, or abusive behavior. For the most part, these qualities are discouraged in this family.

VII. Positive/Negative Feelings: 2

Overall, the tone is more polite than hostile, although warmth, tenderness, and loving, "positive" feelings are not addressed.

VIII. Global Style: 1.5 Centripetal.

The Adams family shows a considerable inner pull, with considerable emphasis on control, expectations for loyalty and dependency, and the obsessional, internalizing qualities of the family members.

Discussion

The classification of this family as borderline centripetal identifies critical themes that can guide the therapist toward effective initial stance and intervention strategies.

Many families with somaticizing, anorectic, or severely obsessional members fit this pattern, characterized by chaotic overt power struggles, a dominant-submissive parental coalition, and repeated ineffective attempts to gain control. These control efforts and accompanying chaos are usually more covert or verbal than behavioral. Generational boundaries are diffuse, and the possibility of triangular patterns of dominance and power maneuvering is thereby increased. Since open warfare is discouraged, members must retreat and protect themselves through patterned rituals and skewed role assignments. Even though love is sought within the family, there is little sense of satisfaction or expressed love and acceptance of the unique individual. One may be praised or damned for one's role performance rather than for one's unique personal qualities.

This case is described in detail in Chapter 10; however, let us offer some general guidelines here. The therapist must join the family emotionally and provide structure to the interaction, dealing openly with power struggles and the tendency to avoid overt conflict. Often, the therapist will need to break up enmeshed dyads (John and Phillip), set boundaries physically (seating distance, blocking), and block intrusions verbally. It is in these families that symptom prescription, honest restraining (we need to progress slowly, as opposed to "quick fixing"), and predicting backsliding and setbacks are useful procedures. (These are the families described most consistently by the Milan group[129] and the "psychosomatic" families described by Minuchin.[107])

The therapist will also need initially to focus attention on the identified patient and progressively to shift the focus of therapy away from the identified patient, thereby diminishing the triangulation and power the symptomatic behavior fosters. The therapist is called upon to help family members express hopes, wishes, and dreams, and to identify current satisfactions and possibilities. The engendering of hope and identification of the potential and possible are important and continual tasks in working with BLCP families.

THE QUAGMYRE FAMILY

This lower-middle-class family began family therapy during the hospitalization of the older son, Nathan, age 16, for "schizophrenia." The other family members include the father, Hiram, 42, mother, Nellie, 38, and George, 12. Nathan had been hospitalized after several weeks of disturbance during which he hoarded food in his room, became verbally and physically assaultive with brothers and his mother, and began "speaking in tongues." This family views itself as quite religious (attending a moderately fundamentalist church); family members became particularly concerned with Nathan's deteriorating behavior when he attacked Mrs. Quagmyre, calling her the anti-Christ. Mr. and Mrs. Quagmyre had noticed a progressive decline in Nathan's performance since about sixth grade, although neither son was ever viewed as an outstanding or socially adept student.

On entering the therapy room, family members positioned themselves cautiously; Nathan waited to see where everyone else sat and then sat at the far end of the room from the others. George sat between Mr. Quagmyre and his mother, who was diagonally opposite from Nathan.

Mother, George, and father placed themselves close together. All members appeared highly uncomfortable in this setting.

After the therapist prescribed the discussion task and left the room, an uncomfortable silence settled in, until Nathan grunted, "Well, what the hell are we doing here, anyway?" This exchange cued the family spokesperson, Mrs. Quagmyre, to slip in: "This lady is going to help [hepp] us be a happier family." (All other eyes were cast downward or aloft.) "We need to tell her what we need to change. George, what do *you* think we need to change?" "I dunno." "Well, what do you think needs changin'?" "I dunno." "Well, you must have some ideas." "*I don't know, mother*!!" From this point, the session deteriorated into random comments interspersed with periods of silence. The few exchanges that occurred between husband and wife were general and disjointed; father's suggestion that "We all need to learn to get along better and cooperate more" met with a challenge from his wife: "Haven't we been trying *that* for years?" Mother made trips across the diagonal to Nathan—to get a cigarette from him and to retrieve an ashtray from the table in front of him. At the end of the 10-minute segment, there was little sense of joining or clarity, much less any definite statements or goals from anyone.

Competence Scale

I. Structure
   A. Overt power: 1.5
      The system vacillates between attempts at control, usually by mother and occasionally by the identified patient, and stereotyped chaotic behavior. There is no sign of consistent leadership; father is powerless in dealings with his wife and children.
   B. Parental coalitions: 1.5
      The marital skew in this family, in the direction of maternal control, is reinforced by the attempts to maintain rigid parent-child coalition patterns. While father has an occasional (and implicit) coalition of the silent and forgotten with George, mother attempts to maintain more overt coalitions of influence and succorance with George. Nathan's attempts to pull out of the coalition with his mother required psychosis; the overt overtures toward reestablishing their coalition were noted in her verbal and physical forays across the room to him.
   C. Closeness: 2
      This intermediate point between the amorphous and indistinct

relational boundaries of the lowest-functioning system and the isolation and distancing of midrange families represents the "overall mean" of this family: There are some members amorphously tied, some attempting to pull out and establish distance, and some vacillating in between. Notably, George's attempts to avoid his mother's maneuvering required effort but left him disengaged.

Several invasions were noted, delivered by Mrs. Quagmyre. These were directed at her husband and at Nathan.

II. Mythology: 4.5

This family talked about itself (on those occasions where there was dialogue) in terms of closeness and cooperation, of encouraging people to grow up and become responsible, and of desiring change. Most of these statements seemed more delusional than actual.

III. Goal-Directed Negotiation: 5

This family was rated as extremely inefficient in negotiating discussion or problem tasks and low in terms of clarity of issue(s), participation of members, and time efficiency. Mother's attempts to structure the task were met with distancing and overt or passive rejection.

IV. Autonomy

A. Clarity of expression: 4.5

Although there were occasional overt "leave me alone" messages (delivered by George initially and Nathan later on), there were no direct and clear statements of personal thoughts and feelings. Mother probed and regulated, father talked in "maybe-sorta-oughta" phrases, and the sons kept to themselves.

B. Responsibility: 4

There is a fairly high degree of blaming others for personal hurts and disappointments. However, the predominant theme, closely connected to the previous scale, is the lack of personal statements.

C. Permeability: 5

Even as individuals speak in this family, other members are gazing away or down; there is very little give-and-take, much less acknowledgment of personal thoughts or feelings. The exception is Nellie, who desperately wants to reestablish connections with her sons; one gets the sense that she does try to respond appropriately, but her timing and intrusiveness prevent any openness.

V. Family Affect

A. Range of feelings: 4.5

Few feelings of any kind are expressed openly in this family; there is a covert invitation to the bland and lonely for all members. The desperation experienced by mother is laughed at or shrugged off. The overall message is that there is much futility in expressing one's feelings.

B. Mood and tone: 4.5

This family appears stuck; there is little interactional energy or intensity. Instead, there is a bland cynicism, at best, and depression, which permeates the atmosphere and family members' dealings with each other. Even Nellie's initial statement that the therapist-lady is "gonna hepp us" is couched more as a threat or command than as a message of optimism.

C. Unresolvable conflicts: 1.5

There is little overt group exchange to begin with, but one gets the feeling that people have been intruded upon and put down, perhaps when they have tried to raise these issues in the past. The stored hurts and unresolved tensions have created a sense of futility and masking of true feelings.

D. Empathy: 4.5

Inappropriate or absent responses to personal statements and feelings were observed in this family. The male members of the family usually showed no acknowledgment of others' feelings (usually mother's). Mother was more prone to respond inappropriately, by hounding, punishing cooperation, or ignoring.

VI. Global Health/Pathology: 9 Severely dysfunctional.

Style Scale

I. Dependency Needs: 4

Dependent behaviors were less evident from the Quagmyre sons than they were solicited from the mother. The solicitation of George's input, some attempts to "baby" Nathan, and suppression of challenges to her arbitrary attempts at leadership and structuring all point to the reinforcement of less mature behavior in her sons.

II. Adult Conflicts: 5

Indirect, covert mechanisms of handling conflictual differences were evident in Mr. and Mrs. Quagmyre's dealings with one another. On the few occasions Mr. Quagmyre spoke, his vague and indirect statements either fell flat or were discounted (vaguely and indirectly) by Mrs. Quagmyre.

III. Physical Spacing: 4

The "inner nucleus" of the family positioned itself closely and carefully, with very little physical space between mother, George and father. Only Nathan placed himself outside the centripetal space, more than adequate symbolism for his psychiatric and developmental condition.

IV. Social Presentation: 1.5

Trying to look interested, cooperative, and pleasant was a theme evident early in the discussion task; the verbally active mother attempted to have her boys sitting up straight and looking appropriate. Both parents allowed Nathan some grumbling and slouching, given his diagnosed psychiatric condition.

Internal scapegoating was noted (shared between Mr. Quagmyre, who was better at dodging barbs and blame, and Nathan, who was also learning to disown the role as scapegoat). George is the likely next candidate, though currently he is his mother's favorite.

V. Expression of Closeness: 2

The word "closeness" surfaced several times in the discussion, both in attempts at goal-setting ("more close") and in describing the current system ("but I think we *are* a pretty close-knit family"). These expressions contrast with the rigid roles and distance observed.

VI. Assertive/Aggressive Qualities: 1

There was a strongly felt taboo in this family regarding direct expression of anger or the assertion of one's will. Again, Nathan was allowed some leeway here, as a result of his illness.

VII. Positive/Negative Feelings: 2

Most feelings are suppressed in the family, but the general tone is to play it safe, keep things under wraps, and produce as much bland positivity as possible. Negative feelings are reserved for the crazy or ignoble.

VIII. Global Style: 1.5

Centripetal family style, shown by a strong, inner orientation; the outside world is viewed as relatively threatening. Control is maintained by emphasizing dependency and guilt manipulation. Feelings are internalized; autonomy and independence are often difficult to achieve.

Discussion

The classification of this family as a severely dysfunctional centripetal family identifies some common themes and can help guide the therapist in developing strategies for family intervention. In such families, the nonexistent parental coalition and attempts to pull the sons into parent-child coalitions signal the need for structuring and breaking triangular patterns. In essence, the therapist must become a stage manager, blocking (more verbally than physically) invasions, defining boundaries, and facilitating encounters with the players. The therapist must also demand clarity and coherence by promoting (and modeling) short and direct statements and by having recipients acknowledge and paraphrase. Fear and isolation need to be acknowledged, as well as the other side of the ambivalent feelings (hostility and dependency). Therapists also gain some affiliative power by comforting and even touching members of these families, who believe they have glue without contact ("air cement").

Examples of intervention strategies with severely disturbed centripetal families are presented in Chapter 10.

THE JAY FAMILY

This family was referred through the court system following the arrest of two sons (John, 15, and Jeff, 13) for auto theft. This was not the first offense for either boy; both had spent time in juvenile correctional institutions. At present, the judge in the case recommended family therapy as an alternative to incarceration.

The family consisted of Fred, 43, recently divorced from Sally, 38, and five children: Jeannie, 18, John, Jeff, James, 12, and Jason, 10. This had been Fred's second marriage. He was a tavern owner, a heavy drinker, and was quite resistant to the idea of therapy. However, since the offspring frequently resided with Fred (moving back and forth between households), he was encouraged to come to the initial session.

Sally was a skilled clerical worker who looked older than her age, despite her attempts to look young (long hair, jeans, t-shirt). A moderate drinker, she was in poor health and had chronic ulcers; several years ago she had had a mild stroke, which affected facial expression and speech articulation.

Jeannie had dropped out of school, been married and divorced, had two children currently living at Sally's (though not present at the assessment), and had been variably employed as a waitress, a topless dancer, and a prostitute. Her legal difficulties in the past included DWI's, hot checks, and eviction for nonpayment of rent.

John and Jeff, as noted above, had experienced several interfaces with the legal system, including auto theft and drug use; both boys were erratic attenders at school and made poor or failing grades. James was mildly retarded and had lived in an institutional setting previously. Currently he was at home. He showed marked "behavior problems" at school and had a legal record for auto theft, vandalism, and running away from home. Jason was bright and doing well in school, with no legal difficulties.

At the initial session, not all members were present, as is typical and predictable in families with this notable record of behavioral difficulty. Present were Fred (because he "had to"), Sally, Jeannie ("why me?"), and the older sons in legal difficulty. Sally left James at home because he "refused" to come; Jason was encouraged to go to school.

Competence Scale

I. Structure
   A. Overt power: 1
      Overt chaos was the common denominator of this family's interaction. No one had enough power to direct conversation, much less control the bickering, random motion, and lack of focus on task. Sally tried to elicit cooperation but very quickly became part of the chaotic mass.
   B. Parental coalitions: 2
      There is no strong parent-child coalition pattern in this family, but there is also a lack of any effective parental coalition. There were verbal hints that Sally's "favorite" is Jason and nonverbal hints of unresolved issues (possibly sexual?) between Fred and Jeannie, but no consistent or stable present coalitions were noted.
   C. Closeness: 1.5
      Overall, the relationships between members of this family are antagonistic and pained. There is marked ambivalence in parent-parent and parent-child dyads, as if there is something desired and sought (love, approval, attention) but never attained, leaving each member frustrated and angry. Hence, the boundaries fluctuate as the needs and situations change; the result is a collection of amorphous and indistinct boundaries.

      Invasiveness was not observed. The predominant mode was chaotic: attack/blame→defend/attack→I'm not responsible. There was not enough structure for members to invade each other physically.
II. Mythology: 3
   There are no grand or even positive illusions in this family about *how*

they function and what is provided. However, there are a few ideas of how the family *is* as a unit in the free-for-all.

III. Goal-Directed Negotiation: 5

Accompanying the lack of leadership and structure is an inability to negotiate. In this discussion, the focus of the task was lost within 30 seconds, as members, both serially and simultaneously, embarked on egocentric blaming and complaining jabs at others, shifting in allegiance patterns depending upon who was under attack most of the time (usually Sally). The result looked like a group of angry five-year-olds.

IV. Autonomy

A. Clarity of expression: 4.5

There is very little clarity in terms of direct expression of one's *own* thoughts and feelings. The vast majority of verbal material (even with expletives deleted) involved terse, angry and blaming statements, along with occasional rehashing of previous transgressions.

B. Responsibility: 5

Across the board, present family members resort to blaming others for any and all actions or blaming distilled spirits for infidelity and hot tempers. In one heated exchange, John and Jeff became embroiled in a simultaneous shouting match about whose fault it was that they were *caught* in the most recent car theft.

C. Permeability: 5

There is little, if any, personal clarity; there is an accompanying absence of permeability. Even with neutral, factual statements or questions ("Remember that, Dad?"), there is little accurate listening, much less openly receptive understanding of another's expressed emotion or world view.

V. Family Affect

A. Range of feelings: 4

The consistent feeling expressed directly is anger; perhaps the most consistent observed affect is frustration. Nevertheless, there is a highly truncated range of feelings expressed in the family. On one occasion, after Sally had been blamed for something by everyone present, she cried, then counterattacked. Even her tears expressed anger and hurt.

B. Mood and tone: 5

Cynicism, pessimism, and the expectation that all future family (and most human) contacts will be hostile and conflictual permeate this family. It would be hard to imagine that this family has any concept of affection, hope, or individual acceptance. Even Sally's empassioned "All I want is some help" carried with it a strong, unspoken qualifier: "but I know that will never happen, so I'll punish you back."

C. Unresolvable conflict: 1

Conflict, whether present and overt or past and stored, is the main fuel for interactional exchange, but severely limits the family's ability to negotiate, plan, and interact effectively. If there were nothing to fight about, there would be no exchange at all.

D. Empathy: 5

VI. Global Health/Pathology: 10 Severely dysfunctional.

The classification of the Jay family as severely dysfunctional indicates major and pervasive absence of coherent structure, leadership, and individual/dyadic boundaries. Attempts to structure the chaotic interaction, if ever present, have long been abandoned, and the concept of a "family" is tenuous or nonexistent and members have adopted an "each person for himself" attitude.

Style Scale

I. Dependency Needs: 1

Any expression of dependency, neediness, or requests for caretaking (if present) are ignored, discouraged, or punished. Perhaps the most "childlike" person in the present group is Sally, whose unanswered pleas for help usually look like a child's tantrum.

II. Adult Conflicts: 1

There is no hidden agenda that these two adults are locked in major conflict; they appear congruent in fighting, in accusing each other, and in producing loud verbal tirades. Since the conflict was so severe (and Fred and Sally were divorced), the therapist decided not to see them together in therapy.

III. Physical Spacing: 1

As much as was physically possible, the Jays spread out around the room, with Fred and Sally directly opposite each other, in corners. Jeannie sat far off in a third corner, and the boys were on opposite ends of a couch along one wall.

IV. Social Presentation: 5

There is little concern for behaving in any socially desirable manner, dressing nicely, or pretending that there is warmth and affection.

V. Verbal Expression of Closeness: 5
In this family, the concept of being close means being dependent and weak. The felt necessity is to be tough and strong and to fend for oneself. The issue is seldom discussed; when it is, the strong denial implies "I'm tough enough to survive."

VI. Assertive/Aggressive Qualities: 5
Fending for oneself in the family implies that you have to fight back every time you are attacked; the sheer frequency encourages and demands aggressive behavior in return. Much like children who are caught in an endless "are too—am not" exchange (where the label sticks to the one who gives up first), these family members fight back or lose.

VII. Positive/Negative Feelings: 5
Feelings of anger, frustration, disappointment, hostility, and irritability are common vernacular. The family was devoid of any warm, tender feelings or overtures.

VIII. Global Style: 5
The Jay family shows a strong centrifugal style, connoting a strong outer orientation, where members look outside the family for possible gratification, where outside superficial relationships are less threatening than close family relationships. There is a strong tendency for acting-out behavior, frequent leave-taking, and tenuous family boundaries.

Discussion

The classification of the Jays as a severely dysfunctional centrifugal (SDCF) family provides the therapist with some initial guidelines and signals the therapist to pull in any loose reins, not get involved in side-taking in the verbal melee, and put on the "structuring" hat (or more appropriately, helmet).

Since the structure is amorphous, it is necessary, even desirable, to work with subsets of the family. The therapist needs to be in as much control as possible in determining who will attend which session(s). Also, the therapist must be in charge of seating assignments and of the starting and ending times of the sessions.

Since the behavioral rather than the verbal is the main token of exchange, the therapist may be required to block angry exchanges physically, to hold and soothe children, and to link words and feelings with behavior. However, if all these maneuvers are attempted with therapist assuming an "I'm in charge" stance, the therapist will quickly become the target for hostility. Hence, it is appropriate to assume a "one-down"[165] position at times, admit confusion and helplessness, prescribe symptoms, and even prescribe setbacks.

The therapist also needs, at critical times, to offer hope, affirm family strengths, reframe hostility as love (or disappointment stemming from tender needs), and emphasize the positive. The recognition and labeling of ambivalence (love-hate polarization) foster some awareness of powerful feelings in these family members.

Finally, working with a cotherapist or a team behind the mirror is a useful and accepted way to balance control and structure with joining and engendering hope.

We shall follow the Jay family further in Chapter 11.

The assessment of this family leads us directly to treatment planning and hypothesis-building, as illustrated in Chapter 7. These clinical examples show how ratings of family competence and style emerge from observation of an interactional sequence without the therapist present. The result is an identification of strengths and weaknesses in the individual family and the categorization of the family into one of our clinically useful groupings. These groupings, as well as guidelines for intervention, will be discussed in detail in Chapters 8, 9, 10, and 11.

Section Two
TREATMENT AND INTERVENTION

7 SCIENCE AND SYSTEMS IN PSYCHOTHERAPY

HARNESSING SCIENCE FOR FAMILY THERAPY

All developmentally oriented psychological theory assumes that the human infant must experience the world in relationship and interaction with others in order to develop a coherent self. This self is inextricably intertwined with the subjectively defined world outside, a kind of figure-ground gestalt of the utmost importance to every evolving human. This self will be unique and different from every other who has existed or will exist. As the self develops, the view of the world outside will also be unique and different from anyone else's. This process of boundary-making, of separating the known from the knower in some coherent fashion, is every individual's task. It is also the task of theorists who concern themselves with the nature of people and the world.

In order to make sense of the self and nature, every culture develops a cosmology (for example, how the world began, how thunder is produced, why crops fail, where people come from, the nature of good and evil), cultural answers to the same questions facing individuals in their organization of the self and the world. Currently, in our western world, cosmology is largely the business of science. Religious explanations of nature and its works have lost considerable power over the last 200 years, although there is residual power in religious statements concerning man's nature. The battles between science and religious authority which have been played out in the 20th century are found primarily in psychology. Psychological concerns with the self, with ego functioning, and with the quality of reality-testing are directly related to the issue of the source of truth. What distinguishes a scientific cosmology from one that is religious? Are they necessarily different? If so, how can one tell the two apart? What is the proper area for science, for religion? Does religion have a place in modern life, and if so is it a sickness or a necessity?

To a rather unimaginative chemist, these may seem unnecessary questions, but they are raging controversies at two ends of the scientific continuum, the science of physics and the science of humans. For years, we have been fascinated with knotty and unresolved problems concerning the essential nature of scientific endeavor. We have received more help from physicists than from biological or behavioral scientists in attempting to get a clearer grasp of how humans determine reality.

Physicists are often concerned about the danger in assuming that scientific pronouncements carry absolute truths. Many physical scientists, along with theologians and intelligent laymen, express their fear that a pin-headed, spuriously certain scientism could reproduce the danger to mankind of earlier centuries; they fear a repetition of a theology of certainty that punished heretics with inhumanity in the guise of virtue.

Many purists in family therapy have an extreme wariness and, indeed, doctrinaire mistrust of research methods and conventional rationality. Keeney suggests that family systems work is not to be understood, evaluated, or bounded by conventional research methods.[86] Tomm expresses doubt about any family assessment that is organized and does not include the therapist as well as the family.[148] These assumptions effectively render any scientific evaluation of family groupings irrelevant to therapy. We believe these theorists discard too much in their efforts to keep family work open-ended, fresh, and innovative. Science, properly understood, is a tool that can be used for humanitarian ends and is indispensable for family work. It is, in fact, a safeguard against human arrogance, arbitrariness, and the damaging of suffering people by blind application of untested theory (or intuition or revelation).

We can give up on science and retreat to the flamboyantly irrational or, preferably, we can make a reappraisal of science, its definition, its limits, its past pomposity and fraudulence, and determine what it can do for us now. Though this question is as relevant to "hard sciences" as it is to psychology and psychiatry, it is in the behavioral sciences that the issues are critical. The attitudes and beliefs that a therapist holds concerning *knowing, explaining,* and *hypothesizing* will directly affect his or her work and effectiveness with patients.

MISCONCEPTIONS OF SCIENCE

We would like first to refute some faulty beliefs about the nature of science that have given a good field a bad name. It is often believed that science (1) is complete truth; (2) is certain; (3) is objective; (4) is furthered by people who are unusually open-minded, using inductive reasoning; and (5) is a useful belief system. These are all fundamentally incorrect.

First, science is not complete truth; rather, it is simply the historical outgrowth of commonsense knowledge. Its outlines are the formal statements of the puzzles and solutions of practical, prescientific humans. For example, science replaces the problem of what is a reasonable belief of a sane person with a formal description of the rules for accepting or rejecting scientific theories.[120] Just as common sense does, science limits its interest to the observable and the pragmatic, and it becomes foolishly pretentious if it claims more. For example, Freud's assumption that religion is evidence of unresolved emotional conflicts[53] or Skinner's belief that internal states are of no significance to the behavioral scientist[131] represent serious and dangerous progressions from elegant common sense to irrational reductionism. Such "progress" yields potentially tragic misinformation that is destructive to people.

Second, science is neither certain nor absolute. The methodology of science allows beliefs to be disproved but never proved. We have the opportunity to use scientific tools to approach truth ever more closely, but we can never expect to have it in our grasp. Newtonian physics gave way to the Einsteinian era, as a new world opened up and the old one collapsed like a house of cards. Science can never produce a rock of Gibraltar, since uncertainty is built into its necessarily open system. Physicists, with theories of uncertainty and redefinitions of time, space, and matter, have attacked almost every assumption of previous scientists and other humans. Stephen Hawking speaks of black holes and naked singularity and challenges the fundamental principle of causality.[80] Whether this rumble assumes the power of a thunderstorm or ripples off into nothingness, it illustrates that the very heart of science, as contrasted with many other disciplines, is tenuous and tentative and its truths relative. Scientific truth is approximate and incomplete, and those aware of the quality of such truth are forced to be humble, leaving to others the certainty which demands intense loyalty to specific ideas and attacks on dissidents and heretics. Korzybski was empathically aware of this increasingly open system of science when he described a 1930 meeting of physicists as composed of "goodnatured Einsteinians and strident Newtonians."[92] He knew that genuine scientific wisdom sees the universe as a mystery which never recedes but rather changes with new understanding.

Third, science is not objective, since it is a product of people—limited, subjective, and biased people—who use their sense organs to develop abstractions that only approximate the nature of the cosmos. With all the mechanical extensions of our sense organs, from giant telescopes to electron microscopes, from radar to computerized tomography, the resulting images are no closer to objectivity. Comprehension and coherence are vulnerable abstractions, devised from raw sensory input. As Korzybski[92] noted, the only objectivity is this incoherent "unspeakable" (preverbal) input that is also rawly subjective, dependent on the varying biological characteristics of individual organisms.

To think of or to describe the real world, one must develop a subjective abstraction. Words are only a bit more abstract than the subjects which they represent. Concepts, individual and shared, are only roadmaps of the awesome reality that is always terra incognita. A chasm exists between people and any absolute comprehension; poets and dreamers can perhaps leap the chasm fleetingly, but scientists in their official capacity can never make the jump.

Fourth, science is not furthered by unusually open-minded people using inductive reasoning. Scientists are as biased, opinionated, and prejudiced as the general population, and perhaps even more so. A decent scientist is always passionate in the defense of his theories. In fact, a scientist who is always "fair-minded" and "objective" may be unable to sustain the enthusiasm and interest necessary for good research. Even with a powerhouse of passion, the scientist's methodology provides incentive and opportunity to change opinions when the data forcibly dictate such change. Watson gave a memorable illustration of this quality of scientists in his descriptions of the varied human attributes and motives involved in the discovery of the structure of DNA.[155]

The scientist does not proceed by blindly taking in data from observations and records of individual phenomena, which then lead to general statements, i.e., hypotheses and theories. This is not the way that the human mind works. Francis Bacon was responsible, in large part, for this romantic nonsense concerning scientific effort; though not a scientist himself, he was a superb public relations man for scientific endeavor, and his insistence on the virtues of pure, untainted observation and on the evils of speculation have affected research and scientists for centuries.[119] Today, we know more about people and the way they think than when Bacon was theorizing about the methodology of science; we no longer assume that any human past the age of six months can observe the world without a priori assumptions, either conscious or unconscious. In fact, there is increasing evidence that even the newborn has biological structures that profoundly influence his or her perceptions. For example, such assumptions as causality and concepts of time and space appear to be intrinsic.[34,139]

Fifth, science is not a useful belief system, for all the foregoing reasons and more. Science can never claim to be the best source of truth and guidance. It does well as a tool, but quite poorly as a faith. It can provide some power over nature, yet very little to assist in developing purpose and meaning. To give up other sources of meaning, such as intuition, visions, dreams, and faith, for some presumed scientific objectivity is to court despair. A sophisticated secular person can elevate science to the level of a faith and thereby diminish life of much that is the source of joy, delight, optimism, and hope.

The reader will probably observe some similarities between the erroneous views of science listed above and the attitudes found in disturbed families. There is a marked similarity between reductionist science and the rigidity and spurious certainty of disturbed family beliefs. Just as 19th-century science broke away from religion, with fear and trembling, and set up a rigid absolutist structure quite like its disavowed parent, many people try to reduce anxiety by absorbing certainty rather than through dialogue with other poor souls. Ego functioning is tentative and probabilistic; it evolves slowly, just as an appreciation of the uncertain and relative aspects of science has evolved slowly.

We believe treatment approaches based on concepts of science that include the misconceptions listed above cannot help individuals grow beyond the limits comparable to disturbed families; in fact, interminable analyses and/or treatment failures result from absolutist, closed-system approaches to human emotional disorders.

Two valuable and original sources of therapeutic insight, Freudian psychoanalysis and experimental psychology, suffer from these erroneous views of science. Both assume objective truth and believe that their respective structures have it. Both tend to be at least impatient—and often harsh—with unbelievers. Both have arrogance, or at least complacency, in the place of a valuable uncertainty. Both tend to wreak havoc on the subjective view of reality: experimental psychologists because of an impatience with so unpredictable a phenomenon as subjectivity; and Freudians by assuming that they understand the subjective and interpret it in a specific, predetermined, systematic fashion that can brook no serious challenge by the patient or others.

A scientist who deals with nonhuman material and believes in absolutes only contributes to a sterility in that field, the languishing of progress, and resistance to new theory. However, if a scientist or therapist is dealing with human material, the Procrustean bed can become bloody. Closed-system pseudo-science then behaves much as old Procrustes the woodcutter, stretching and cutting humans to fit his beds with an insensitivity to the damage that such fervently held absolutes can deal. Examples of this phenomenon are unfortunately frequent:

Skinner states (seriously, I am afraid, not in hyperbole) that proper attention to conditioning can lead us "beyond freedom and dignity";[132] orthodox Freudians become pessimistic over the unsolvable problem of man's aggressive/destructive nature and society's unsuccessful fight to control it.

Since the shakily scientific disciplines that concern themselves with the nature of man deal with articles of faith, rather than with theory that may be altered or scrapped, and since they quite violently disagree with one another, how are disagreements between various behavioral schools negotiated? Most of the time they are not, since adherents of the different cults seldom participate in useful dialogues. Freudians, behaviorists, existentialists, organicists, and family therapists can spend years next to each other on the same faculty, never treading on one another's territory. If they do, agreement is quite likely to be reached by political (power) means. This use of power and status is inevitable if human truth is seen as absolute. With such a viewpoint, one simply cannot negotiate in good faith without risking a terrible threat to personal identity, a condition quite similar to poorly functioning families, whose members attempt to gain closeness and agreement through intimidation rather than through respectful dialogue.

We believe a better understanding of the nature of the scientific method will encourage family therapists to realize that they, too, can join the scientific community, and that this community can be protective of human values rather than threatening the joyful creativity of either therapist or patient. Science can be both a useful servant in the effort to alleviate suffering and a dependable watchdog, protecting the less powerful from the enthusiastic arrogance of healers who shun examination of their work by systemic assessment and follow-up studies. Such an appreciation will lead to the abolition of schools and cults in family therapy and result in a synthesis of the valued contributions of many current theories and treatment approaches.

WHAT SCIENCE IS AND HOW IT IS VITAL TO FAMILY THERAPISTS

As the outcome of commonsense knowledge, science: (1) is concerned with increasing man's power in the material world by making sense of things; (2) deals with the refutable and the pragmatic and is, therefore, limited; (3) is an abstraction, a map of reality; and (4) is essentially a method. Let's take these one at a time and look at them more closely.

First, as science increases man's power in the material world, there is an effort to make sense of things. Such sense has to do with substance and relational contexts.

It is ironic that reductionistic science—the splitting up of complex phenomena into elementary components or units in an attempt to discover the laws governing the parts so to understand the complex from the elementary—was so successful that this methodological shortcut became identified with the whole enterprise. The success of reductionism (Von Bertalanffy calls it Galileanism[153]) obscured an intrinsic quality of science: its dealing with patterns and relations. General systems theory would not have been novel or much of an advance had there not been a long period of mechanistic science reducing the complex to the elemental and leading to the erroneous belief (sometimes stated, often implicit) that the whole is nothing more than the sum of its parts.

Such reductionism has plagued psychology since the beginning of its formal study.[108] In order to gain scientific respect for psychological science, early and contemporary investigators have often felt obligated to follow the Galilean method and study man as an intrapsychic phenomenon, or as a stimulus-response interactional structure, or as a chemical equation. With general acceptance that scientific endeavor deals with structure and relations, the scientific study of sick and well humans as complex, biological beings, enmeshed in a significant social system, can assume its rightful place. Procrustes can return to cutting wood instead of people.

Second, science deals with the refutable and the pragmatic; therefore it is limited. Do not expect a scientist to tell you whether wars should be fought or fiercer weapons developed or whether an atomic power plant should be placed in your town. A scientist might give you the odds of success, but important personal or social decisions are more than scientific or technical—they are related to values, consensual subjective reality, and social power. Scientific information is important but not decisive in this arena.

Similarly, do not expect a psychotherapist practicing a scientific discipline to decide whether a patient should get married, get a divorce, have a lover, or be rid of one. Such decisions, although difficult, are areas of personal choice not to be found in the wisdom of any human other than the one involved, and no amount of therapeutic expertise makes this any more or less so. Indeed, the professionalism of a helper is inversely related to the frequency with which advice is given. The poor therapist who gives many directives is much like one's Aunt Lucinda, who usually knows what everyone should do. A skilled therapist can use the assessment of families to determine when directives are needed and useful and when they get in the way of family members' change, growth, and increasing autonomy. By joining the family system and knowing at what functional level that system operates, a therapist can most effectively help the family to become unstuck, resolve conflicts, and effectively carry out needed negotiation. Thus, family assessment becomes a vital source of data to guide a behavioral scientist/therapist in joining, negotiating, healing.

Third, science is an abstraction, a map of reality. We are in Korzybski's debt for getting us out of the sticky objective/subjective dichotomies of existentialists squaring off against behaviorists and organicists. The only objectivity humans have is the raw sensory input before they integrate and abstract.[92] Objects are lower order abstractions from words, and concepts spiral upward in increasingly abstract symbolizing—for example, pencil, table, self, motherhood, patriotism, love, God. Every human has a unique self and a unique world affected by biology and experience. No man has objective truth, scientific or otherwise, and the individual's subjective view of the world is as close to "reality" as anybody's alleged objectivity.

Harry Stack Sullivan's beautiful term, "consensual validation," with which he replaced the Freudian concept of "the reality principle," shows a profound understanding of science and of human development.[145] Freud's reality was an appeal to an assumed universal, an objective absolute, that reflected the science of the 19th century. Sullivan captured in his replacement phrase the essence of 20th-century science, with its awareness of uncertainty and continuing change through dialogue with other observers. Here we see the rationale for a fundamental tool of family therapy—the "reframing" of events to more hopeful and more useful concepts. A "bad boy" becomes a valuable distractor from parental pain; an angry punitive father becomes a caring parent expressing love in a way that can be improved. These reframed concepts are no more or less "true" than the ones previously held by the family; they are simply more useful in allowing effective problem-solving.

The processes of developing ego strength and of being scientific (they are quite similar) do not consist of finding objective truths. To believe so can lead individuals and families toward the promotion of illness rather than toward emotional health. Rather, these processes consist of negotiating a shared perception of useful truths in respectful dialogue with others (the "validation" process of consensual validation!).

Becoming sane may be a somewhat different process, depending on the degree of authoritarianism in the social structure. Consensual validation is the common factor in scientific exploration and in the development of ego strength. In an open society, scientific research may be rewarded and open discussion of individual differences at least tolerated. Becoming sane, then, can include such ego-promoting dialogue with peers. But in closed, authoritarian societies, sanity may be promoted by being wise enough to concur with the socially powerful, a much different process from respectful negotiation. It is fortunate that, even in totalitarian cultures, there will be smaller groups of friends and families with an openness that allows ego development.

A family therapist must be aware of similar requirements in joining a family. One must be respectful of the world view, basic assumptions, and modes of operation of family members. Negotiation is modeled for family members by the successful negotiating strategies and techniques of the therapist.

A few may have difficulty with this relativistic definition of scientific knowledge and of ego development. Perhaps, for example, a physician specializing in pathology who has wandered into this book by mistake might demur, pointing to a cluster of cells seen through a microscope and saying, "Those cells are not a consensus; they are either cancerous or they are not." However, unless this expert has labeled pathological specimens countless times quite like other pathologists, no one will seriously view the expert as such. If our specific pathologist insists that he or she is closer to objective truth, then a research endeavor must ensue. If experiments support an aberrant opinion, these data are brought up in dialogue with fellow pathologists and the process of consensual validation (or scientific research) continues.

Since scientific, cognitive knowledge is an abstraction, there can never be wholeness or completeness in such knowledge. A map of a terrain can be of immense help to a traveler, but it is always rather dull in comparison to the real thing. We will always need to rely on dreams, fantasies, poets, artists, theologians, and philosophers to help us get a bit closer to the terrain itself. Science will lead us astray if we depend on it for answers rather than guidance, for reality rather than a skeletal structure. Nonetheless, systems-oriented, uncertainty-embracing, approximate, and value-conscious 20th-century science is far more helpful to and respectful of humankind than its mechanistic 19th-century predecessor or any prescientific philosophy.

Fourth, science starts with a problem and develops a theory which is vigorously criticized in a dialogue of equals, in a necessarily open system. The method of science is a refinement of the effort to learn from one's mistakes. This is essentially all that it tries to do, but it attempts to create rules and discipline that permit the job to be done better and more consistently.

Francis Bacon was quite hostile to speculation and insisted that (despite the human inability to do so) one should approach nature with an open, unbiased mind. He argued that people have a strong tendency to interpret data in the light of their own prejudices. For example, if a man believes that all history is a class struggle, then whatever he observes or reads of human interaction will be interpreted in the light of this belief and will only strengthen it.[120] If one possesses notions that can always be confirmed by his observations, he can learn nothing new.

This empty exercise of pseudo-experiments may not only limit observations, as the example above, but also affect behavior. For example, a parent who believes in the innate savagery of humanity will understandably attempt to control his own evil impulses and those of any children by harsh discipline. Such behavior then leads to the very reality—surly hostility lying in wait for an opening—that fits with the theory. On a broader societal level, harsh government policy leads to hidden resistance. Repression leads to rebellion, which leads to repression: theory unchanged, learning nil. This is a circular self-fulfilling prophecy.

What a predicament! If humans are so enamored of their theories that all data can fit into them, and the effort to expunge all theory from mind and to learn directly from the book of nature is impossible, then things sound rather bleak. This situation is similar to the current family therapy scene. Ardent enthusiasts of various methods—"strategic," "structural," "Milan"—are convinced of their advocacy with little regard for what kinds of families would be helped (if any) and how one would determine the failure or clear deficiencies in any touted method.

Popper[120] can be of assistance in this dilemma. He advocates the following approach: First, embrace and respect theory; rejoice that man's abstracting and symbolizing capability provides such delightful playthings and tools. Second, insist that all those hoping to have their theories considered scientific describe observations which, if occurring, would *refute* them. If all possible events fit the theory, it cannot claim to be a part of scientific dialogue. It may be promoted with enthusiasm, power, threat, or even violence, but certainly not with experimentation and respectful discourse. This understanding is crucial to a clear delineation of the difference between theory and dogma. It is important to understand this in order to distinguish between the scientific and the doctrinaire.

For example, if a Freudian theorist cannot describe possible family interactions that would indicate the lack of patricidal wishes in a particular male child, then such theory is out of the realm of science and has become secular dogma. If a learning theorist cannot describe experimental results that would refute a belief in the unimportance of subjective choice or instinctual drive, the belief is dogma. If a family therapist cannot outline results of using a preferred method that would indicate the method is not helpful with this family or this group of families, then assertions of usefulness are out of the realm of scientific discipline. Such embracing of theory as truth throws the field back into a prescientific morass where Freudian psychoanalysis has languished—where truth is determined by authority rather than data and one is a disciple of a cult rather than a respectable clinician carrying on an open-ended dialogue with peers in a constant search for improvement.

Third, Popper instructs, accept observations as supportive of the theory only if they are severe tests of that theory and if sincere and capable efforts to disprove it fail to do so. This means in clinical work that control groups are necessary and that outcome studies must be sophisticated and follow, as much as is feasible, the rigorous position of excluding random change and including relevant negative results.

Popper's simple rules lay the groundwork for honest scientific dialogue and describe the requirements for scientific progress.[119]

Now, let us see how one can practice the scientific method according to Popper. Remember that this method is simply an elegant outgrowth of common sense, in which men learn from their mistakes.

First, we start with a problem either practical or theoretical. We then devise some solution, usually inaccurate.

And then we criticize it. We test it with experimentation. We work on the problem; we become thoroughly acquainted, thoroughly immersed, married to it.

Wrestling with this problem makes us an expert on it.

We invite others interested in the problem to criticize our best efforts at solution.

We carry on this critical discussion within the three rules mentioned earlier. The process is productive and endless: problems, theories, criticisms . . . problems, theories, criticism. . . .

Now let us look at some of the systems requirements for such problem-solving effort. First, the participants must be relatively free. They must have enough overt personal power to express individual opinions, to share these openly with others, and, if need be, to challenge current socially approved beliefs. In addition, participants must be equals. Criticisms of theory can only be potent and effective when carried on in an egalitarian atmosphere. Unequal power squelches such dialogue quickly, as the personal security of the participants becomes more important than the search for truth. Finally, for such a human interactional system to develop, one that includes openness, confidence, and relative personal freedom to think and communicate, there must be a genuine shared respect for the individual person's subjective reality and creative and productive potential. This description of the context of effective scientific productivity is also a description of the optimal milieu for ego development, as our family material will indicate. The climate necessary to develop capable scientists or capable people with adaptiveness, ingenuity, and good sense seems to be the same.

One can take this description of the scientific method and do a decent job of family therapy! Of course, therapists' personal characteristics, training, identification, models, and knowledge of some coherent theory are important, but much of the damage, as described by Bergin,[25] that some therapists do to patients will be avoided and the potency of family therapists will be augmented by learning and using scientific methodology.

This use of scientific methodology can be done in at least two ways. A clinician can join with others in a formal research project, attempting to determine who is helped and who is hurt by a clearly defined intervention approach. Examples of this are more and more frequent. Alexander,[5] Goldstein,[58] and Falloon[46] come quickly to mind as producing elegant examples of such enlightening and methodologically rigorous work. But clinicians may also use the scientific method with family members, inviting them to become peers in exploring problems, developing theories (reframes), and criticizing the results of using the new ways to understand and approach living problems. A therapist will soon learn the family's operating assumptions and will also develop a hypothesis or two. The therapist may offer these to be considered and criticized by family members. In such a contextual invitation to negotiate, the therapist does everything possible to develop an atmosphere of equal power, of openness and mutual competence, so that the process will be satisfying and successful. By doing so, the therapist proffers an opportunity to experience intimacy, possibly the first that the family members have experienced.

This scientific approach to family therapy, with its invitation for family members to become participants in problem-solving, can be a valuable model for all psychotherapeutic endeavors. Dealing with human pain, suffering, dreams, and possibilities, the scientist is the humanist, with respect for the intrinsic dignity and value of the people served. Learning is growth when it comes from shared exploration rather than indoctrination.

A FAMILY SYSTEMS APPROACH TO PSYCHOTHERAPY

Our overall approach to family therapy includes family assessment, the use of the scientific method described above, and a family systems orientation. This family systems approach to psychotherapy has many theoretical and pragmatic advantages. Systems thinking can integrate previously conflicting theories of treatment and data that apply at different levels of human experience. Such an approach is not only quite compatible with but also demands an appreciation of human biological data and theory, of human developmental data and theory, of individual psychic life, of family dynamics, and of larger human systems. The approach offers a psychotherapist many options to provide the common healing factor—that of increasing closeness and intimacy to significant others—which is necessary in successful treatment of people and relationships.

Every mental health discipline and fad claims the "right way" to do psychotherapy. Freudian, Adlerian, Jungian, behavioral, cognitive, gestalt, paradoxical, prescriptive; seeing people alone, as couples, as families, as groups, as environmental units: All are sometimes designated the only or the best way to help suffering people.

There are even more new competitors in the field, with buzzwords on their lips such as "co-dependent" and "adult children of dysfunctional families." These practitioners/evangelists are usually modestly trained and somewhat antagonistic to traditional mental health professionals. They often have very firm beliefs in biological causes that are doctrinaire rather than data-oriented. Some family therapists are fond of cryptic paradoxes or deliberate absurdities and use somewhat obscure and capricious interventions that can be comprehended only (if at all) by an alert and properly unfocused "right brain." Outcome studies on these newer approaches are, as far as we know, unobtainable.

Freudian and Jungian psychoanalysis, though still strong theoretical schools, are out of the running as techniques in psychotherapy. Too long, too costly, with no clear-cut evidence for efficacy, they are falling back into overt cultism, with true believers substituting for the unavailable data regarding effectiveness.

Short-term interventions relying on Freudian psychoanalytic theory are quite in vogue, with the short time interval itself considered some evidence of utility. However, the current psychoanalytic interest in character disorders[2,141] is not going to help the cause of increasing practicality of analytic treatment.

In unwinding this confusion, aspiring or current mental health professionals can choose the power route—determining *who* has the social power and, making that decision, going with that group. Or, alternatively, we can go with the group that has little power and attack the establishment, assuming it must be right since it is oppressed. This is a quite traditional way, i.e., powerful vs. persecuted or disdained, to struggle with and take sides on issues. Prior to the scientific revolution, there was no real alternative available.

If we wish to do better than this, how would we go about it? We can bring the dialogue into the 20th century and prepare for the 21st, replace the naive 19th-century rationalism, and arrive at a paradigm that depends on pragmatic results—the basic scientific premise. We can direct our best efforts at a determination of who should get which psychotherapy for what, and then work very hard on follow-up studies to learn whether our hunches and our clinical work stand up to careful scrutiny. With this approach, theory is respected to the degree that it is supported by data available to all for discussion. In reaching for a new comprehensive paradigm for psychotherapy we will present several intertwined and significant constructs that have supportive data. These include:

1. A useful way to conceptualize psychotherapy is that all types, including individual psychotherapy, are variations of family treatment, and that therapists must be responsible for their rationales and for choosing individual, couple, family, or group treatment.
2. The treatment of people with severe mental illness is more effective when done with a family systems approach.
3. A family systems approach includes the basic premise that there are many levels organizing people's lives—from interacting neurotransmitter substances and neural organization through intrapsychic mechanisms, couples, and families to institutions and societal structure. *Each level interacts with and influences the others.*
4. Most people enter psychotherapy with primary complaints about spouses and family members. When they do so, the therapist has an increased capacity to help and a reduced risk of harm by psychotherapy of multiples rather than individuals.
5. If individual psychotherapy is selected, transference and countertransference difficulties are minimized with a scientific, family systems approach.

All Psychotherapy Can Be Considered Family Therapy

We are born into families and live in relationships to and with others. Without a supporting network, a "family" of sorts, we become emotionally ill. Restoration to health requires a reestablishment of family.

For example, Pattison charted the daily contacts made by groups of normal adults, neurotics, and psychotic people and observed a clear and ominous decrease in contacts correlated with the presence of emotional illness and with its severity.[114] Emotional illness is directly correlated with isolation and distancing. "Family" is necessary for health then—not necessarily a traditional family, but a group of people who are committed to supporting one another and sharing their significance.

In choosing psychotherapy strategies, one should first consider the treatment category, that is, whether it should be individual, couple, family, or group. This is a critical choice and yet so often ignored—people do what they have been trained to do.

One of us (WRB) had a sad discussion with a sensitive and scholarly psychoanalyst. The discussion followed a presentation of a young woman with marital problems; the recommendation by those presenting the patient had been for her to enter into individual psychoanalysis. The psychoanalyst was informed of the Gurman, Kniskern and Pinsof data[65] regarding better outcome and less risk with marital or family therapy when the presenting complaint is one of marital or family discord. It was disturbing to find that he was not aware of the data, but it was downright painful when he said, "Well, I guess we just do what we are trained to do."

Here was a kind and intelligent mental health professional with years of experience giving a quite honest and unguarded answer. But such an answer will not do. Can you imagine the professional and malpractice problems radiologists would have if they refused to use CAT scans or magnetic resonance imagery techniques because "We simply do what we are trained to do?" We must find a better rationale for our various psychotherapeutic endeavors.

There are many compelling reasons to see a patient in individual treatment, of course. The single adult who has successfully left home but has not yet established a committed sexual relationship is a frequent subject for individual work. In this instance the psychotherapy will be "family therapy" if it (quite properly) centers on helping the individual gain living skills sufficient to move apart from a family of origin and to make a new family network (ultimately aimed at eliminating the need for a psychotherapist), in order for the person to develop hope, confidence, and good morale. Carl Whitaker has suggested that individual psychotherapy might be indicated with family members after the family therapy is successfully completed. Forty percent of the patient/client hours of those who call themselves marital and family therapists are individual therapy hours.[63] This suggests that even the most family-systems-oriented professionals are quite invested in doing individual psychotherapy.

However, in this era of intense but difficult efforts at cost containment, it is clear that psychotherapy *in hospitals* drains society's dollars more than does *outpatient* psychotherapy.[49] It is also clear that a treatment approach that includes the family can dramatically reduce the number of people who must be treated in hospitals,[49,54,94] as well as reducing the time in hospital,[57] much to the dismay of many profit-based inpatient facilities. Both treatment efficacy and cost containment are necessary responsibilities of modern mental health professionals, and the automatic assumption of an individual approach is becoming less defensible on either basis.

Efficacy of a Family Systems Approach to Severe Mental Illness

The treatment of people with severe mental illness has repeatedly been shown to be more effective when based on a family systems approach. Concepts of individual psychotherapy are inadequate and frequently useless in helping these people. May and coworkers, in a comprehensive study of schizophrenia, found only questionable advantages resulting from the use of individual psychotherapy in addition to adequate drug treatment and suggested that some types of individual psychotherapy frequently induced regression in these patients.[100] Various careful studies of family intervention, however, have shown significant, even dramatic, improvement in patient well-being and ability to remain out of hospital when treatment of the family is the chosen psychotherapeutic strategy.

A series of papers by Wing, Leff, Vaughn, and coworkers studying families of schizophrenics correlates recidivism with the presence of certain family processes.[32,33,150] They have shown that families differ in levels of a complex quality they term "expressed emotion" and that a therapeutic reduction of this expressed emotion in the family is quite feasible and reduces the frequency of rehospitalization.[95]

Goldstein and coworkers demonstrated the dramatic effects of a simple and direct form of family therapy with acute schizophrenic patients following first hospital admissions averaging 18 days. With six sessions of family work and adequate drug treatment, recidivism in six months was reduced to zero—compared to 30% in the group receiving adequate drug treatment but no family treatment.[58]

The treatment is truly an exercise in the scientific method. The family is informed that the patient has a mental illness and then there is an invitation to brainstorm about stressors that have led up to the illness. Then, prospectively, the family is invited to consider future stressors that the patient may encounter and to work together as a team in developing plans and strategies to reduce these stresses. The work is simple, elegant, and effective. Falloon and coworkers have reported an investigation of family treatment of chronically ill schizophrenic patients, most of whom were of lower socioeconomic status. Working with these families in a similar problem-solving and mutually brainstorming fashion resulted in dramatically lowered stress for the family. These tangible gains were stable and continued throughout follow-up into the third and fourth years.[47] Davenport and coworkers have reported impressive data concerning people with manic-depressive illness. When family members are included in treatment efforts that involve more than simply maintaining adequate lithium levels, there is a satisfying reduction in family breakup, job loss, and psychiatric catastrophes, including suicides.[39]

These studies strongly suggest that mental health professionals who wish to help people suffering from severe emotional problems need a family systems orientation and family therapy skills as a part of adequate training.[62] There also needs to be an overhaul of treatment and of therapists. "We were trained that way" is no longer adequate or acceptable.

Many Interacting Levels

A family systems approach includes the basic premise that there are many levels of organization in people's lives—and that each level interacts with and influences the others. We know that individual psychiatric illness, such as depression, can be induced by a lower, i.e., biological, level problem such as congestive heart failure or a meningioma and that treatment at the individual psychic level is relatively useless or counterproductive if the major contributor to dysfunction is elsewhere.

These multiple system level interactions have been a particular interest and focus of research at the Southwest Family Institute for some years.[13] We know that clinicians frequently encounter a complex relationship among family system, individual dynamics, and physical problems.[15,17] Our SFI research group has been focusing on the interrelationship of a child's developmental disability and that family's patterns of adaptation.[9,76] We have utilized these families in the further development of family assessment instruments, since it is our belief that family assessment is as important as individual diagnosis in understanding these interacting system level factors.

It is not as well appreciated, though quite well documented, that individual psychiatric illness can be induced by a higher level, i.e., dyadic, family or social problem. Certainly, a child's severe behavior disturbance can be the result of conflicted parents keeping the marriage intact through scapegoating the child;[106] a previously stable worker can become suicidally depressed by the loss of family role and social identity following a prolonged lay-off from a job.[61] Therapy at the individual level will be relatively ineffective or even counterproductive if the major contributors to dysfunction are at a different system level.

Psychotherapy of Multiples as Treatment of Choice

Psychotherapy of multiples is the best choice when people enter treatment complaining of problems with spouse or family. The Gurman and Kniskern data briefly mentioned earlier[64] support this position conclusively. Most individuals seek treatment complaining of problems with family members. Adequate outcome studies show a higher percentage of treatment success if they are seen as couples or families, when compared to individual psychotherapy. Further, there are seriously greater risks of decompensation and psychiatric emergencies when only individual treatment is provided for these family complaints.

The therapist sequestered with one patient is more vulnerable, as is the patient. Depressed and manipulative patients in such situations are encouraged to capitalize on the power of this helplessness. Continuous threats and/or allusions to suicide, for example, can make treatment efforts ineffective and subject to the control of the disturbed patient, as the isolated therapist becomes anxious and fearful. The focus needs to shift from intrapsychic forces to networking and group support.

The primary shift from individually oriented psychotherapy to a contextual or family systems orientation is manifested by the extreme value and emphasis placed upon people's supporting each other in social networks, as well as a sharp reduction in the belief that the therapist is the source of healing. The family therapist becomes the catalyst for change, even a consultant to the family.[162] This allows a more equal dialogue and fosters the scientific method of treatment—a dialogue with respected peers regarding problems, ways to deal with the problems (theories), and results (criticism). Family members are potential allies, who can be useful partners in treatment efforts. If there are none available, then therapists can insist on the patient's joining a therapeutic group. In a previous publication,[10] one of us (WRB) described the interpersonal pattern of impotence/omnipotence, which, though normally seen in a mother/infant relation, is an important aspect of emotional illness. Opening up the treatment system and inviting others to participate actively diminishes the likelihood that such a destructive dyad will continue.

Our world currently has many more divorces than in years past, many more single-parent families and many more blended families. These families are more apt to be centrifugal than centripetal. Yet all of the individually oriented psychotherapies have been developed for the individual products of intact, centripetal families, an average expectable environment for people who are verbal, believers in words, respectful of authority, not prone to impulsive and destructive expressions of negative feeling. We have many families with little emotional glue, who need help in organizing a caring supportive network for their members. Victims of even the most severe mental illnesses, e.g., chronic schizophrenia, are hopelessly lost without family. Such programs as the Fairweather project acknowledge this need for developing a family network by turning hospital isolates into group members and discharging these people together into a group living arrangement, a sort of family. These results are a clearly superior alternative to discharging isolated chronic schizophrenics into a social void.[150] Such programs are few and limited, and the public sector will not take the lead in expanding them. We professionals must direct others to family-systems-oriented mental health programs which offer greater efficacy and economy.

Reducing Transference in Individual Psychotherapy

For an individual to feel emotionally well, there must be a supportive network of people who show by action that this person is significant and valuable. Some emotional closeness must be experienced with a few of these supporting people. Sometimes a therapist will make the judgment that it is necessary to model this healing closeness by individual work. The treatment is a transitional phase, a kind of "Linus's blanket," with the goal of providing an experience that can be replicated in the patient's life with family and friends.

Individual work is focused on catalyzing a significant new learning and obtaining this vital supporting network; the emphasis is on identifying needs and learning to meet these needs through relationships with fallible, frustrating, delightful humans.

Such an approach views transference as ubiquitous but, if too intense, compromising to treatment effectiveness. Family-systems-oriented individual psychotherapy focuses on the patient's evolving competence. Transference intensity is discouraged because it interferes with rather than facilitates the work at hand. No evidence in the literature on psychotherapy research shows that intense transference is necessary or even useful in successful psychotherapy.

Inviting the patient to be a fellow investigator, identifying needs and problems, and developing effective solutions that work in the world outside the office, is valuable in avoiding an exaggerated view of the therapist's role or qualities. The psychotherapist's purpose is defined as assisting people to re-experience the intimacy and the reward-multiplying joys usually most prominent in the inception of a family relationship, as in love or as a new parent. In this way the therapist acts as a technician of relating rather than as a central character in the drama, thus reducing the transference problems. Anyone who has treated a married person of the opposite sex as an individual and then treats that person or a similar individual as a therapist of a couple will notice and usually testify to the striking reduction of heavy emotional pulls and sticky intensity with the therapist.

Group therapy can be considered an additional way of providing the closeness to be found in individual psychotherapy with a minimizing of transference difficulties. Using a therapy group in addition to the individual treatment can provide an artificial family with rules that are more humane, more caring, than those of the family from whence the patients come. The group is a highly effective way to break up destructive transference resistance, which flourishes in dark secret places and withers in the light of the social network.

For example, a 32-year-old housewife/socialite with a dramatically alcoholic husband came into treatment because of depression and difficulties coping with her husband. Repeated efforts to bring her husband into private sessions were unsuccessful. In a short time the patient developed a powerful neurotic transference to the male therapist and attempted to use intensity of feeling to control the treatment activities. Since the husband was one of those rare spouses who refuses to appear, the therapist invited the patient to enter group treatment in addition to individual psychotherapy. After some initial reluctance, she shared with the group her feelings about the therapist and was able to refocus her attention on the practical solutions to living that were needed but previously unavailable.

CONCLUSION

This chapter is an introduction to a particular viewpoint about psychotherapy. This viewpoint is based on applying current concepts of science and of family systems. A dialogue develops in the therapeutic process that is open-ended, uncertain, and exploratory, with respect for those who come for help. Data from the family structure and interaction as well as from the family members are sought and used in formulating solutions to presenting problems.

This is a brief summary of the model of psychotherapy basic to this book. It is faithful to the concept that a scientific approach to human material greatly enhances the probability of people's being treated with dignity and respect. Yet, utilizing a formal scientific approach, this method of therapy can be critiqued, as can all others, and the question of which groups of families benefit from the method can be addressed and at least partially answered. As we have tried to practice this way, we have experienced the excitement of people respecting each other, working hard on a problem, and sharing the exhilaration of finding solutions. We shall describe these effects in the next several chapters.

8 SOME GENERAL CONCEPTS REGARDING FAMILY INTERVENTION

Our clinical research is woefully incomplete; doing follow-up studies in a busy clinical setting is fraught with perils to procedural purity. However, we do have useful data in which we can place a reasonable amount of confidence. These data lead us to some general observations about family intervention as well as specific suggestions regarding procedures useful with the various family groups described in Section One.

In this chapter we cover the general conclusions regarding treatment of families derived from family research and clinical observations. The clinical statements are those of a family-systems-oriented psychiatrist with over 37,000 hours of face-to-face clinical work who has used the assessment method since its beginnings in supervising over 200 mental health professionals. Here, as throughout the book, we attempt to make the implicit explicit through research—moving "clinical" experience out of the shadows and displaying it for all to see and evaluate. Although we have only partly completed this work, we approach the ever-receding goal proudly.

Stereotyped interventions are not particularly useful. Our clinical research supports the view that different family groups, like different patient groups, require specific attention to their unique attitudes and problems and to varying techniques and procedures that are determined by the assessment. Chapters to follow will expand on this thesis. Nevertheless, there are several *principles* that hold true for all family treatment. These are the subject of this chapter.

THE "MAGIC" OF PSYCHOTHERAPY

There is a profound ambivalence in the field of mental health. Psychotherapists wish to be scientific, yet also wish to be seen as artists whose products are experienced rather than quantified. This is understandable, even laudable. Healing is more than science, yet it becomes quackery when totally divorced from scientific rigor. Competent therapists fluctuate between the limits of a scientific discipline and the infinite possibilities of inspired intuition.

A point at which these two necessary but contradictory aspects of psychotherapy come together might very well be described as the phenomenon of magic that keeps us (and all other psychotherapists) in business: *the development of sufficient closeness whereby one person's hunger feeds another.*

That's it. That's what keeps us all in business—all us individual psychotherapists, all us marital and family therapists, strategic and psychoanalytic and structural and whatever! If we can help troubled people get close enough to somebody in their network (building a network if it is absent), we can add to the available vital emotional food. And it comes from others' emotional need!

The hope for families and family members resides in this bit of magic—get two people close enough *without losing the awareness of separateness* and the hunger of each is the food of the other.

When people are distant, alienated, when they feel small or powerless, they fear the vulnerability and need in others and dream of finding loving, competent, god-like people who give without needing in turn. When these same people experience closeness and intimacy, the need of one person feeds the other because it is experienced as warmth. A number of years ago, one of us (WRB) defined warmth as "human need, honestly expressed, with a recognition of the limits of the other."[10] It is the closeness that allows one hungry person empathically to determine the limits of another.

Let's try an example or two. A mother with no bonding to her child will see that child as a monster demanding her soul as well as her milk; obligation and guilt can drive her to mother, but the child's needs will be seen as depriving. One step closer and the child's needs are seen as similar to the mother's—human, not monstrous—and satisfying that need is a great source of gratification. Adequacy—as a woman and as a mother—is affirmed by the infant.

Or the newborn's father is threatened by the child, whose needs will take the father's woman away. The child's needs are in direct competition with the needs of the father. One step closer and the father sees the infant as his enlarged fulfillment and mother's feeding infant is concretely experienced as feeding father as well. Father can then respond warmly to mother, and a three-handed game of hunger being fed is demonstrated.

Measurements of closeness, intimacy, sharing, and the like do exist.

In our own scales used to measure family functioning, both those used by outside raters and by family members, the degree of closeness can be given a numerical value.

The artist, however, is interested in creating an experience—damn the numbers. This artist/psychotherapist knows that closeness comes from experiencing with another the raw humanness that we all share. Human relationship structures, though necessary, inevitably attenuate that experience; parents are sharply differentiated from children and forget what it is like to be a child; people in a sexist society or family are trained to sharply differentiate male from female, so that the opposite sex is experienced not as a fellow human but as an enemy.

So structures that poorly serve the humans that exist within the framework of those structures are challenged by the healer, whether this be strategically, structurally, logically, emotionally, or magically. And, with luck, closeness evolves and the hungry are fed by another's hunger. Then the magician moves on.

PRINCIPLES OF INTERVENTION

In helping family members to achieve this healing and feeding closeness, several important yet basic principles are worth noting.

1. *You can't give to others what you don't have (choosing and facilitating choice)*.

It is important to remember that an isomorphic quality of family systems and individual systems is conflict. At the individual level it is called ambivalence. Personal ambivalence and family conflict are ubiquitous, inevitable, and unrelated to pathology. However, the ability to *resolve* conflict and ambivalence is the hallmark of family or individual health.

(a) Systems don't change themselves—people change systems. Therefore, individual action by the therapist or one or more family members is necessary to produce system change.
(b) The most effective therapeutic interventions increase the abilities of family members to choose, to resolve ambivalence, and to negotiate with others in achieving a greater degree of satisfaction and living. In short, an increase in individual autonomy and choice-making is synergistic with and indicative of a useful family change.
(c) If the therapist is controlled by a rigid and limiting ideology, treatment of the system in which the therapist is embedded cannot move in the direction of greater individual or family health.

A developmental theme underlies all of these clinical assertions. Human development inevitably moves toward separateness, the differentiation of self from others and the leaving of one's family to develop new relationships that are stronger than the family of origin ties. Symptoms in families and in individuals are signs of "stuck" positions—patterns that repeat over and over without movement toward growth and individuation.

The most valuable aspect of any treatment is the experience of something new in interaction—something that frees, that points toward hopeful possibilities, and that increases patient morale. This is inevitably assisted by modeling on the part of the therapist—modeling of a spirit of and skill in negotiation. These experiences allow family members who are stuck in assumptions about the inevitability of failure in achieving desired goals to develop their own negotiating skills and to know greater autonomy and successful choice-making.

Bergin, in assessing individual therapy, found that people in treatment either got very much better or very much worse than controls.[25] Though he took Eysenck to task for viewing psychotherapy as essentially useless,[44] Bergin challenged psychotherapists to find which of us make people better and which make people worse, or which of our patients we help and which we make dysfunctional. This same message is quite appropriate to family therapists. There are many practitioners enamored of techniques that have no clear evidence of utility. At the same time there are carefully researched methods of family therapy that show remarkable results in severely dysfunctional patient populations. These methods are clearly solution-oriented, open-ended, and offer participants a maximum of opportunities to express opinion and choice.

Both Goldstein, working with the families of acute schizophrenics,[58,142] and Falloon, addressing the needs of families with chronic schizophrenic disorder,[46,47] have shown that involving family members in the shared projects of exploring stress inducers and developing possible solutions to reduce the stress on the patient helps patient and the family to cope more effectively. These therapies can be seen as practical exercises in applying the scientific method, if the method is basically considered a dialogue among peers who make observations, who discuss their meaning, and who determine consensually interventions designed to effect favorable results.[10]

2. *Suffering may be unavoidable but is not necessary or useful.*
Many families and not a few therapists have the notion that progress is marked by emotional pain and suffering. Little, if any, research data

support such notion. Healthy families are marked by good humor and a pleasant optimistic atmosphere. The degree of family dysfunction is highly correlated with the amount of painful, despairing, harsh, depressed, and/or angry affect present.[97]

This concept may be illustrated by imagining two basketball teams— one badly coached, badly trained, and accustomed to losing, the other well coached, well trained, and accustomed to winning. Skill in basketball or in human relationships is accompanied by a pleasant feeling tone. Generosity of spirit and supportive, reassuring feelings result from good morale, which is a by-product of confidence and a sense of mastery.

That same concept applies to therapists as well. "Burnout" is frequently described as an ever-present risk with clinicians who work with severely dysfunctional families. Burnout is the result of trying to do too much with too little, taking on responsibilities that cannot be discharged effectively, defining goals for the self and for the family members that neither are realistic nor result from negotiations. Such interventions lead to unmet goals and therapist pain and suffering. This inevitably afflicts the families in treatment, for they cannot feel enthusiastic or joyful with a suffering therapist. Negotiating clearly defined goals that all participants believe to be attainable and are willing to share responsibility for is a powerful step in achieving good morale and good results.

3. *The therapist is to give and expect decent treatment.*

The first inkling of what family members can expect comes with the initial interview. Is the therapist aware of the importance and techniques of joining or does he or she have little appreciation of this important aspect of treatment? If one is too technique oriented or system conscious, to the exclusion of the people reaching for some help, family members may feel that they don't count. On the other hand, members of poorly functioning families are sometimes cynical, hostile, openly contentious, and even insulting to a therapist. They will be suspicious of overt demonstrations of warmth.

A reasonably good procedure, which both reassures patients of their significance and dignity and maintains the same qualities for oneself, is to keep steadfastly to the development of a *contract based on the needs of the people in the room*. This very much includes the needs of the therapist as well as the needs of the family members. Therapists, like all humans, require a certain dignity and respect in order to feel good and respond to others warmly and supportively.

Therapists have developed many techniques to deal with difficult patients and families and still maintain dignity. Rather than detail these techniques, let us tell a story which captures them in metaphor:

Long ago one of us (WRB) was a young father with a young son. The father had a workbench with many tools in the garage and had built a similar but pint-size workbench with tools for the three-year-old son. Both were working away one Saturday morning when the father, who was very disorganized, couldn't find his hammer and impulsively reached down to the small workbench for his son's tiny hammer. The boy drew himself up to his three-foot height and said, "I will let you use my hammer."

In one fell swoop the three-year-old had taken the initiative and control of the situation, even though he was outmatched and overshadowed.

This the therapist must do—maintain dignity without overplaying the hand that is dealt. When this happens, the therapeutic experience can offer dignity, respect, and freedom to family members.

4. *Every successful family therapy is an experience in observing multiple levels of systems and how each level influences the others.*

Severe physical or emotional illness is a profound factor in family dynamics. For example, developmentally disabled children place great stress on families; this cannot be overestimated when we attempt to understand presenting family dynamics of families who have a developmentally disabled member.[9]

Economic hard times and job losses can derail a previously well-functioning family. In our original healthy family studies,[97] one optimal family dropped dramatically in family functioning on a three-year follow-up. The father had lost his prestigious but hard-to-replace job and mother had been forced to work. Father was drinking rather heavily, mother was resentful, and the children were anxious and irritable.

Stresses due to biology, physical illness, and social forces can be as significant as a sudden outburst of psychosis in paralyzing family coping methods. However, increasing family system adaptability can help families overcome awesome stress from other system levels. Even in healthy families this is dramatically evident. A 13-year-old girl, in the first bloom of adult feminine attractiveness and sexual power, can influence the family dynamics powerfully. Mother can be rivalrous in a way that she doesn't understand and has not been previously; father may either shun his daughter phobicly or cater as adoringly as a courtesan to a queen; this has a remarkable effect on the couple dyad as well as on other aspects of the family system.

5. *Helping people handle loss is always a part of useful intervention.*

Depression,[116] psychosis,[89] substance abuse,[36] and sexual problems[126] are individual emotional symptoms that have been related to un-mourned or poorly mourned losses. It is safe to say that loss and a failure to overcome its threatening aspects are part of every emotional problem. Successful psychotherapy of any sort can be regarded as addressing these losses either directly or indirectly.

Direct approaches have been described by such clinicians as the Pauls,[115] Stanton and Todd[135] and Coleman.[36] Sometimes a family presents with such obvious need to mourn that a sensitive therapist will respond and address that need immediately.

Indirect approaches include any technique that increases family members' morale and a sense of being close and safe. Mourning cannot be completed alone; successful recovery from a significant loss always requires the sharing of feelings surrounding the loss. Only when we help family members resolve their conflict can healing from loss take place. Additional loss can be better accepted when alternative sources of satisfaction can be identified and hoped for. For instance, if adolescents are assisted in separating from the family, the old wounds of a lost parent or sibling or grandparent can better heal.

Losses are inevitable; they may be crippling unless mourned well. Mourning requires someone close to share the loss. Helping families function better can be done by approaching unspoken feelings regarding the loss directly. But feelings regarding losses can be expressed more easily and mourning better accomplished when a family is functioning well and has little chronic unresolved conflict. Techniques are available to intervene at any point in this circle.

6. *Helping families solve problems and mobilize resources is superior to acting as a "change agent."*

This principle is probably more controversial than the preceding ones, since a rather sizable body of family therapy literature implies or states that the therapist is the actor, the proactive force changing things around and treating the family. Common sense, research data, and the bountiful increase in self-help books, however, suggest otherwise. Once again, the most clear-cut demonstrations of family therapy efficacy are those where the therapist brings family members in as partners, mutually identifying difficulties and solving problems.[47,58] This reduces any pesky belief in a therapist's omnipotence and emphasizes a reality that healthy families have always known—that it is important to be able to depend on each other in the family and to make good friends in the larger community whom you can count on in times of trouble.

Outcome research in family therapy is paralleled by findings in individual psychotherapy. Cognitive therapies and interpersonal therapies that emphasize the power of the patient and/or the patient's milieu in resolving conflicts and symptoms produce better results than analytic techniques that accentuate the significance of the therapist (e.g., developing a "transference neurosis").[109] If a family therapist wishes initially to use a large overt power difference to create change, the effort must be short-term. Longer-term treatment with a large overt power edge inevitably encourages either family coping mechanisms that center on the therapist or a rejection of the therapist's methodology. Most family therapy is relatively brief and/or egalitarian in comparison to individual techniques, so the potential problem of dependence has been less significant than with intensive individual therapies.

Wynne and coworkers have developed a concept and approach labeled "family consultation" that emphasizes the importance of empowering family and family members.[162] They assist families in solving current problems, finding community sources of help, and altering coping strategies effectively. These concepts can help all of us resist burnout, reduce our omnipotent fantasies, and become more open to a variety of treatment styles.

7. *Having a treatment plan based on family assessment is essential.*
No competent therapist does treatment without assessment. If one is given the opportunity to "treat" by a license, by an institution, or by a family, then the assumption is that one treats something that is identifiably wrong.

It isn't really a question of whether one *assesses*, but, rather, whether one uses a "public," clearly defined method or one's own private method. And, if the method is private, is the therapist aware of doing the assessment?

The older generation of family therapists, such as Ackerman, Satir, Whitaker, Minuchin, and Nagy, have followed a historical pattern seen in the pioneers of individual psychotherapy. They have all been, in Freud's colorful phrase, *conquistadors*—bold adventurers exploring a new territory with danger all around and wearing armor needed for protection. The armor in this instance has been reassuring and comfortable technique. After the territory has been gained, settlers come in and make friends with the natives, learning their ways and coexisting with them, possessing increasing respect for the characteristics and patterns of the individuals, families, and groups in the territory. Today the therapist no longer needs to rule by conducting, but can guide by reacting and joining. Formal assessment of families allows for rational alteration and variation of techniques and strategies.

8. *The setting or context is significant in choosing treatment techniques.*

In a public setting serving a specific population group or in a preferred provider organization under contract to cover a specific number of lives for a fixed amount, the emphasis will be on short-term treatment that addresses symptoms as rapidly and effectively as possible and sends the clients away. This has the positive effect of encouraging therapists to remain dispensable; however, there is a continuing risk of not joining with the family sufficiently and not helping family members cope well enough to avoid further troubles. These halfway efforts at treatment may send patients later to inpatient units, bypassing therapists in the hurry-in-and-out clinic and producing a greater health care cost and a greater cost to the patient's welfare than would a more intensive family-centered approach.

Insurance companies' statistics show that, in 1986, only 40% of psychiatric inpatient claims also had outpatient claims for the same year.[159] This strongly suggests that less than half of inpatients in psychiatric hospitals had an initial trial of outpatient therapy or decent outpatient follow-up. Frequently the most conventional and easiest approach is the most expensive. As family therapy becomes more respectable and understood, it can stand as a bulwark against quick definitions of a family member as the ill person and contribute greatly to family and individual family member competence, as well as reduced costs for mental health care.

In a subsidized or private setting where the clients are in the driver's seat, emphasis is much more likely to be on growth-oriented therapy. Marital therapy to improve relationship skills or family therapy to help the overall family functioning will often be requested. This allows, even demands, that therapists get to know their clients, and vice versa. Warm and genuine relationships, still within the bounds of ethical, professional, and therapeutic rules, are often experienced, in addition to the satisfaction of a job well done. Intuitively, one feels that, in a world where kind, close, and genuinely respectful relationships are at a premium, this experiencing of one in a treatment setting is therapy at its best.

On the down side, of course, is the potential for patients to "settle in"—to become dependent on treatment, with therapeutic goals either so nebulous or so forgotten that they cannot be met. This is much less frequent when several family members are seen, probably because it is more difficult to mobilize the whole family week after week. In individual therapy, it is not uncommon to see patients making the trek to a beloved therapist rain or shine, month after month, for years and years, with dubious results.

Hence, the setting strongly influences treatment contracts. It is important for a therapist to keep in touch with peers and administrators who can have an effect on these settings. This leads to our next and last point.

9. *Follow-up is essential to the improvement of treatment methods and therapists' skills.*

Psychotherapy research is out of favor in Washington circles these days (if it was ever in), yet program evaluation and cost-effectiveness are in favor all over the country. This produces some strange results, since federal grants may pay for poor or sometimes reasonably decent outcome research, as long as it is developed and maintained under the heading of program evaluation and/or cost-effectiveness.

There is a widespread wailing and gnashing of teeth over the sad state of mental health care and the commercialization of psychotherapy of all sorts. Psychiatric treatment is big business now. It is often alleged that we psychotherapists just want people and corporations to continue to pay us and have faith that we are competent and on the side of the angels.

As mental health costs have soared from 10% to 18% of the total health care dollar in the last six years,[159] and as the total of health care costs spirals upward, there is an understandable desire of administrators and payers to control—i.e., to reduce cost and to insure value for expense. Harkening back to Bergin's discomfiting data that many patients get worse if they are treated, the honorable and scientifically curious therapist cannot help but see a bit of zesty challenge in the current state of affairs. Yes, many of the administrative efforts to control costs and to determine efficacious treatment have been foolish, heavy-handed, and even draconian at times; however, the goal of getting needed services to the public at a decent price is compatible with our goals as therapists.

Even as solo practitioners and certainly as members of a treatment-providing organization, we can develop some sophistication and some data regarding the outcome of our work. A standardized telephone call six months after treatment does not take much in the way of time, but it can pay large dividends in learning from one's clinical experience.

At our own family institute, the research is not subsidized; it comes right out of the clinician's total time. But there is satisfaction in adding a bit to our knowledge of how to treat families. We believe that follow-up and analysis of results will eventually become a regular part of clinicians' activities.

BROAD CATEGORIES OF HELP FOR FAMILIES

"Garden Variety" Family Therapy

The typical modality is for a clinical family to meet, with all members present, with one or more therapists conjointly. The main goal of intervention is systemic change that will maintain therapeutic gains in the identified patient(s), through increased clarity, role and boundary changes, generational differentiation, leadership enhancement, etc. This is where the majority of the "schools" of therapy (identified by the diverse chapter headings in textbooks)[64] are classified. The therapist joins, structures, challenges, paradoxes, and/or loves the family. As the remainder of this volume will elaborate, different families require different qualities and procedures from therapists. For example, the more dysfunctional the family the more important structuring becomes. CF families require more power differential and structuring skills than CP families at a similar competence level, because CP families respond better initially to joining and supportive maneuvers and attend more to the magic of words rather than overt behavior.

Therapy Team (Behind-the-Mirror Approaches)

These approaches, which utilize active therapy teams, some in the room with the family,[160] some observing and intervening from behind a one-way mirror,[128] form a structurally and relationally different stance with the family, increasing the power differential between therapists and family members. This stance may be necessary with potentially violent clientele and is very useful in dealing with chaotic or loosely structured families. Hence, more disturbed families and those of more CF (often lower social class) style are most likely to benefit from such structural power differential. On the other hand, many borderline and midrange CP families are extremely uncomfortable with the lack of joining and distance signified by the faceless observers.

Fostering of Resolution of Unmourned Losses

Whether with a whole family present or with an individual, the context of these interventions is a therapist working with a patient/client to foster adaptation to crisis or loss.[116,135] The temporal nature of the loss may be short-term (death of a loved one in the past year) or long-term (abuse or rejection during childhood). The signal for such intervention involves current relational difficulties, depression, or situational anxiety. The goals are to foster expression of feelings, especially anger (in CP families) or sorrow (CF families) toward acceptance of a loss. In more disturbed families (or families with more disturbed individuals), the therapist must also structure the interventions surrounding the use of denial, projection, blaming, or psychotic maneuvering used by the patient to stave off the painful passing of time. These time-binding mechanisms of more disturbed systems prevent the eventual acceptance of separation and loss.

The Therapist as Consultant to the Family

This class of interventions deals with the provision of information and support to families in stressful circumstances. The therapist provides information on how to support an ill member and consultative skill/stress management principles to the system or available subsystem.[162] These consultative interventions are most appropriate for lower functioning families and families of lower socioeconomic levels (usually more CF). They help families to understand what to expect through the crisis period and to build strategies for coping with the crisis or illness.

At one level, psychoeducational programs such as Falloon's[47] are geared toward providing information and support to families with schizophrenic members, helping them know what to expect and how to best care for the patient and themselves (no dramatic movement in family system "functioning" is expected). Wynne et al.[162] provide examples of a family consultant model in cases of physical illness as well as in psychiatric debilitation. Likewise, family consultants have been used for family support and problem management in child placement programs,[71] where the stability of the placement of a disturbed child depends upon the family's adaptation to that child's behavioral and emotional difficulties.

At a potentially high level of system functioning, the therapist/consultant may become teacher and socratic facilitator in such enterprises as parenting skills, multifamily group enrichment classes, and preventive skills development (such as communication skills classes). These are targeted typically for midrange or better functioning families.

It is quite useful for a therapist to keep all of these possibilities in mind and even to be on the lookout for ways to help that might not easily be classified under any of these categories.

The following outline summarizes our current concepts regarding intervention and connect the general observations of this chapter with the more specific approaches suggested in the following chapters.

I. Considerations for different levels of family competence
 A. Severely dysfunctional families
    1. Assist family members in making sense to one another; develop coherent discussion.
    2. Clarify context of treatment and of relationships.
    3. Define expectations of participants in therapy.
    4. Bring up the opposite of whatever single feeling or attitude is expressed, thereby making a place safe for acknowledging and expressing ambivalence.
    5. Offer hope whenever possible.
    6. Yet acknowledge one's own despair when it occurs; this is occasionally useful, even necessary.
    7. Use team and behind-the-mirror approaches when available.
 B. Borderline families
    1. Be ready to derail efforts at controlling therapy and therapist.
    2. Use story telling, whimsy.
    3. Use indirect methods of intervention frequently, such as predicting setbacks, urging family to go slow, carefully prescribing symptom.
    4. Reach for the painful feelings of the more overtly powerful family members.
    5. Use team and behind-the-mirror approaches when available.
 C. Midrange families
    1. Invite partnership.
    2. Develop power only to give it away.
    3. Join in a closer fashion, with more shared feelings.
    4. Respond to expressed desire for greater intimacy between family members; these family members have the potential to find it.
II. Considerations for different family styles
 A. Centrifugal families
    1. Use physical intervention, e.g., move between hostile combatants.
    2. Directly control physical placement, e.g., increase or decrease space between family members.
    3. Use positive reframing frequently.
    4. (And thereby) emphasize the denied positive side of ambivalence.

5. Confuse when there is a spurious certainty that could produce an attack.
6. Avoid the use of "paradoxical" interventions; there is little "glue" in the system to hold it together—an important factor in the success of this type of intervention.
7. These families come in crisis; focus on the immediate problem and its solution.
8. Begin with and maintain an overt power edge; this will usually last for short treatment periods.
9. Do not expect to work with the whole family. Deal with those who can be reached.
10. Do not concern yourself with being close or open with family members.
11. When words are used, try in every way possible to have behavior that matches and accompanies the words.

B. Centripetal families
1. Expect the whole family to be present when requested.
2. Use concepts; words are respected, as is authority.
3. Encourage separateness.
4. Use positive reframes sparingly.
5. Encourage expression of negative feelings relatively often.
6. Look for and encourage dissipation of family secrets.
7. Investigate loyalties; who is owed what by whom?
8. Beware of families "settling in," becoming dependent on therapy and therapist.

9 THE TREATMENT OF MIDRANGE FAMILIES

Both midrange mixed (MR mxd) and midrange centripetal (MRCP) families are frequently seen in family therapy. The midrange centrifugal family is rarely, if ever, seen. These MRCF families are not sufficiently maladaptive or symptomatic to draw the attention of external forces such as schools or law enforcement agencies, which in turn may pressure their members to come into treatment. In addition, since they tend to mistrust words and are wary of authority, they are highly unlikely to appear in a therapist's office of their own accord.

Treatment approaches for MR mxd and MRCP families can be considered together. We have found that, though their stylistic differences need to be taken into account, treatment approaches do not need to be altered significantly.

UNDERLYING ATTITUDES AND EXPECTATIONS OF THE THERAPIST FOR MIDRANGE FAMILIES

Power struggles are not a real threat with these families if the therapist is reasonably gentle and does not attempt to impose attitudes or behavior markedly foreign to the historical family patterns. In other words, these family members can be expected to be reasonably cooperative, without letting past experiences derail or undermine the treatment process.

While it is useful to show respect for the dignity and worth of each person in the room (including the therapist) in any treatment experience, it is doubly important with this group of families. It is not necessary to be tough, to demand an overt power difference, or to hide one's strategies. Indeed, such tactics can easily lengthen treatment or even diminish the chances for success.

With these families, the basic challenge is not how to gain enough power to be effective, but simply how to empower the family members. There are challenges in the changes inherent in growth and development, aging and death, that require significant interpersonal skills. These families are just short of the skills necessary for such challenges.

One can reasonably expect success in the treatment efforts in MR families. Our own clinical studies show clearly that the more competent the family is rated at the outset, the greater positive change is shown in follow-up. This is consistent with theoretical considerations. The more adaptive and less fixed or stuck the family is, the more movement can be expected from a treatment experience.

These are the families that make a practice possible! They usually come willingly and have a good prognosis. There is generally a pleasant and enjoyable atmosphere while these families are being treated.

The symptoms of individual members of MR families include depression, moderate acting-out, various substance abuses, sexual dysfunction, school problems, and occasionally acute transient (schizophreniform) psychotic episodes.

The system symptoms more frequently encountered are couple conflicts, severe enough at times to lead to divorce, incomplete separation of spouses from families of origin, conflicts between parents and children over desired behavior and performance, and increasingly, conflicts over the care and/or disposition of aged parents.

Setting

In a busy, overburdened public clinic, short-term intervention is a necessity, not a choice. For midrange families, potential problems in therapy often center around avoiding dependency on the therapist and normalizing and affirming characteristic family behavior that was troublesome. As an example, a family may come in with a child whose school performance is less than the child's potential would indicate. Following an evaluation, the child may be defined as healthy but simply possessing different goals from those of his parents.

On the other hand, in a private practice setting one often has the luxury of meeting family requests for extended work. The child in the above example might be defined as being the "stalking horse" for the family—having developed moderate symptoms as a way of bringing the family into treatment so that everyone can explore goals, needs, and developmental directions. Neither of these approaches is "wrong" in some absolute way. Each approach can be useful to families, but each would be maladaptive when practiced in the wrong treatment setting. (In our family institute, all trainees are deliberately provided with opportunities to work in both settings during their supervised treatment experience; either setting alone, we believe, would be apt to produce technicians with insufficient appreciation of the usefulness of various techniques and the importance of context.)

Joining

Midrange families are most apt to incorporate the social stereotypes of the broader society.[10] Therefore, it is important that a therapist look and act like an orthodox professional in dress, manner, and behavior. The "good" therapist must have as many degrees on the wall as possible, as authority is respected (though, in the case of MR mixed families, not necessarily taken too seriously).

These families will typically come as a unit if this is requested, and it is important for the therapist, in joining with the family, to have a genuine and warm encounter with each member, making eye contact and a real effort to empathize. In talking with the family members during a first visit, the therapist models a negotiating position in an "illustrated lecture"—providing an experience in reaching a consensus between therapist and family member as to how that family member views the problem(s) and the reason for coming to treatment.

This joining is done and redone throughout the therapeutic process. If an overtly powerful family member feels unheard and disregarded, the family may be prematurely lost from treatment. If a member with little overt power feels *rejected*, the therapy can deteriorate into a group of grown-ups saying "ain't it awful"—covert power is effective in demolition if not in constructive action.

In the course of therapy with MR families, a straightforward, easy to understand approach will be rewarded. A therapist will do well to offer a rationale for treatment maneuvers that is clearly grasped by family members. This disclosure of rationale and strategy is evidence of joining and trust-building desired by MR families.

For example, a structural move of changing the sitting place of two or more family members will be readily accepted if that request is accompanied by an explanation such as, "Dad and mother, you seem to have a hard time getting together on this issue. Perhaps if you are sitting next to one another, you can more easily talk over your positions and become more comfortable."

Or, "People tend to notice another's behavior they don't want; however, the behavior that leads up to the unwanted actions is often not noticed. In the next week, I want all of you to write down the instances of behavior in members of your family that you don't like, and then write down as many things as you remember that you and others were doing prior to that unwanted behavior."

Or, "Excuse me, John, but I want to interrupt right here. You are pretty clearly upset with Sally, but the way that you're saying it is puzzling to me. I think when you say that Sally takes after Madonna rather than after her mother you are saying she does some things you don't like, but it isn't very clear. Could you tell her and me what's the beef?"

Or, "I would like for father to take the responsibility for disciplining Sarah until our next session. Mother and Sarah seem to be so frazzled in trying to relate without explosions that a period of respite may help them both back off, to get out of the ring."

CONTROL ISSUES IN MIDRANGE FAMILIES

From the start, it is useful to approach the family's efforts at negotiation with an emphasis on each person's wishes and desires. It is not easy to rehabilitate the concept of "selfish" with these families; there is too much familial and cultural negative freight attached to the term. So we usually operate on the principle of assisting each family member in achieving a greater degree of enlightened self-interest, without going against strongly ingrained beliefs that a good person is unselfish. Frequently, our reframing of selfish is "being responsible for oneself." However, this is not always so.

It may be useful to tell a story to a family group with whom a therapist has developed some rapport. This story can be along these lines: Three-year-old Molly has a little friend her age over to play but is hoarding all her toys and not letting her visitor play with any. Mother says, "Don't be selfish, Molly. Share your toys." What mother is saying, of course, is a little different from what she is trying to get across. She is really saying, "Don't be stupid, Molly. If you don't give the kid something to play with, she'll go home mad, you'll be miserable all afternoon, and so will I." Mother is attempting to teach enlightenment rather than unselfishness.

The emphasis on what the family members individually want is crucial to helping them move up the ladder of competence and negotiating capacity. Midrange families have a rule that "Loving means controlling" because people are basically bad and "my advantage comes out of your hide and your advantage comes out of mine." When family members experience some successes in working out problems to the satisfaction of all, they are close to the healthy family rule: "Your advantage is mine, and mine is yours. If you suffer damage, that diminishes me." When such rules are sensed and the possibilities of everyone's winning are clear, the midrange family is close to reaching for intimacy and closeness rather than control. This is part of the fun and good prognosis with midrange families—intimacy is possible without prolonged treatment efforts.

"Unilateral bargains" is an oxymoron that is usually found in family conflicts and is quite noticeable in midrange families. The phrase refers to assumptions in one person's head of a bargain or contract with another that has not been made direct or verbal, but is nevertheless quite real to that one person.

Unilateral bargains often originate in the coming together of the couple to make a family. Each carries specific family rules and expectations from the family of origin into the new relationship without discussion. The failure of the partner to meet the terms of the unilateral contract results in a sense of betrayal, rejection, and open or hidden unresolved conflict. These unilateral bargains lie behind the development of individual symptoms as meaningful responses to family needs and dynamics.

For example, a surgeon and his wife presented with their oldest son as the problem because of his poor school performance and his refusal to do homework. Mother was furious with her husband because he was gone so much, though he had been in a residency and had been gone about as much when they first married. Her father was an accountant with regular hours who was home on a generally predictable schedule. It didn't take long to discover that the "erring" son was faithfully expressing his mother's anger with the father, since the father was terribly but impotently angry about his son's lack of interest in school. The son's contempt for the father's years of scholarly effort, which made him an absentee parent, was a variation on his mother's frustration. The father, of course, felt virtuous in his attention to patients. The unilateral nature of the presumed bargain between the parents came to light rather quickly.

The lateral approach, that of inviting family members to become colleagues in problem-solving, allows for a wide variety of interventions with oftimes a sense of lightness and joy in interaction. For instance, genograms[102] allow family members to pursue family patterns, losses, successes, and failures over generations, and to compare and contrast the families of both parents. In this way an atmosphere of exploration can be developed and the opportunity to make meaningful corrections in patterns enhanced. Family sculpting is another rich source of information regarding perceptions of each family member. Any revealed differences are opportunities to develop an enriched shared reality that is more sympathetic and less oppositional.[125]

It is important to remember that midrange families desire control as well as closeness. This is true even in families with badly misbehaving children, as one of the ubiquitous midrange family rules is "Loving *means* controlling." Therefore the therapist "goes with the flow"—offering control. No MR family ever comes to treatment because there is too much control; rather, it comes because someone perceives there to be too little. Part of the necessary negotiations will involve successfully increasing control of what can be controlled and accepting what cannot. Total control of others is not possible, but a good relationship will provide a considerable degree of influence.

The parents are roughly in the same position as a politician, interested in developing and maintaining power in order to properly carry out the assigned role, yet always having to exercise the art of the possible. Parents must be aware of power coalitions, develop consensus, and adapt goals that are related to the interests and the abilities of the people governed, i.e., the family members.

It is our view that many midrange families that come to treatment now would not have needed to do so a generation before. These parents rely rather heavily on authority and intimidation rather than negotiation, since they parent much as they were parented:

"Spare the rod and spoil the child."

"Children should be seen and not heard."

"My dad helped us serve the Lord by using a stout paddle."

"Children should want to do their chores."

"I expect the best from my children whether they like it or not."

Part of the current dilemma is that there are many more families with both parents working and commuting long hours. This leaves little time for parent-child interaction. It is a truism of conditioning that punishment is only effective when it is surrounded by positive reinforcement. If the punishment or amount of control without choice is too high compared to available positive, warm and empathic interchanges, the very punishment or intense efforts at control become a reward, thereby fostering the behavior the parents want to eliminate. Consequently, therapy of MR families with poorly behaving children often involves modeling and teaching skills in behavior alteration through negotiation, which by definition includes the choice of all persons involved. In addition, the focus often shifts from the behavior of the child who is identified as the trouble to the way in which the parents work through their negotiations regarding the handling of that child. A typical exchange between such parents is:

"You're too strict."

"No, you're too lenient."

"Well, I'm lenient because you are too strict."

"Well, I'm strict because you are too lenient."

It is not hard to affirm both parents in such a mess—sometimes it is good to be strict, sometimes good to be lenient. The problem is when to do which. If we agree that nobody knows how to raise children (an assertion we will readily buy or sell since adaptation is a continuing changing process), then both parents have valuable observations and intuitions to bring to the job. The focus becomes the process of negotiating requirements, rewards and punishment, limits and freedom that both parents can find acceptable and together can make effective.

In studies by our earlier research coalition[97] observing family interaction patterns, it was noted that healthy families that had about the same parenting techniques as midrange families (termed "adequate" families) had no observable differences in child-raising effectiveness from the so-called "optimal" healthy family. This was because, though they seemed to present rather poorly, they cared about parenting and put a great deal of effort and time into the activity.

It is valuable to normalize the parental conflicts over discipline and limit-setting, focusing on process rather than content. Attending to each parent's views of reality and suggestions for solutions and emphasizing the value of negotiating decisions that both parents can cheerfully support enhance almost all treatment with intact (i.e., not divorced or re-married) MR families.

Educative efforts are most apt to be useful in this group of families. Trusting words and authority to a greater extent than other clinical families, they respond to parent training, couple enrichment courses, and communication skills training. Such educative efforts may supplement or, as a timely intervention, replace conventional family therapy.

SPECIAL ISSUES WITH SINGLE-PARENT AND BLENDED FAMILIES

In recent years, as the divorce rate climbs and the remarriage rate climbs as well, increasing numbers of midrange families present either as single-parent families or as step or blended families. These present the therapist with some particular problems that are repetitive and hence predictable.

Single-Parent Families

It is important to realize that a single parent has a hard time doing very well at parenting. The job is lonely, with no one to talk with about major decisions, which are terribly ambiguous and unclear. The results are uncertain and often—even usually—available only a long time after action has been taken.

Therefore, it is important to offer single parents parenting skills in addition to any formal family therapy. This is one way the single parent can come into contact with others in her (85% of single parents are female) situation. Therapy often will go well if there are single-parent support groups or ongoing parenting classes available. Talking and sharing pain, insights, and successes with others provide these hard-pressed parents with hope, interest, and a sense of success and competence in the parenting endeavor.

Family therapy may often be family consultation for the MR single parent—helping this needful, hard-pressed, lonely person find emotional support as well as technical insights. The children, too, may be assisted in finding social structures that provide competent, useful, and enjoyable interactions with adults. Churches, community agencies, and volunteer groups are all useful at times, and the capable family therapist will be aware of these local possibilities.

Single parents, who manage money alone, frequently with little background in handling so little money carefully and effectively, often need economic counseling. Family therapists are advised to become knowledgeable and interested in the gritty business of budgeting, planning ahead, covering the necessities and saving a bit not only for emergencies but also for celebrations.

Blended Families

Excellent texts are now available on the subject of blended families; see, especially, Visher and Visher[151] and Sager et al.[124] Until relatively recently these families have received little systemic study or attention. Now, as they become increasingly prevalent, researchers and therapists are realizing that they have special needs and problems that require special handling. These include: (1) multiple opportunities for triangulation; (2) conflicts between the children from previous marriages; and (3) conflicts with parental authority. The possibilities for triangulation are endless. Previous spouses do not disappear and, especially if unremarried, can and do feel left out, poorly treated, and deserving of more than they receive. Male ex-mates often feel abandoned by the children and may threaten family rules by indulging children during visiting privileges. Female ex-mates, if possessing custody, are routinely concerned about financial stability and feel that the ex-husband is not providing enough for his (and her) children. The current wife, on the other hand, has many reasons to be threatened by the demands that both the ex-spouse and the children make on her husband. The husband feels, understandably enough, that he is pulled in several directions, with little possibility of anyone's feeling that he is doing a competent, let alone superior, job. If each new parent brings children into the marriage, there is a powerful tendency to develop, through triangulation, chronic resentment regarding the treatment of *my child* in contrast to *your* child.

Exquisite attention to the couple's relationship is needed to head off these developments or to remedy them when they become evident. In never-remarried nonlabeled families, it is clear that the marital bond is critical in developing and maintaining negotiating ability throughout the family. This vital bond suffers greater challenges and hence deserves greater attention in blended families.

Conflicts between his and her children can be seen as a symptom of the triangulation that sets parents at odds, as well as an issue itself. Two people, each with children, who fall in love understandably hope their children will also care for each other and that the resultant larger family will be a warm and loving group. Unfortunately, they may, with the midrange family rule of "loving means controlling," attempt to dictate this feeling: "This is your new big brother; I know you will love him just like you do your sister." Such efforts are misguided. If therapeutic help is sought during the formation of a blended family, the therapist will do well to counsel caution and going slowly.

In interviewing healthy or nonlabeled blended families in workshops around the country, one of us (WRB) has been interested in the family members' own views of how they became a comfortable working unit. Without exception, one point is made by the children: "When we first got together Mom and Dad asked that we be civil. It was only after a while that we found we really cared about one another." To a great extent oppositional attitudes and behavior can be avoided if these perceptions are heeded.

Conflicts with parental authority are perhaps inevitable in blended families. Frequently a female single parent looks with relief to the lover who becomes her husband to help with or even take over the role of disciplinarian. In most families, especially midrange families, the father's role is expected to include being the "heavy," the enforcer. It is not surprising, then, that both adults would expect the male to move right in and begin to shape up the discipline, which in many single-parent families is a bit ragged. This frequent error often requires unwinding in later years. Inevitably, with these expectations, the children of single parents grow to dislike or even hate the stepfather, and he is uncomfortable and ineffective in being a father to them.

It is important for the parents to know that discipline in the first year or so needs to remain in the hands of the biological parent, with greater and greater numbers of shared decisions regarding limit-setting and discipline developing over the course of many months. After about two years, when the new parent has had a chance to develop a decent relationship with the children, discipline can be shared and even skewed toward the father.

The theoretical background for this recommendation is quite simple and clear: Punishment is only effective in reducing or eliminating unwanted behavior when it is surrounded by positive reinforcement. If the new stepparent moves in too fast with disciplinary efforts, there is no opportunity for the bonds of enjoyable shared experience to develop and a cartoon emerges of loving biological parent and wicked stepparent.

The time requirements mentioned for adaptation are deliberately vague, since there are variations due to many factors, especially the ages of the children when the stepparent arrives on the scene. Generally, there is a shorter transition time with younger children.

CASE EXAMPLE

The concept of inviting family members to become "fellow scientists," working with the therapist in identifying desires and needs of family members and helping them spring into reality, is perhaps best exemplified by an interview of a midrange mixed blended family, the Faraways.

This assessment had been made by using the 10-minute segment mentioned in Chapter 6 of this book, which begins by asking family members to "talk with each other about what you would like to see changed in your family." In this way the stage is set for a successful contract to be negotiated and for moving from "Who's to blame?" to "What do we do?" and from "Who's sick?" or "Who's bad?" to "How do we operate better as a family?"

This blended family consists of the parents, Carl and Brenda, and three children—Michelle, Carl's biological daughter, age 15, Walker, age 14, the biological son of Brenda, and Peter, age eight, the child of Carl and Brenda.

In evaluation the parents explained that they were there because Carl had found Michelle in her bed having sex with a male 15-year-old whom neither of the parents knew. This was the culmination of a number of disturbing events in the family. Some of the other concerns included enough conflict between Carl and Brenda that a month ago Carl had left home for a day and a half, getting away "to think"; at that time he seriously considered leaving the family. There was chronic conflict between Carl and Walker over Walker's responsibilities around the house—cleaning his room, carrying out the trash, etc.

An extremely long history of conflict between Brenda and Michelle was reported. Brenda resented having to be a mother to Michelle and honestly stated that she had rejected the girl early in their marriage of nine years. Recently, however, the conflict had seemed to abate somewhat.

All agreed that Carl was hard to talk to and had a hard time talking. Brenda was usually frustrated over her unmet needs for relationship and contact with Carl. In the course of an interview with the family, conducted by a visiting family therapist who uses the principles we have discussed, several hypotheses were developed and offered to the family. Clinical data were collected that supported these hypotheses. Two of them will be discussed here:

1. *Michelle sensed the distance between Carl and Brenda and dramatically acted to bring them together.* Supporting this was the fact that this was, indeed, what happened. Carl and Brenda had great difficulty in coming together and developing an emotionally tight, common approach, but after Michelle's escapade, they talked and worked together.
2. *Walker also had found a way to bring father into the family—by not doing things and getting father angry at him.* Again, the data supported this. Carl did tend to be noncommunicative and, as Brenda said, "Well, he doesn't say much to Walker unless Walker isn't doing something right."

The therapist circled back several times during the interview with these hypotheses, confirming them with further data to all the family members' satisfaction.

With the pressure off the "bad kids," attention was drawn to the hunger of Carl and Brenda for closeness, and they were physically moved closer to each other. As they spontaneously touched each other and held hands like high school lovers, both happily focused on the ways they could talk more, share more, and desire more from each other.

Of course, the data could just as easily have supported many other hypotheses. Michelle is a little slut, Walker is a lazy bum. Carl is overwhelmed at work and must come home to deal with willfully wanton and hostile, ungrateful children. Or else mother has rejected Michelle, destroyed her self-esteem, and pampered Walker, who in turn helps her by goading her noncommunicative husband and therefore punishing him.

Such hypotheses would lead nowhere because they destroy hope and confirm everyone's worst fears. Implicit or explicit in all useful therapeutic work is the idea that people are basically decent and have respectable motives. Further, if people can get together they can solve a lot of their problems and better tolerate those that cannot be solved. Everyone is needful, and with a certain degree of closeness that need and hunger can feed the other.

Therapy with the family was successfully accomplished along the lines suggested here. Carl and Brenda's relationship became a major focus of treatment, with Carl frequently being congratulated for having chosen such a fine partner as Brenda to help him overcome his loneliness and self-defeating reserve. He had "married against his neurosis," i.e., he had chosen someone who made it difficult for him to withdraw.

Brenda was affirmed in her honesty regarding feelings, both positive and negative. This made it easier for Carl to trust her, to risk getting close to her.

Michelle responded well to the closer relationship of her father and stepmother. She allowed Brenda more of a mothering role and Brenda accepted that role. Her sexual acting-out ceased, though she continued to test limits such as curfew times.

Walker posed a bit more of challenge. It was possible, however, to have Carl, Brenda, and Walker negotiate some mutually acceptable rules regarding chores. This was only accomplished after Carl was much closer to Brenda and hence less resentful of Walker.

Working with midrange families, a therapist can usually tap the creativity of all participants. Further, the family members' wishes, goals, and responsibilities remain their own. The family keeps the initiative as well as the responsibilities. Our clinical research indicates that therapists do best in treating these families with a modest overt power difference, a maximum disclosure of strategy, and a comfortably open, relatively unguarded relationship. Treatment approaches that describe and emphasize concepts, such as Nagy's contextual therapy,[29] are useful in this group of families. Family of origin work as developed and promoted by Bowen[30] is an effective approach to these families as well.

10 BORDERLINE AND SEVERELY DYSFUNCTIONAL CENTRIPETAL FAMILIES

In developing treatment strategies for families with limited adaptive capacity it is necessary to make a clear distinction between centrifugal and centripetal families. Not only do borderline families differ significantly from midrange families in their requirements for successful treatment, but the approach to borderline CP families is also quite different from the approach to borderline CF families. Additionally, in their demands on the therapist borderline CP families differ qualitatively from severely dysfunctional CP families.

This chapter discusses interventions with the borderline CP family and with the severely dysfunctional CP family. Chapter 11 will deal with the treatment of centrifugal families. These assessed differences in family groups are valuable in planning strategies, in being aware of special problems and pitfalls, and in developing reasonable expectations for families and for the therapist.

BORDERLINE CENTRIPETAL FAMILIES

In doing hospital consultations, an experienced family therapist will frequently be presented with a family from this group, usually with half smiles on the faces of the referring staff members. "Aha! Let's see what you can do with these people, O Wise One!" These are the troublemakers, the tough cases, the drive-one-to-distraction families. Why? For at least two reasons. First, this family group worships control over all else—over satisfaction, over apparent success, perhaps over a place in heaven. These family members are constantly attempting to control one another and, unlike their CF counterparts, they experience just enough success to spur them on to ever more strenuous efforts. There is little awareness of the possibility of intimacy or interpersonal closeness. When these families reach out for help, it will be for one of the members, not for the family as a whole. And, of course, the family assumption will be that the helper(s) will control the member who is deemed to be out of step and, in turn, be controlled by the family member who is most successful in exerting overt control within the family. This sets up a series of frustrations for everyone. Such a family can chew up naive or unwary therapists and (figuratively, most of the time) eat them for breakfast, if not brunch.

When assessment indicates that one is dealing with this kind of family, there are several principles to keep in mind. First, everyone is suffering. In such a family it is extremely tempting to forget systemic thinking and find villains. Usually the most tempting target is the family member (almost always a parent) who most stubbornly insists on directly controlling everyone and everything that moves. Finding a villain is a big mistake, of course, since it will set up a confrontation that will result in the family's leaving treatment. The overtly powerful family member is frustrated and miserable but not without impact.

It is necessary to go below the power struggles and tap into the underlying feeling tone of the family group and the individual members. These people hurt! All are on very short rations of warmth or intimacy.

Second, there is a strong need to support the overtly powerful member, even though this often goes against the humanitarian impulses of a therapist. Since these families are involved in interminable power struggles, they will usually present some form of the rescuer, persecutor, and victim cartoon show. (Cartooning is a term we use to describe rigid, narrowly defined, stereotyped, and repetitive roles played out in concert by the family members. In the comics, Beetle Bailey is always the goof-off, Sarge is always the obese bully, Lt. Fuzz is always the bubbleheaded wimp. The humor of cartoons lies in the predictability of the characters; when this occurs in real life, it is tragedy.)

A natural tendency, then, is to try to help the victim and reduce the control of the apparently powerful one. However, this is not wise. Everyone is controlling everyone else in these families; everyone is victim and, in another sense, everyone is villain. Developing a strong alliance with a "victim" is not therapeutic and discipline is required to back off and treat everyone with both respect and some seasoned wariness.

It is in the borderline centripetal (BLCP) families that scapegoating is most apt to occur and to be stubborn and stereotyped. This is due to the following reasons:

1. Midrange families are significantly more adaptive and, though capable of scapegoating, are less apt to perseverate in the maladaptive activity.

2. Severely dysfunctional families are unable to maintain a consistent agreed-on overt power hierarchy, which is essential for consistent scapegoating of a member.
3. CF families have such tenuous control and poor generational boundaries and so pervasively use blame and attack that *everyone* in these families has a turn at being the scapegoat.

If one attempts to rescue the scapegoat in the BLCP family rather than helping the family realign the system, the therapist has been co-opted by that system rather than maintaining a meta-position to the family in a manner that can induce change. Years ago, Fred Ford, a family therapist once associated with MRI in Palo Alto, said, "My idea of family therapy is to be Fred Ford in the middle of a family."[52] This could never be more true than in BLCP families; such a system exerts maximum pressure on therapists to be somebody other than themselves.

It is important, then, to join with the family by not attempting to reshuffle its overt power structure. This means necessarily developing a good liaison with the overt authority while avoiding being co-opted into the system. This requires a move below the power struggles into the affective life of the family. Everyone feels, and is, deprived. The most overtly powerful person in the family can most easily thwart and discontinue family therapy; therefore, the therapist must address that person's emotional needs quickly and usually first.

Case Example

Brad Sr. and Martha have two children, Brad Jr., age 14, and Leslie, age 12. Brad Jr. has always been a handful. Currently, his school performance is poor, he is sullen and negative at home, and he has recently shown clear signs of being involved in alcohol and marijuana abuse. He has also driven the family car without permission on several occasions. Leslie has been a model child, quiet and cooperative, with good school grades. Martha is a pretty, rather sad-looking woman with aristocratic bearing; she seems ineffectively to be pleased with Leslie, covertly appalled at and covertly bonding with Brad Jr. Brad Sr. is a hard-driving, successful surgeon who feels harried at this self-defined job of making money and controlling his family by denigrating his wife and bullying his son. The bullying brought the family to treatment, as the father broke his hand in an altercation with Brad Jr., preventing him from doing surgery for a time.

Developing an alliance with Martha, with Leslie, and with Brad Jr.

presented little challenge. However, to join with Brad Sr. required some sympathetic probes into his feelings, such as, "You seem to be working so hard and getting so little out of it." "Do you feel sometimes that you are being cheated with all this energy and not much results?" "You obviously care so very much for your family! Do you ever ask yourself, 'What's in it for me?'" "I see you struggling and working; I would like to see you getting more for yourself from all that effort." This approach slowly brought Brad Sr. into the fold.

A frequently used motto of therapists treating BLCP families is, "People don't come to see me because they are controlling. They come because they want to control things and are notably unsuccessful." The successful therapist gives people what they want, though it may come in a form different from the initial expectation. It is no crime to want to control. All people try to control those things that they care for intensely. A diver will fight hard to maintain the integrity of the air supply. People will fight wars over water rights and food sources. The problem for all families, and for borderline families in particular, lies in the fact that what family members want to control in their close relationships requires the other person's choice:

"I don't just want you to take out the garbage. I want you to *want* to take out the garbage."

"I don't want you to study because I say so. I want you to study because you see that it is necessary and you want to succeed."

"I don't just want you to be an agreeable sex partner. I want you to see me as desirable and want me."

Here lies the maddening dilemma for the overtly powerful member of a BLCP family: His or her only mechanism for control guarantees defeat.

Children have a most instructive game in this regard. It is called Paper, Scissors, and Rock. As two players compete, they simultaneously make hand gestures that indicate a rock (fist), paper (flat outspread hand), or scissors (forefinger and middle finger thrust out wide). Scissors cut paper, paper covers rock, and rock breaks scissors. Each has power, each has vulnerability. It is just so for strategies in life and relationships.

Passivity or inaction has its vulnerability, but it can defeat overt control efforts every time. Being ineffectual is not much fun, but it can whip anybody who tries to change the situation. Conversely, being efficient and goal directed is useful, but it will bite the dust when addressing aspects of another person's being that are necessarily and particularly his/her own responsibility.

Hence, it is in the BLCP family that a therapist must reserve the most potent indirect (side door, back door[165] methods). Prescribing symptoms,[68] prescribing setbacks,[5] and blessing the status quo[69] are all useful methods to prevent being defeated in pinheaded (linear) power struggles and in maintaining control. It is always useful to keep in mind Carl Whitaker's injunction to have the initiative in the family and the control in the hands of the therapist. This, of course, means control of sessions; the control of the family is vested, along with the initiative, in that family.

A useful way of thinking about so-called "paradoxical" methods of intervention[158] is that these are ways of maintaining control of sessions with families who are on a control rampage—attempting to control when focusing instead of satisfactions, needs, and fears would serve everyone much better. It is not necessary to consider these paradoxical means as therapeutic themselves; rather, they are approaches required to maintain control by the therapist in the manner of the children's game of Paper, Scissors, and Rock. In order to derail the out-of-control direct control efforts of these family members, indirect methods must be used.

Case Example

A grim and tense family entered treatment because of their 16-year-old daughter, Mary. She was rebellious, flaunting previously respected family rules, and had had sexual escapades with a variety of boys the parents did not know. Neither John, her father, nor Marsha, her mother, was able to speak two sentences without the other disagreeing (politely, of course), but it was clear that John usually had the last word. Two younger children, Seth, 14, and Holly, 12, were considered normal. That is, they did as they were told.

The assessment placed the family in the BLCP category. Treatment began with John and Marsha's listing the failures of previous therapists to help and insisting that the current family therapist do something quickly to stop Mary from doing these bad things.

It became apparent that John and Marsha had some long-standing conflicts between them. Sex had virtually ceased in the last five years; arguments were barely held in check during the treatment sessions and then only when John and Marsha agreed on Mary's problems. Further, it was evident that Mary had no intention of altering her behavior pattern. Though she had been docile during earlier years, now she was defiant. She had the capacity to make her parents into raging neuters as she went her personally threatening, self-defeating, and rebellious way.

In the third session, after making an attempt to hear from everyone and join with each, the therapist chose to offer what could be called a paradoxical intervention.

She observed mildly that perhaps Mary might need to continue her rather frightening behavior pattern until such time as John and Marsha were able to get together a bit more regarding their own relationship. Continuing, she said that this would certainly work a hardship on Mary and was not recommended, but it might be necessary for the moment.

Such a tactic is never required in midrange families and is rarely, if ever, necessary or even useful in severely dysfunctional families. It is an effort to prescribe the status quo when family authority figures are clearly interested in defining an adequate therapist as one who can do what they have found impossible—in this case, to control Mary.

With a redefinition of time-limited goals, the therapist can maintain or regain control of sessions and go about the business of reaching for family members' needs, wishes, dreams, pain, and hurt. In this case, after the desperate attempt on the part of John (and Marsha, too, secondarily) to control this therapist was dodged, a more genuine effort of family members to be responsible for their own lives was pursued.

Much has been written of paradox in therapy.[129,158] The literature has spawned some faddish therapies that encourage therapists to be less than genuine, less than honest in their relationships with family members. This is an unnecessary and potentially mischievous use of paradoxical interventions. These are best seen simply as *necessary tools* for maintaining control and keeping a family in treatment. The therapy can then address important issues and avoid tactics that have already been shown to be maladaptive.

A motto at our institute is: "Paradoxical interventions are only effective when they are not paradoxical, we say paradoxically." That is, prescribing of symptoms or the status quo or predicting setbacks is not a cute gimmick but a genuinely felt statement of the therapist's belief about what is happening within the family at that moment and the therapist's desire to have the family recognize what is happening without being lectured. It is not necessary to use such tactics in families not so wedded to a crazy effort at control. Such dedication suggests the frightening specter of chaos behind the attempts at control and indicate the vulnerable position of the family system. There is a need to respect that family pattern of adaptation and to expect slower change than is possible with midrange families.

In our outcome research at the institute, we have developed assessment tools for families and for therapists. The assessment of therapists requires that each list at the end of the third session the degree of closeness, the degree of overt power difference, and the degree of disclosure of treatment strategy desired in working with a particular family. We believe these three variables—power, closeness, disclosure—are key in most of the varieties of family therapy in the published literature. When therapists' ratings with this borderline CP group are compared to those with any other group of families, we find that therapists wanted to have the greatest amount of distance and the least disclosure of techniques with BLCP families. They also want to have a greater overt power difference than with any other CP family group. It appears, therefore, that our therapists are sensing the pitfalls in being too straightforward, too open, or too close with BLCP families.

After the control battles between helper and helpees have been neutralized, treatment can proceed along the lines of the overall pattern of effective family intervention defined in Chapter 8. A therapist must focus on individual hunger and needs and reframe the previously ridiculous and impossible control efforts as near misses in caring, useful, attainable control. If spouses, parents, and children are not seen as inevitably oppositional, then control can occur with the agreement of the controlled. That is, in concrete terms, family rules will be respected when adolescents have some input into their structure and composition.

In breaking up the efforts to torpedo therapeutic control, there are several other methods which have proved useful in addition to the aforementioned paradoxical techniques. Story-telling is one that is hard to teach but can be extremely powerful. Nothing can better deflect a raw demand for the therapist to come into the snake pit with the parents than a reflective story that has a telling point that is not immediately evident. Stories about the therapist's own family,[160] Chinese struggles with tyranny, and tyrants' struggles with maintaining order—all of these can be used to play Paper, Scissors, and Rock successfully with frantically control-oriented families.

One technique mentioned by many family therapists[67,158] is taking a one-down position. This can be extremely effective in avoiding the pitfall of becoming the knowledgeable expert whom the family defines as adequate only if he or she fixes things. We have termed this useful technique "playing the game of limbo." In Caribbean countries, a pastime is the competition/game of seeing who can writhe lower under a crossbar without falling on the ground. When family members present as helpless, it may be necessary for the therapist to admit helplessness and confusion. Never, of course, should the therapist bite the dust with such admissions.

Humor is another powerful tool in coping with BLCP families. Humor (not wit) always goes hand in hand with perspective, with backing off from the fray and seeing more, seeing farther. This talent is dramatically lacking initially in BLCP families; they are so caught up in power struggles that perspective eludes everyone involved. Humor and story-telling are, of course, natural allies. A good therapist for these families can maintain perspective, see past the control battles, and help the individual members define themselves, their boundaries, limits, needs, goals, and capabilities better than they have done before.

Borderline family members are always on the edge of, if not in, depression. This is because depression in individuals always includes two factors—feeling helpless and feeling alone. The family members always feel relatively alone, but the control battles offer a tenuous feeling of being powerful, rather than helpless. Even the pitifully emaciated 70 lb. anorectic daughter of a BLCP family can feel powerful in defeating parental directives to eat. As the therapist avoids being co-opted and controlled by the family members, as the family members are reminded of and refocused on their needs and emotional hunger, overt depression may develop in some member. It is important to emphasize the possibilities of being together, of being on the same side, in order to avoid new depressive symptomatology.

In previous publications, we have described the extreme importance of ambivalence in human illness and health.[10,16] Ambivalence in humans is isomorphic with conflict in families or other human systems—it is inevitable and it is ubiquitous. It is neither healthy nor ill; it simply is. The degree of emotional health can be measured by the degree that ambivalence regarding highly significant issues in life—job, relationships, beliefs—can be resolved for significant periods of time. Individual pathology reflects, among other things, a failure to resolve ambivalence. Family rules have a powerful effect on the ease or difficulty with which members resolve these inevitable mixed feelings. BLCP families make it rather difficult for members to accept and resolve personal ambivalence.

It is for this reason that therapists must make a special effort to be the voice for denied opposites. When the overt controller seems most intent on being powerful, the therapist brings tears to eyes by noting how much of a load this controller is carrying and how little reward he or she seems to reap. When the member who is defined as deviant shows the most alienation from the family, the therapist can note the faithful living out of parental predictions, the loyalty and tenacity shown in remaining within the family structure even though the emotional toll is steep.

Case Example

The Adams family (see Chapter 6) consisted of Phillip, 52, Agnes, 50, John, 25, and Sherry, 20. Sherry was the identified patient, with a five-year history of anorexia. She restricted her food intake and severely abused laxatives regularly. Efforts at outpatient treatment had not been successful. Currently, the patient had low plasma potassium, and abnormal blood pH and weighed 86 pounds with a 5′4″ frame.

The family was seen and assessed on admission. Phillip was an aggressive industrial psychologist who energetically sermonized, interrupted, and controlled the family discussion but not the family behavior. Agnes was a well-dressed, slightly obese matron who seemed to have a permanent look of subdued and sullen anger. She spoke sparingly and carefully. John, who still lived at home though having graduated from college three years previously, was working and was viewed by the parents as an ideal son who was docile and agreeable. They were not disturbed by his remaining at home and his frequent unexplained absences. (Later we learned that Sherry kept his secret that he was heavily abusing amphetamines and ecstasy.) Sherry was a wreck. Hair disheveled, almost incoherent at times, she alternately remained silent and rambled on about the idiocy of her going to the hospital.

It was clear that father attempted to maintain a kind of sanity by tremendous efforts at controlling all the family members. Mother usually responded by silence, punctuated by sympathetic and conspiratorial looks to John or Sherry. John was the most controlled of the group, appearing calm and unflappable. Sherry was the most effective in breaking up Phillip's monologues—by putting her head down, hands over ears, or by stubbornly maintaining one of her ramblings.

The family's 10-minute interaction segment was rated as a borderline CP family (competence 8, style 1.5) and work was begun. Sherry was admitted to the hospital and the family was scheduled for twice-weekly sessions. Sherry adapted well to the ward routine. Her individual therapist learned quickly that she had many of the usual anorectic characteristics—she was depressed, scattered, angry, fearful of sexuality and of closeness, and nearly devoid of peer support.

It became quickly apparent that Phillip was no ordinary parent. He had connections with the chief executive officers of his company, which controlled the family health insurance, and he successfully arranged full insurance coverage for Sherry's hospitalization although she was not going to college and was not eligible. He also had connections with the hospital chain that owned the unit where Sherry resided and threatened repeatedly to use his considerable influence in various efforts at control. He began to question every aspect of Sherry's treatment, making frequent threats to go to higher authority or to remove her from the hospital.

The treatment team elected to respond to Phillip's need for control by merging the family sessions with the team treatment meetings. The family members were defined as important members of the treatment team, and each person had a say in Sherry's treatment plan. In this way Phillip got what he apparently desired—entry into the treatment plan—but the treatment team was able to maintain enough control so that hospital ward functions were not rendered chaotic. The shift in the treatment group composition assisted in making evident the underlying struggle between Phillip and Agnes. They did not agree on any aspect of the treatment. Agnes, feeling the support of a larger group, began to express some pent-up feelings regarding Phillip's treatment of her, as well as of their daughter.

In addition to family therapy, the couple was seen separately at that point. It was quietly suggested in these family sessions that perhaps Sherry needed to go slowly in treatment because a quick recovery would put too much pressure on Phillip and Agnes. Although this was not accepted openly, Phillip's insistence on a quick recovery for Sherry subsided. John became more verbal in the family sessions and, in an emotional outburst, confessed to amphetamine abuse. It was as if he were taking over Sherry's role as the spotlighted miscreant. At any rate, the family secret was out, dialogue was enhanced, and all four members of the family were indicating common but unmet human needs.

As the struggle between Phillip and Sherry subsided, the conflicts between Phillip and Agnes were addressed and John's needs were recognized. Sherry adapted to the program and her weight on discharge was 108 lbs. Further work was indicated, but this family had bounced up from borderline to lower midrange in competence, as determined on discharge assessment.

Control efforts usually run amok, with resulting intermittent zany or poorly regulated transactions, both verbal and behavioral. Since satisfaction is thought irrelevant or unattainable, the opportunity to resolve ambivalence through attending to one's own wishes, needs, and hunger is quite limited. In this example the therapist refocused the family members on goals which were more attainable and more satisfying and avoided being drawn into the family paradigm of grim control battles.

It is evident that special therapeutic maneuvers are required with borderline centripetal families in order to keep the therapist in control and the family possessing the initiative. Useful approaches include Minuchin's structural therapy,[104] based on his pioneering work with families of anorectic patients. Minuchin's techniques are useful in focusing the family tension on concrete here-and-now behavior, which makes it easier for the therapist to stay in control.

Whitaker's "symbolic-experiential" family therapy[160] can be helpful; story-telling, abrupt shifts of emphasis, and carefully selected shared fantasies can all be useful in derailing family members' control efforts and avoiding direct conflict with these members. Haley's "problem-solving" therapeutic approach[68] is also helpful in maintaining control of encounters with these families.

SEVERELY DYSFUNCTIONAL CENTRIPETAL FAMILIES

Severely dysfunctional centripetal (SDCP) families are not as frequently found as they were in a previous generation. As the pressure of emotional deprivation creates a sort of boundary between individuals, more families are seen as centrifugal. The hallmark of SDCP families is the continuation of symbiotic, poorly differentiated boundaries between family members long past the time of early infancy and early motherhood when such symbiosis is necessary, developmentally appropriate, and adaptive. These families search vainly for *coherence* and yet avoid it equally energetically. This brings us to a second dramatically evident quality of SDCP families—the presence of marked expressions of opposite and strongly held feelings without awareness of their discrepancy.[12,20]

One of us (WRB) began studying family dynamics in 1960 because of the demands of treating these families and their emotionally impaired members. In succeeding years, it has become apparent that a systemic approach is more useful in guiding the treatment of these families and individuals than in determining etiology or causes. That is to say, in a SDCP family with a schizophrenic family member, reduction of boundary confusion (overinvolvement is another term for this) and of the negative criticism resulting from the overinvolvement will allow the patient to remain out of hospital and to enjoy enhanced social functioning[32,150]; however, such research results do not in any way suggest that the boundary problems *caused* the illness. Quite the contrary, it is just as easy to hypothesize that having a family member who is in so much pain and so maladaptive will invite, from loving kin, the various responses that limit the ill person's potential for functioning well.

This truly systemic viewpoint can destroy the damaging, false myths of so-called "schizophrenogenic mothers"[4] or families[3] that were prominent in the family literature of the 1960s and 1970s. These concepts have been profoundly offensive to family members who must take care of severely emotionally ill members.[62,161] The organization of these family members, the National Alliance for the Mentally Ill, has stimulated the family therapy field to embrace a more sophisticated and comprehensive systemic view. Avoiding linear concepts of simple cause and effect is more than a slogan; it also prevents therapists from doing harm to family members who must struggle and cope with mental illness.

A systemic understanding of severely dysfunctional families allows a therapist to assess the patterns of interaction at the moment, develop treatment strategies, and avoid excessive concern with how the patterns came to be. In the course of treatment, the family may show unmourned losses creating chasms between members, mental illness in a member, profound changes in economic circumstances, and overwhelming demands from changing cultures. Recognition of these important factors can be most useful in planning treatment.

SDCP families are despairing. It is painful to be in their presence. The hopelessness is expressed indirectly, since negative feelings are unacceptable. Long silences, vagueness, inability to address problems, and pervasive leaden affect are all ways of jointly communicating despair. This hopelessness and its companion, an abiding belief that openly expressing feelings will severely wound or even destroy a family member, must be successfully challenged in the course of treatment.

As in other family therapy ventures, joining with each person is vital. Working with SDCP families can be conceptualized as a clear-cut exercise in the scientific method. A good therapist will join with and enlist the help of all family members in defining what each member is attempting to attain or achieve and in developing strategies to reach those goals and the teamwork necessary to implement the strategies.

Since all family members—all people for that matter—have ambivalence, its resolution is an important task in any family therapy. The unresolved ambivalence in SDCP family members is so dramatic and marked that it requires special attention. The family rules inhibit direct expression of negative feelings, hence the difficulty of resolving mixed feelings is markedly increased. Good therapists make it clear that their offices are safe places to express mixed feelings and will gently but firmly assist members in expressing the previously unacceptable. To do this we adopt Minuchin's "Yes, but" technique:[104]

Father: "We love our son so much even though he is different; we hate to see him hurt by the rejection of people outside the family."
Therapist: "You clearly love him and go out of your way to protect him. But I imagine that at times he is a burden. Being human, I expect you could resent the effort and time required to care for your son."

Adolescent family member: "I just want to grow up and work to make a living and have a family."
Therapist: "I am sure that you do. But I would imagine that, when things are tough, it is tempting to just stay at home where it is more predictable and safe."

Unless each family member can experience mixed feelings as acceptable to the self and to family members, there is little ability to choose, to select a path on the basis of the preponderance of feelings.

"I want you to grow up, but I am so scared for you." "I love John, but I do get tired of being a parent." When it is clearly safe to say such things, to have mixed feelings, it is possible to resolve them and choose. Such choosing is the basis for the development of a self. It clarifies boundaries between family members and allows previously impossible negotiation. The resulting interaction produces *change*, a vital ingredient in recognizing the passage of time.

Families who are stuck in unacknowledged, often unrecognized, and certainly unstated ambivalence are also stuck in time. The inevitable biological changes of growth and development, aging and death, are not synchronized with the family's life. Growing up becomes an empty concept. Death cannot be accepted, and unmourned losses abound.

As a therapist assists the family in accepting mixed feelings, there is a greater feeling of vitality in the sessions. This one change offers the opportunity to experience encounter, a powerful phenomenon that occurs as people share their innermost feelings (always mixed) in a relatively unguarded way and find them acceptable, even welcomed.

In working with SDCP families, we often have a feeling of cogwheels that are disengaged, spinning away but producing no movement of the whole. All are caught in the family "force field" but are infinitely and awesomely alone. These families have taught us that intense encounters with others are required to develop a coherent self. These encounters can be nonverbal, as is the usual pattern of relationships with one or more very young children, or verbal, which requires the skills of adults and older children. While language is well suited to facilitate closeness and encounter, it can also be a powerful tool in avoiding these experiences. CP families depend on words. A good therapist will sense when words are becoming sterile and losing their impact. When this occurs, breaking up verbal defenses against encounter can be accomplished by stage managing—directing physical movement, as in "structural" work[134] or family "sculpting."[125] In these techniques, physical proximity or distance is orchestrated and touching can be facilitated.

The particular task in treating SDCP families is to achieve *coherence*, which is only possible through people's getting across to each other their unique perceptions of reality. Though coherence is devoutly desired by family members and means a respite from feeling all alone, it is also feared as potentially quite destructive. Only when many open and direct encounters of feelings have occurred with enjoyment and healing rather than chaos or death can these family members begin to trust their own feelings and the innermost feelings of their loved ones.

Severely dysfunctional families desire (but fear) coherence. It is useless to attempt to assist these families in achieving control (as in borderline or midrange families) or closeness (as in midrange and healthy families) until coherence in dealing with vital issues is frequently rather than occasionally present.

The therapist, in addition to making a place in the world safe for ambivalence, will focus on the achievement of coherence:

"Did you hear what she said?"

"Tell me what you heard."

"Is that what you intended to say?"

"How would you change it so you could be heard as you want to be heard?"

Underlying these efforts is the therapist's belief that people are basically decent, that differences are not insurmountable and can be worked out, that recognizing the ubiquity of mixed feelings can help people get on the same side, and that every situation or circumstance has possibilities and miseries.

The difficulties these families have in coping are daunting to the members and to the therapist. More than with any other group of families, it may be useful, even necessary, for the therapist to admit confusion, helplessness, even despair. This is no gimmick or clever strategy. It simply is the honest truth. This "technique" has long been recognized as useful in severe human difficulties.[48] It brings helper and helped closer, obliterates power differences, and dramatizes the need for all family members to be empowered, to reach for every coping ability that can be mustered. In SDCP families, there usually are family rules blocking or severely hampering the development of competence in one or more members. Therefore, the therapist honestly needs a powerful tool in altering the developmental inhibition.

Increasing family awareness of the importance of member competence challenges the view that there is something evil about leaving home. If parents wish to do things together outside the family, they are rewarded rather than punished. If children wish to go outside the family for friends and for enjoyment, this is normalized, not pathologized.

A frequent pattern among SD families—that of victim, rescuer, and persecutor—is discouraged. In this triangular scenario, a family member is seen as a victim, another as a persecutor, and a third as rescuer. Of course, the family rarely agrees as to whose role is whose, so that unspoken conflict continues even on the basic definitions of who is playing what. The therapist, naturally, steps into the role of rescuer and must effectively refute that definition or be incorporated into the family structure, becoming just as futile as those being "helped." Being confused or despairing is a shield the therapist uses to avoid being placed in the rescuer role. This not only implicitly empowers family members but also prevents the therapist/rescuer from being redefined as persecutor at a later time, when problems continue and miracles do not occur.

As the therapist becomes part of the family and avoids any stereotyped role, such as rescuer or persecutor, there is great pressure on the family system to redefine itself in new and potentially useful ways. Biology is on the side of treatment, since growth and development, aging and death are shared realities that cannot be effectively redefined or denied.

Empowerment of family members through the development of greater skills in negotiation is the goal of a good therapist. Modeling this negotiating ability is a basic tool in this process, and searching for the wants and needs of individual family members develops the context of family negotiation. The despair felt by family members is associated with pervasive feelings of being alone and feeling helpless. As dialogue and negotiation of differences and of separate goals occur, helplessness is replaced by competence and aloneness by sharing.

The therapist does not require a great overt power difference in doing effective work; initially one needs to organize and structure a previously chaotic and incoherent situation, but this requires just enough power to remain in control. Any more power will backfire; the therapist will walk into the rescuer role and nothing in the family will change significantly.

There is not much closeness between therapist and family members in the initial treatment phases. These people are no more able to be close to a therapist than they are to each other; feelings must be hidden, desires unspoken. Closeness, on the other hand, is always a two-way street. This is one of the reasons that SDCP families are considered by most therapists to be "draining"—there is a sense of being as alone as the family members are. Having colleagues or friends available to talk about the ongoing work is most important.

Co-therapists can help, if this is feasible. Behind-the-mirror supervision or teamwork has a double edge with SDCP families and is less frequently advisable with this group of families than with BLCP or any CF families. Although this set-up provides help to the therapist, the powerful Oz-like structure can encourage the continuation of family victim-persecutor-rescuer games, unless this possibility is carefully attended to by the treatment team. Likewise, it is contraindicated to be obscure about strategies with these families or to resist disclosing them. They have more than enough confusion, mysteries, withdrawing, and ambiguity in the family system. The therapist does well not to add more.

Since these families are not so well organized as to be effectively controlling, going off in a corner and plotting strategies that family members have no part in developing simply recreates, rather than diminishes, some profoundly maladaptive family patterns. The outcome studies that we have available to us regarding intervention with such families clearly indicate that open, straightforward efforts at problem-solving produce good treatment results. Goldstein, working with families with acute schizophrenic patients,[142] Falloon and co-workers, addressing the problems of families with a chronic schizophrenic member,[47] and Anderson, working with similar families of chronic schizophrenics,[6] all suggest that a level of overt power difference just capable of structuring the work, avoidance of attempts to obtain or emphasize closeness, and an open, friendly but business-like discussion of problems and potential solutions are effective with this group of families.

In addition to the cognitive reorganization of family structure, roles, and relationships, with the resultant reduction of distance, it is usually valuable at some point in treatment to encourage socially appropriate touching—spouse to spouse, parent to child. Touch is a powerful tool in reaching across an emotional gulf; if the timing is right, the therapist's permission can help members leap that gulf. Often one can empathically experience the yearning of one or more members to be touched, to have a hand held, to have an arm on one's shoulder; directing this movement at such a time is a part of the therapist's art. Encounter heals, and desensitization of the fear of encounter is necessary in this family group.

Case Example

The Quagmyre family was evaluated (see Chapter 6) as severely dysfunctional and centripetal. The family consisted of Hiram, 42, Nellie, 38, and their sons, Nathan, age 16, and George, age 12. Following hospitalization for "schizophrenia," Nathan had stopped taking the prescribed Thorazine. He showed no evidence of any thinking disorder at this first or any subsequent family sessions; rather, he was sullen, withdrawn, and angry with both parents and the world. He seemed to embrace the despair and hopeless attitude that the other family members refused to acknowledge openly but showed in their faces and in their inability to develop clear and effective plans of action. Nathan did, however, show some warmth for and interest in his little brother George.

The therapeutic goals of the family were defined as getting Nathan off drugs and getting the family back to "normal" (it was found that Nathan had indeed been using marijuana regularly in the preceding six-month period). The therapist made a mental note of the poor alliance between Mr. and Mrs. Quagmyre and the dearth of negotiating skills observed in the family. There was a pervasive lack of clarity in the family members' speech and no one was comfortable with any expression of ambivalence. In addition, it seemed important to empower Mr. Quagmyre to be more effective in the family so that he and his wife could set limits effectively. Finally, it appeared that George was quite emotionally entangled with Mrs. Quagmyre and she was attempting to find some closeness with him rather than with her husband.

Nathan had dropped out of school prior to his hospitalization. He disliked studying, had few good things to say about school, and reported no warm memories of his educational experiences. It was quite clear that he required a more satisfying social role and some effective social network.

The parents agreed on one thing—that Nathan was the problem in the family. The therapist took this as a starting point and suggested that they all work together to devise a way that the rest of the family could help Nathan achieve what he was after.

Nathan was definite on one thing, that he did not want to go back to school; his mother was equally definite that he was going to, and his father made ineffectual efforts to be on both sides. The therapist saw this as an opportunity to bring out the presence of mixed feelings and to increase the clarity of each person's feelings and perceptions. With a little coaxing, both Mr. and Mrs. Quagmyre were able to agree they really didn't want Nathan to go back to school if he was only to fail again; on the other hand, Nathan was able to state that he wanted to be able to support himself when he was grown and that he probably needed some kind of skills in order to do so.

George helped by talking of his own ambition to be a radio announcer. Any hopeful, future orientation in this despairing family was welcome and valuable.

With Nathan and his parents somewhat on the same side—that is, they all wanted Nathan to succeed as an adult and they agreed that some vocational skills would be needed—contact was made with the public school and a vocational program was found to be practical and tentatively acceptable to Nathan.

After this promising beginning, family treatment hit a snag when Nathan was found to be smoking marijuana again, with an accompanying deterioration of functioning in the new school environment and in his mood at home.

In the session when this information was disclosed, Nathan became defiant, challenging both parents to do something about his marijuana use. Mother attempted to tell Nathan he really wanted to stop, but Nathan would have none of it. Father tried to support mother, but in a sadly ineffectual way.

The therapist thought she saw despair and fear in the parents. They really couldn't make things right. This observation regarding their underlying mood was made gently, and both parents began to cry.

Mother: "We can't give up. We've got to try."
Therapist: "Yes, you work hard, but sometimes you can't do for others, no matter how hard you try. Don't you feel it's OK to show Nathan that you care, but you're helpless and scared for him?"

Both parents agreed that they did feel that way. The fight and surliness left Nathan for a while; his shoulders dropped and he stared at the floor. George was very quiet, looking in turn at each face in the room.

Therapist: "I also am feeling helpless and I have some fear. I think we need some more help. I think Nathan could use some more help, too. Nathan, would you go to a NA group? A group made up of people your own age who want to grow up without drugs?"
Nathan: "I might."

Nathan did begin to go to a NA group; mother and dad were asked to take him to the meetings and while he was there to spend their time talking together about their mixed feelings. They were told that very few times do people feel just one way about important things; most feelings come in pairs, and they can get closer if they can share mixed feelings about their lives, their family, and their children. George was to take care of himself while the parents were gone.

After Hiram and Nellie dutifully talked to each other, it was proposed that the weekly family meetings be augmented by a weekly session involving the two parents.

It was easier for Hiram and Nellie to disagree clearly in the marital sessions. Initially, they were most afraid of "looking bad" by having strong open disagreements in front of the kids. At this point, the therapist had ambitions to get Hiram and Nellie closer, to assist Hiram to feel empowered as a parent and as a spouse, and to diminish Nellie's extra involvement with George. She often behaved as if George had more strength and sense than did her husband.

With the therapist's help, some real encounters occurred between Hiram and Nellie. He was able to say that he resented her controlling him and keeping him from being an effective parent. She was truly amazed at this perception, responding, "I've always had to move in and do what I could because you wouldn't."

The therapist, of course, quickly pointed out that they were on the same side and wanted the same things. The encounters they both had dreaded became actually enjoyable as they found they came out stronger and closer.

After 12 marital sessions and 26 family sessions, Nathan was finishing a term in a vocational school and going to NA. His behavior was tolerable but not easily acceptable at home. Mother and father were talking more and feeling closer. George was talking to his father more; they were sometimes playing catch in the back yard.

Mother and father were still frequently angry at Nathan for breaking rules such as curfew times. "Grounding" was the major sanction used. The format once again became weekly family work; the therapeutic activity consisted mainly of clarifying, focusing, helping each member to express both sides of feelings, and encouraging, even badgering, the parents to get together on decisions regarding discipline.

There were eight more sessions, with improvement in the parents' limit-setting effectiveness. They were much more infrequently "playing a hand that they could not win," i.e., setting limits they couldn't or wouldn't enforce and then backing down. Nathan and George talked frequently in the sessions, sometimes agreeing with the parents, sometimes loudly expressing indignation over unfair rules.

When the therapist left for a two-week vacation, she made an appointment for after her return which the family did not keep. A follow-up phone call found mother assuring the therapist that things were better with the family and saying that they had decided to go on their own for a while.

Restructuring, redefining roles, increasing coherent encounter, and helping individuals resolve ambivalence are all vital to working with SDCP families. It is quite satisfying to see previously despairing people leave treatment with hope and a sense of competence, no longer expecting rescue. The relatively simple, straightforward approaches of Carol Anderson and co-workers,[6] Michael Goldstein and co-workers,[58] and Ian Falloon and co-workers[46] can be quite helpful to therapists working with these families. In addition, the concrete, experiential approach of Minuchin[106] is valuable with these severely dysfunctional centripetal families and with the borderline CP group as well.

11 BORDERLINE AND SEVERELY DYSFUNCTIONAL CENTRIFUGAL FAMILIES

Centrifugal family members trust neither words nor therapists; they have difficulties with authority of varying degrees depending on their competence level. They are open in their conflicts but deny warmth, fear, and human needs. They are much more visible to the community when in trouble than when functioning reasonably well.

This discussion will address borderline and severely dysfunctional CF families together and will not address midrange families at all for the following reasons:

1. MRCF families are rarely seen in treatment. Since CF families distrust words and therapists, and MRCF families' functioning capacity is reasonably high, they do not voluntarily come to treatment, nor are their members sent by the school or work place.
2. Clinically, we have not been able to separate intervention techniques that differ clearly from BLCF to SDCF. Though the family groupings are sufficiently different and separable, the techniques of working with the families seem quite similar. It would be needlessly complicating to separate them in this, the treatment section.
3. Our research into intervention and outcome does not differentiate the SD and BLCF groups. Though the functioning level of these families is a significant factor in treatment outcome (more competent families do better), style is more important when we come to select interventions.

STRATEGIES WITH CENTRIFUGAL FAMILIES

These families are hard to corral—they only reluctantly come to treatment, usually with external pressure, and it is hard to get the whole family together. Indeed, a joke around our institute is "Get all members of a CF family together for three visits and they are cured!" Family

174

therapy settings that insist on having the whole family for all treatment sessions will simply screen out this group of families; they will not cooperate initially in that regard. Intervention methods must allow for the presence of a varying number of family members.

It is also frequently hard to define the number of persons in the family. Is the man who frequently stays overnight in a SDCF single-parent family a member of that family or not? Is the 17-year-old child who has been in residential treatment settings since age 13 still a family member or not? Are the unwed 18-year-old daughter and her child, living outside the home, still family members? Clinically it is important to note that helping the family clearly to define its members is not only a useful but also a necessary maneuver; at times it is the procedure that effectively treats the family.

If a therapist is put off by rudeness or open hostility, he or she will find it hard to join with these families. There is clearly a relationship between the therapist's experiences in his or her own family of origin and the ease or difficulty of joining with CF families. Most family therapists have come from CP families and have to reach a bit, with a good amount of supervision, in order to become comfortable with these CF families. Sometimes a family therapist trainee has come from a CF family, or at least from a large and mixed family with many memories of open conflict and of jostling among siblings. If this is so, CF families may not be intimidating but rather somewhat enjoyable. It is often hard for a clinic administrator not to pigeonhole such clinicians to work with the CF families and subtly develop a specialization among therapists. This is efficient but does not expand the horizons of the therapists. A balance must be struck between assigning families to those clearly most able to handle them and assigning families that challenge therapeutic skills and broaden the capabilities of therapists. In private practice, one must decide similarly: Do I limit my practice to those I am comfortable with, or do I wish to give myself the chance to become uncomfortable and to seek supervision for families with whom I am overly anxious?

These CF families will definitely change the outlook of therapists from CP families, and since they are increasing in numbers in this country, it behooves all of us to learn more of the nature and treatment of this group. BL and SDCF families are physically chaotic as contrasted to BL and SDCP families, who are verbally chaotic. Behavior is the preferred mode of expression and the expression preferred is hard, negative, and tough, rather than fearful, gentle, loving, or warm.

Ambivalence is denied, just as in BL and SDCP families, but therapists must tease out positive feelings rather than negative ones. Making a safe place for ambivalence is just as necessary as in CP families, but the reframing is of a different nature: Family members discover love, not anger; they disclaim fear, not independent strivings.

It is just as important to address boundary issues in CF as in CP families, though they are expressed somewhat differently. Verbally, members routinely deny attachment, yet behaviorally they show a markedly inadequate differentiation. Children leave home angrily only to return with no expression of warmth, chagrin, or regret; spouses separate and return with yoyo-like predictability.

Control is desired by parent or parents, of course, but is quite impossible to obtain in the SDCF families. It is also hard to come by in the BLCF group. Their miserable failure in efforts to control contrasts with the more frequently effective control seen in CP families.

Needed coherence in these families is attained by increasing effective behavioral controls. A basic therapeutic tool is positive reframing; hostile outbursts, personal attacks, and intense conflict are redefined as the expression of caring, love, and warmth. Passion is passion. To hit out is to reach out; the need is disguised but not totally hidden! Such redefinitions may confuse, and also inhibit blind, impulsive action. This sets the stage for the claiming of mixed feelings, as well as their beginning resolution.

Frequently, these families submit to treatment because one member is "held for ransom." A juvenile referred by police or judge, a father with assault charges from a family dispute, or a mother with shoplifting charges is sometimes diverted from the criminal justice system to family therapy. It is frequently possible to pronounce the erring behavior an effort to call attention to the pain in the family and to obtain assistance. This is consistent with our goal of reframing negative behavior as positive motivation.

Perhaps it is useful here to restate some basic assumptions about "truth" in family life. First, no one will ever know motives—of oneself or another. This is a murky swamp that is entered with no guarantee of return. It is much wiser for a therapist or family member to begin with the assumption that the people one is working or living with have decent motives.

Second, truth, as Harry Stack Sullivan succinctly defined it, is "consensual validation."[144] That is, it is the consensus of interested parties, an artifice, an invention of humans rather than a constant to be discovered. Third, the good therapist selects truths according to their potential usefulness, their ability to instill hope and keep the process of treatment from grinding to a halt or becoming static and stuck.

Fourth, since truth is defined through consensual validation, an important part of offering useful truths in treatment is having them accepted and made a part of the family reality. This requires sensitive attention to the particular family mores, beliefs, and customs. One should never play a hand one cannot win and never overplay one's hand. One should offer new realities, truth, reframes, or interpretations only when the family can accept them. Otherwise, one might strain the therapeutic alliance and, in the case of CF families, drive them away.

For example, it might be possible to have a CF family tentatively accept that a delinquent offspring is calling attention to family pain and making a cry for help rather than being worthless and mean. This is because the behavior clearly resulted in an offer of help; the motive could be as easily determined this way as any other way. If, however, a therapist chose to suggest that the delinquent behavior was an effort to bring the parents together, this might well be too much for the parents to stomach. After all, they might reason, he has shown no interest in the parents' needs and relationship previously. Such a reframe might be rejected along with the therapist who offered it. It is important to keep the development of new realities close to the data, address the ubiquitous mixed feelings, and be part of a plea to induce better family functioning and relative trust in members.

Frequently, a family member may refuse to come to sessions. With CP families, the usual approach is to reach out and ask the member for help. With CF families it is often more effective to ban the person from sessions, saying something like: "He is not ready for family work yet." Challenges are often more effective than appeals for assistance. This is an example of going with the family patterns while assisting in their change.

The need for coherence is as great in these families as in other severely dysfunctional families; the methods for obtaining it are somewhat different. Behavior is much more prominent than words in CF family messages and dialogue; therefore we must keep it in mind when attempting to increase coherence. For example, it is possible to be drawn into the family belief that coercion and denial are more effective than sensitivity and empathy. For instance, the family arrives three-quarters through the scheduled time of a session. Of course, a conscientious therapist may be tempted to create havoc with office scheduling and continue on into the next session, thus rewarding the lateness by showing "concern." In this way, family members learn once again that authorities are fools, unable or unwilling to set reasonable limits out of fear of creating an uproar. Intimidation is shown once again to be more useful than thoughtfulness.

Limit-setting in the sessions is most important. The therapist must either keep order or insist that the parents keep order. Accepting behavioral chaos is not useful. Here, cotherapists, team approaches, and physically controlling, separating, and restraining family members are all legitimate and frequently necessary tools in developing "behavioral coherence"—a relatively quiet and safe working environment.

Redefining behavioral chaos and aggressive provocative challenging as grief, fear, or neediness has at least two values. First, since it may well be true, such redefinition allows the other side of ambivalence to surface. The vulnerable is acknowledged and addressed. Second, it attaches to unwanted behavior a motivation that is frequently so distasteful to the perpetrator that the behavior is derailed or inhibited.

CF family members do not like to show that they grieve, that they are frightened, and that they have needs. It takes some real effort on everyone's part to reach personal and family acceptance of childhood needs that we all possess and continue to have—the need to be cherished, to be held, and to have love and dignity. One mostly focuses on the simple, the basic, and the observable. Words are only grace notes in the underlying behavioral melody of CF families.

As limit-setting is addressed, the unclear generational boundaries become evident. Parents lack effective authority; they frequently lose any semblance of parenting and get "in the face" of a child more as an angry peer than as a grown-up. Part of any work with CF families is the development of parental dignity and increased parental effectiveness. Helping parents set limits is a small but vital part of developing ongoing coherence and structure where negotiating is possible and makes sense.

CF family members do not enjoy each other very much. They look for satisfaction outside the family. One measure of improvement is the discovery that one can have good times at home. Assignments of age-appropriate games is often useful; parents and children can find joy in each other's company. To facilitate good times, memories of early enjoyments can be pried out of parents or children. It is easier to admit softness, hunger, and need if tender moments and feelings are couched in each member's childhood memories rather than in the present.

Child abuse, like substance abuse, can be found in any of the varied family groupings, but it is particularly apt to be a part of CF family life. Children are usually beaten because they act like kids—they show fear, dependency, ineptness,[136] all the qualities that CF families find awkward and embarrassing. It is both legally and morally necessary to intervene actively in any ongoing abuse; this is just one more example of attending behavior and being extremely active when working with CF families.

It is necessary though difficult to avoid arguments with CF family members. Their behavior is often provocative, and the temptation is always to impose more limit-setting or direction than the family members can tolerate. It is important to remember the apocryphal French politician who, when observing the crowd surging to the city hall, said, "I must follow them for I am their leader." One needs to make efforts that are compatible with the family's current side of the ever-present and unresolved ambivalence.

Statements like these are helpful: "OK, we can assume for right now that Jason is just a bad boy. Now what do we do?" "It is a very frustrating situation. I'm not surprised that someone gets mad enough to lash out physically. Doesn't seem to do much good, though." The feelings can be blessed and then redirected. "How can these frustrated feelings be expressed without anybody getting hurt?"

Confusion is very useful in treating people who act badly and can hurt others. A spurious certainty is necessary for harmful action. Homicide or suicide requires this harebrained—yet unchallengeable—certainty of the moment in which no hesitation or contemplation intrudes. Reframing behavior that seems hostile as caring and loving not only helps develop fuller, more human dimensions in the family members, but also causes confusion and a useful uncertainty in people who often have acted quickly on simple, even simpleminded, explanations of family members' actions.

Case Example

A separated couple with a long history of tenacious and painful fighting had a violently aggressive 14-year-old son, Jake, who was bigger than his father and had physically attacked the father on several occasions. In an individual session, Jake was able to express his feelings verbally. He began to cry with some empathic probing of the sources of his rage, and he spoke of the many times he had been emotionally torn to pieces as his parents verbally and physically fought when he was smaller. As the boy was successfully encouraged to talk about what he felt as he attacked, the family was brought to relative calm and the parents were able to understand what was going on inside Jake. His father and mother softened their stance of defining the boy simply as a bad seed that needed to be put away.

This story suggests another technical point important in treating CF families—do not be afraid of splitting them up and working with subsystems. A rebellious adolescent may require a new and empathic person to allow tender feelings to emerge. Parents may need to work on getting control of their children in a marital session. Often a therapist can act as a consultant to the parents in their efforts at child-raising, rather than insisting that all the work be done with the therapist present.

Single-parent CF families are a special challenge. These parents (almost always female) are overwhelmed, have generally poor parenting skills, and receive little support from any broader social network. Single-parent support groups and parenting classes, in addition to formal family therapy, are frequently vital to producing good results.

Therapists do not expect to get very close to these family members, and they are less apt to disclose treatment strategies than with CP families. There seems to be no compelling reason not to disclose these strategies, however. It is useful to be straightforward with these families; there is relatively little emotional glue present. Prescribing symptoms or predicting setbacks can produce unwanted destabilizing effects.

A marked overt power difference between therapist and family members is useful and can be sustained during treatment, since these families characteristically come in during crisis and leave when the crisis is over. They are not apt to stay in treatment when things are going reasonably well. There will usually be a number of treatment episodes, produced by crisis, and each experience in therapy can increase comfort, trust, and negotiating abilities just a bit more.

Case Example

The Jay family (see Chapter 6) consisted of divorced parents, Fred, 43, and Sally, 38, and five children—Jeannie, 18, John, 15, Jeff, 13, James, 12, and Jason 10.

This was Fred's second marriage. He owned a tavern and was probably alcoholic. Sally was a clerical worker in poor health with a duodenal ulcer and a previous mild stroke.

Jeannie had dropped out of school, been married and divorced, and had two children. She had worked as a waitress, a topless dancer, and occasionally as a prostitute. She also had been arrested several times for DWI's and for hot checks.

John had erratic school attendance and performance which became worse after a severe drug overdose. Jeff also was erratic at school. Both these older boys had police records, including auto theft, drug use, and time in a state correctional institution. James was retarded and had lived in a state school. Jason, the youngest, was bright and went to school regularly and had no police record.

The presenting problem was that the older boys were arrested for auto theft.

The beginning task of the therapist in this case was to assess the family and identify what members of the family could be motivated to attend and make use of therapy. The older children and Fred were generally unmotivated to attend therapy even though the judicial system was clearly supporting therapy as an alternative to confinement. Sally, on the other hand, was motivated. She saw herself as attacked by her ex-husband, her children, the school system, her creditors, and her health.

Early assessment of the family as severely dysfunctional and centrifugal was relatively easy, even though we never had a session with all seven present. The fact that the family was so chaotic and negative was one indicator; another was Sally's inability as a custodial parent to obtain the children's attendance by use of either power or relationship. When parts of family did attend in dyads or triads, their interaction was angry, cynical, and unprofitable. Communication was unclear and responsibility was rarely taken for individual thoughts or feelings. Sympathy and understanding of others were not exhibited.

Initially, Sally and all the children were asked to attend family therapy. This direction was quickly abandoned for two reasons. First, it could not be accomplished. The boys switched residences regularly and the parents were too hostile to exchange and negotiate simple information regarding therapy times and transportation. Second, family therapy would have been unproductive with that many hostile members in the room, since mother's ability to exercise any control was minimal.

Therapy began by working with the mother individually and moved to working with mother-child dyads. Sally was placed in a support group for mothers of acting-out adolescents. Three of the children were frequently seen in an adolescent group when they were not incarcerated. Therapy was often structural in nature. The generational boundary was reinforced on a regular basis.

Early therapy was often crisis-oriented out of necessity. During and between crises, one job of therapy was to introduce structure, power, and support in Sally's life. Therapy included much teaching, e.g., teaching her how to use logical consequences of behavior with children, ex-husband, and friends. She was encouraged to further structure and simplify her life. This was a difficult concept for her to internalize, as evidenced by her decision to save money by sharing a lease on a condo with a schizophrenic, recovering alcoholic woman and her son! Such impulsive decisions were frequent and followed by crises.

Besides the structural issue of appropriate power for the mother, another key issue for this family was communication. At first, therapists simply interrupted chaotic interaction. One example of such interruption was the shift from seeing the family together to working with different individuals of the family in group or individual sessions.

Next, chaotic interactions were transformed into understandable conversations. To bring dyads of the family back together on an irregular and changing basis the therapist began by connecting them around issues of an informational and crisis-solving nature. After chaos was limited and information could be shared, the process moved to reframing attacks into caring and vulnerability. Limiting chaos and impulsivity and adding structure and simplicity came slowly, as did the willingness to express vulnerability instead of anger. Setbacks were often predicted and did occur. The therapist's job was to see strengths in the midst of confusion and to continue to engender hope for members who had given up.

Besides helping Sally meet crises, develop structure, and discover appropriate use of power, her group experience was also a powerful place to experience support and nurturing and to grieve over her own chaotic and abusive childhood. When she was encouraged to grieve over the past and learned how to accept support, she was capable of setting limits and nurturing her own children in ways she had not been able to do previously.

As Sally organized her own life, the therapist working with the family found that it was possible to include more members of family in a session. Family members began to be capable of voicing vulnerability and caring. Therapy moved from providing structure to encouraging expression of relationship. At one particular poignant moment, Jeff shared with John how frightened he was when John convulsed after a drug overdose. Jeff was able to detail what he had to do to save his brother's life and how much he wanted his brother to survive.

A later crisis was caused by the mother's refusal to take responsibility for her two grandchildren, even though refusal meant that the grandchildren would be given up for adoption. This was again a structural boundary issue. Jeannie had expected that the mother would be responsible for her (the daughter's) finances, health, and children. The mother's own resources, including her health and her finances, were limited. This was a difficult decision.

This issue was used by the therapist to encourage members of the family to express feelings of sadness, vulnerability, and connection, while setting limits. The family's ability to deal successfully with such a difficult issue indicated that change had occurred in this family during the 20 months of treatment.

Other behavioral indicators that this family have moved toward greater overall family health include the following:

1. Jason, at age 12, was successful in school and uninvolved with the law.
2. The number and severity of crises were greatly reduced.
3. John and Jeff were no longer breaking laws.
4. The family had learned to enjoy some family activities.

The children's father and Jeannie, the sister, were never directly involved in therapy. However, the other family members found themselves better equipped to deal with them.

These centrifugal families have been insufficiently attended. Psychotherapy is quite a verbal endeavor, and most theorists have focused on concepts and techniques for the centripetal groups. There are some useful exceptions, however. These include Zuk's *Process and Practice in Family Therapy*,[166] Minuchin et al.'s *Families of the Slums*,[105] Stanton and Todd's *The Family Therapy of Drug Abuse and Addiction*,[135] and Alexander's *Functional Family Therapy*.[5]

COMMENT

Suggesting recommended treatment approaches for these various family groupings does not, of course, cover all the variables that are significant in therapy. Ethnicity is important and will require alterations and adaptations of treatment approaches. McGoldrick, Pearce and Giordano have provided some guidelines in their *Ethnicity and Family Therapy*.[103] Boyd-Franklin's, *Black Families in Therapy*[31] is valuable in offering assistance in treating this ethnic group. Specific gender issues are helpfully addressed in McGoldrick et al.'s, *Women in Families*.[101] Walters et al.'s *The Invisible Web*[154] is also useful in this regard.

Treatment techniques are constantly evolving. We believe that the relatively simple, clinically useful, and solidly researched assessment method described in these pages is necessary for that evolution to be fruitful and increasingly productive.

12 . . . AND THE RICH GET RICHER

Social economist Jeremy Bentham has suggested that society should be organized so as to provide the greatest good for the greatest number. However, certain commodities have been historically unequally allocated: "people who know a lot generally value additional knowledge and skills more than those who know very little,"[82] a condition which tends to create an unequal distribution of "knowledge" as a commodity due to unequal demands.

Much the same observation can be made of the mental health and family therapy fields, in which services have been skewed toward the healthier, the better functioning, and the more competent individuals and families. All through this volume we have emphasized that family competence can be viewed along a continuum, and that growth and the potential for competence are cornerstone concepts of assessment and treatment. Therefore, ideally, we would hope to be able to see comparable levels of growth and gain across all levels of family competence, especially when one tailors the therapeutic approach to the family. Sadly, this has not been realized. Throughout the literature, gains in individual[56] and family therapy[65] are unequally distributed across competence levels: Healthier people and families tend to make the greatest gains in therapy.

But this message also carries an optimistic note regarding the cost of improving family life: If all kinds of therapy can help fairly competent families, perhaps these families can choose less intensive (and less expensive) enterprises, such as group, didactic, or enrichment workshop activities.

It is becoming increasingly apparent that interventions such as parent training, marital enrichment, and consultation services are as meaningful and effective for *some* families as intensive family therapy is for others. Those therapists (like the authors) who have conducted "family life education" classes, parent training seminars, or couple enrichment activities have noted a significant enrollment of people who would probably not be seen in clinics or on private practice rosters, much less in public or court-referred family therapy clinics. For many of these clients, "education" and "training" become acceptable descriptors of skill enhancement, since they do not "need" counseling or therapy. Conversely, there are always a handful of individuals in training or group enterprises who are hopeful for a "quick fix" or become "group groupies." These less competent individuals often become the problem patients and monopolizers described by Yalom.[164] Our research and experience suggest that many of the multiperson/multifamily education and training approaches are designed and appropriate for upper midrange and better functioning families, but typically have limited utility in dealing with dysfunctional or highly stressed groups of families.

One of us (RBH) has been involved in conducting and evaluating parent training procedures for a number of years, with biological, blended, single-parent, and foster families. We have studied different types and modes of training,[78] compared individually trained parents with group-trained parents,[77] and studied the temporal durability of skills and behavior changes over time.[70] The most impressive aspects are the individual differences in parenting skills that these participants bring to these training groups and the influence of individual skill level on the acquisition and maintenance of new skills. Regardless of race, social class, or family type, certain individuals in these training groups have terrific intuitions and skills in working with child and family matters and are confident and optimistic in their approach to parenting and quick to pick up certain skills and practices. Much like the star students in the classroom, these competent people gain insights, new ideas, and confidence, and become the teaching assistants in the class. Unfortunately, some participants in parent training classes are less skilled at the outset, and appear to have greater difficulty acquiring new skills and knowledge.

In our work with foster parents, we were able to test these observations empirically and systemically, using observational and self-report instruments to tap parent-child interaction, parent attitudes, knowledge of child development and needs, and individual motives for becoming a foster parent. At the outset of training in two different groups,[70] parents were rank-ordered in terms of a composite skill index. These ranks were unknown to trainers. Post-training assessments of each parent provided a basis for comparison of rank at the completion of a 10-week training sequence. Across both training groups (N=25), there was remarkable consistency in ranked skills across the training period: 24 of the 25 individuals maintained the same rank (Tau = .96, $p < .001$). Everyone improved to some extent, but the higher-ranking parents were still better at the close, and the lower-ranking remained so. We also found, not surprisingly, that the better-ranked parents actually gained more during the training (Spearman-Brown $r = .416$, $p < .06$). These data are strongly supportive of the notion that the rich get richer in these training programs. The poor do not get poorer, but they do not gain as much and are still comparatively poorer than their more skilled counterparts. Those parents who apparently "need" training most typically gain less than the more talented parents.

We have found similar results in our evaluation of families entering family therapy at the Southwest Family Institute. For whole families, the greatest predictor of therapeutic gain (as measured by observational, self-report, and therapist rating) was the observational competence score rated at the beginning of the first session. The more competent the family at the outset, the greater the therapeutic gains; the more dysfunctional the family, the smaller the gain. Midrange families have much of the necessary structure and moderate flexibility to make considerable headway, while the most dysfunctional families are rigid systems that are more difficult to loosen and redirect toward competence.

With this in mind, let us discuss several intervention strategies globally defined as training or enrichment procedures, which are most useful for the better functioning families (midrange and better). These include parent training, marital enrichment, and family assessment procedures.

PARENT TRAINING

For what has been termed the most important job in society—the job of parenting the next generation—the objective "job benefits" package is relatively slim. There is no pay, little vacation time, and little systematic education. Parenting is an intuitive interpersonal process that evolves from experience, a working relationship with one's spouse (if present or involved), and one's own family of origin.

Parents have assigned to their charge these offspring, whom they may or may not find attractive, competent, compelling, too much or not enough like themselves or like neighbors' children. They are expected to know, by some process, how to discipline, enculturate, and nurture children through their developmental processes. They may have few trustworthy role models or advisors.

"I told myself I would *never* do to my children what my parents did to me," we hear again and again, "but I *found* myself _____." For most parents, difficulties in the parenting process do not stem from willful maliciousness, but from frustration, lack of experience, or lack of knowledge. Parents are also more isolated from extended family and the sense of community than even two decades ago. Hence, the rationale for parent training interventions includes: providing support and a reference group for parents, providing a knowledge base in child development and theoretical perspectives on parental guidance and discipline, and attempting to reduce frustration levels. A very important result reported by many of the participants in our groups is making overt the covert, automatic, or unconscious: These parents become more *aware*, sometimes painfully aware, of what they have been doing.

The goals are admirable, and the results of parent training are positive, but we cannot expect parent training to be panacea for correcting shortcomings in all parents and children. A brief review of some of the major findings clarifies this summary statement.

First, the effectiveness of parent training is determined partly by course content and partly by the skill and experience of the instructor(s). We have found that training techniques that are primarily behavioral in perspective have an impact on behavior and disciplinary problems in parent-child interaction, while reflective (communication, feeling, and attitudinal focus) procedures typically affect parent attitudes and empathic communication skills.[78,147] Behavioral procedures have shown greater durability over time, after the training sessions have ended, presumably giving parents useful general tools to carry forth to novel situations.[70,147] Combination approaches, such as STEP[40] or Abidin's Parenting Skills Training,[1] emphasize both affective/relational and behavioral/disciplinary domains and are effective in both arenas.[77]

The outcome of parent training groups also depends somewhat on the skills of the group leaders as models, as facilitators, and as creators of hope and growth. Comparisons of parental skill gains in training groups conducted by therapist/leaders of higher- vs. lower-rated facilitative and reinforcing skills show that parents do better when they are trained by highly skilled people.[70,147]

Second, the context of parent training can also influence its results. One contextual question is whether training should occur in a group or with an individual family, even in the home. One of our studies[77] found no overall differences in measured and observed skill gains between group trained and individually trained foster parents at the close of training, but the individually trained (at home) parents reported greater satisfaction and greater perceived effect on the children than did the group trained parents.

Another important contextual issue involves the heterogeneity or homogeneity of parental needs and concerns. Some of our training groups have been targeted toward parents with retarded children,[147] foster parents for emotionally disturbed children, parents with ADD (Attention Deficit Disorder) children, and the like; others have been open to anyone interested. We have found that groups that start out with a shared universal reference point jell more quickly, share more appropriately, and progress more collaboratively than randomly constructed groups. A parenting group recently conducted by one of us was comprised of a single mother, a grandmother, a couple with an adolescent son, and a couple with very young children; while all participants benefited, the group lacked the sense of shared universality[164] that is apparent in more homogeneous groups.

Third, parent training can be a useful adjunct to more intensive family therapy.

For some families, particularly those of midrange or lesser competence, parenting groups can be a useful adjunct to family therapy, providing some behavioral controls, clarifying expectations regarding parent-child behavior and roles, and fostering growth in structure and generational boundaries. These initial steps may be accomplished through the group training experience, paving the way for the more specific and intensive work to be done in therapy.

For example, a single mother with two children (Mrs. Promom, from Chapter 6) sought family therapy because she was frustrated with her children's noncompliance and negative attention-seeking, her isolation from meaningful adult relationships, and some significant family-of-origin difficulties. The therapist recognized early on that the children provided consistent and powerful buffers for this mother. She would/could not address important therapeutic issues, but instead joined the children in a chaotic "three-child circus," alternately blaming and feeling sorry for the children. She was referred to a parenting group, in which she quickly learned the role of positive attention, making clear her expectations, being comfortable with leadership, and clarifying the generational issues related to responsibility and problem ownership.[40] These gains proved invaluable for the family therapist in furthering the growth of family and promoting the development of consistent generational boundaries and more affiliative attitudes in the family. It is noteworthy that the initial gains were accomplished in the group training context, at markedly reduced cost and professional time.

Finally, certain core elements of parental awareness and skills central to successful parenting can be promoted for a lifetime or for shorter duration through parenting education interventions. Some of these

more important elements are cornerstone concepts of family competence, promoted in the context of group training.

Most participants report an increased awareness of personal needs,
expectations, and behaviors. It is a telling exercise for many to listen to a
tape recording of a dinner conversation and monitor the frequencies of
critical vs. other comments to the children; "catch them being good"[23] is
a theme we stress early on. The focus on problem ownership[40] helps
parents learn awareness of owning responsibility for personal behavior
and disowning others' problems. The discovery that "discipline" stems
from the basic concept of discipleship and is not necessarily related to
punishment paves the way toward teaching and negotiation. In essence,
these discoveries help promote responsibility, clarity, and autonomy, all
cornerstones of competent families.

Another general theme that is universal to positive outcome in parent
training involves openness, sharing, and group problem-solving.[8] As
participants develop a sense of trust and sharing, collaboration and negotiation skills evolve; the teamwork taken from the exchanges in the
group serves as a model for negotiation and collaboration with spouses
and children—also imperatives in family competence.

A third major theme of useful parent education emphasizes spontaneity and "creative consequences" in parent-child interaction. Many of the
actual or perceived "behavior problems" have resulted from all members' getting stuck and frustrated with a particular mode of behavior or
punishment. In one training group conducted by one of us (RBH) several
years ago, an older couple with a teenage son reported great frustration
over the son's dawdling and resultant missing of the school bus. The
father, a truck farmer, left the house before sunup each morning; his wife
would attempt to move the boy along quickly in the morning and get
him out of the house and on the way to the bus stop in time. Since there
was only one vehicle (father's truck), she could not get him to school
when he dawdled back after missing the bus. She would place the call to
father's work station, and father would drive back to the house, deliver
the boy to his junior high school, rant and rave, and return to work.
Ignoring the behavior, which could be advocated from operant theory,
was not a viable option, since truancy proceedings were likely if the son
missed another day.

In the parenting group, ideas from participants were solicited, and the
term "creative consequences" emerged. The next time this behavior occurred, the father agreed to take a little extra time getting back to his son,
using the time to get extra dirty and fully acquire the scent of manure.
Nothing was to be mentioned to the boy in the truck, but they were to

walk into the school arm in arm for all to see, timed exactly for the change of classes. One-trial learning occurred with that maneuver, and not one angry word or physical gesture of punishment had taken place.

Another highly important theme of parent training programs is the uniqueness of the individual child—in analyzing the nature of the problem behavior, in planning useful interventions, and in anticipating unique rewards for each person. The most successful training endeavors emphasize that careful rewarding, finding the positive, and using what each person *likes* as rewards are all important. But it is not the new video game or bicycle or cash that lies at the core of successful rewarding—it is the spontaneous moment of shared human delight between parent and child that sparks growth and facilitates competent family interaction.

With these common perspectives contributing to the parents' understanding of children and the reciprocal and interactive nature of family behavior, it is not surprising that parent training procedures also affect the family at large[70,127] and enhance marital satisfaction.[127] Hence, interventions that recognize and reinforce systems thinking and are geared toward promoting competence, autonomy of members, and responsibility are close kin to "family therapy."

MARITAL ENRICHMENT PROGRAMS

Enrichment programs are most typically targeted for married couples, focusing on that particular subsystem of the whole family. As with parent training, such interventions affect the whole family's functioning through enhancing competence and couple satisfaction. Although there is no evaluative literature available on the effects of these intervention programs (generally or specifically), we believe they are similar to parenting programs in that better functioning couples acquire more skill, recharging of emotional fuel, and appreciation for each other than do less competent couples. Enrichment procedures may actually be counterproductive with certain borderline and dysfunctional couples who maintain a tenuous alliance through rigid complementary relating or illusory closeness, especially when verbal clarity, mutual disclosing, trusting exercises, and demands for intimacy are involved.

Globally defined, marital enrichment programs are usually conducted in a group format, ranging in size from several couples to several hundred (as in the Forum). They may be offered hourly over several weeks or be concentrated into several evenings or a weekend. The procedures employed are many, but usually involve steps that facilitate open, direct communication, helping couples engage in mutual problem-solving and negotiation, take personal responsibility for thoughts and feelings, understand personal contributions to current interactional themes (including, in some, family-of-origin analyses), and break down defensive barriers so that the affiliative side of the relational ambivalence can emerge. Some enrichment programs focus heavily on reciprocal dyadic behavior through exercises and tasks, while others rely more on the cognitive and affective awareness of the individual. (One quite competent and savvy wife and mother reported back on her experience of one church-sponsored, full-day couples encounter: "One more 'touch and look into each other's eyes' exercise and I was going to be out of there!")

Testimonials from couples going through such enrichment experiences indicate that their affective involvement with and understanding of their spouses have increased; many report that they have "rediscovered love" and "learned not to take (him/her) for granted." Moreover, a most consistent and common undertone surrounds the couple's renewed emphasis on teamwork, communicating directly rather than through or around children, and having and taking time for each other without interruptions from children. Consequently, these enrichment experiences are useful and productive interventions for fairly competent couples needing a "booster shot" of a positive sense of their marital relationship. These interventions can also be useful in reinforcing appropriate generational boundaries and supportive couple teamwork in midrange and some borderline CP groups.

For example, Mr. and Mrs. D., an upper-middle-class dual-career couple, referred their older daughter, Margaret, for "continual defiance, sassing, and a negative attitude." The daughter, bright, attractive, and shy, was polite and respectful to all except her mother, who interrupted, invaded, intruded, and generally spoke and felt through this 15-year-old. She wanted the best for Margaret socially, academically, and personally, and took it upon herself to inform her about how to talk on the phone and other matters. Margaret is no pure saint in this exchange, playing helpless and incompetent at times (picking out clothes, making decisions) and alternately blasting her mother for intrusions (the reason for referral). Mr. D. is a master at avoiding highly charged encounters by not listening, going for walks, or retreating to his wide-screen TV. He sometimes sides with Margaret, sometimes with Mrs. D., and usually takes no side; his favorite person is Liz, the younger daughter, who is bubbly, sociable, and keeps her distance from mother.

As we began to disentangle the generational issues in this midrange CP family, it became apparent that there was a great deal of loneliness and lost collaboration in the parents. The further Mrs. D. felt from her husband, the more she invaded Margaret. The couple was encouraged to attend a couples enrichment program conducted over two adjacent weekends as an adjunct to family therapy. The renewed trusting affiliative attitude and teamwork that the couples group provided facilitated a sense of strengthened parental coalition, allowing whole family therapy to progress at a more rapid pace.

The relative lack of systematic research on the outcome of these enrichment enterprises is probably attributable to few attempts to measure systemic functioning in individual participants; this measurement is further complicated by the group format, in which many couples with few common threads converge (except, perhaps, in church-sponsored groups). These constraints—systems assessment, short time interval, many individuals, some clinical and some nonclinical participants—make "research" difficult. The challenge to all of us therapists/trainers/researchers is to develop appropriate scientific methods to answer questions of both utility and professional curiosity: Do these procedures work, for whom, with what family constellations, for how long?

ASSESSMENT AS INTERVENTION— COMING FULL CIRCLE

We have asserted that assessment and intervention are inseparable elements of clinical family work; we also believe that *for some families* formal assessment plus resultant feedback *is* intervention. Certain better functioning, unstuck systems can utilize feedback to engage in corrective behavior. These families are typically in the upper-midrange or more competent ranges, have an investment and pride in their sense of family, and show enthusiasm in gaining feedback about their family. Some of these family members have impressed us as being the ultimate scientists: Looking at their own strengths and weaknesses with an open mind, with faith that effort, determination, and positivity can reap more, with faith and trust in outsiders (and our instruments), and with the all-important realization that everything human is fallible and unpredictable. These are not all highly religious people (defined in terms of church or synagogue attendance), but most seem to have a belief in a higher order than the human one and in transcendent values[16] that make striving and gaining important.

In the prototypical setting, a family comes in, initially voluntarily for research purposes, and undergoes a series of observational and self-report family assessment procedures. The scores and ratings are summarized and presented to the family (within minutes or up to the next week). Bloom[28] has found that immediate feedback is most useful and appreciated by families; his "Colorado Family Checkup" uses multiple on-line response terminals (all self-report), which provides immediate scoring and profiling (across members).

Assessment by observation or self-report has certain limitations, with both positive and negative qualities. There is no doubt that assessment information reflects deliberate and voluntary behavior or responding that occurs because the participants know that they are being observed. Healthier families show more competent system behavior in this context, and dysfunctional families show more repetitive, stereotypical, "stuck" behavior. Hence, better functioning families may show competent ratings which may be higher than a family average over time. The ratings represent what is *possible* with some effort.

So what do family members do with feedback? If it is congruent with family realities, suggests strengths in the areas in which the family perceives itself as doing quite well, and offers suggestions about where to improve in certain areas that have been overlooked by or obscure to the family, then it is useful and growth-enhancing feedback. The focus on the positive and possible suggests room for growth, which is why feedback based on assessment is more useful and stimulating to better functioning families than to dysfunctional ones. The process that follows is probably different for each family, but some feedback-initiated internal self-monitoring generally occurs. Many of our (and Bloom's) families come back periodically and enjoy seeing how they measure up.

As trainers of therapists/assessors, we are also impressed by "trickle-down" competence enhancement. As fairly alert and competent individuals learn family assessment procedures, they become more aware of their own family qualities; hence, family assessment may serve to help the families of the assessors as well as the assessed, reminiscent of Reissman's[122] "Helper Therapy" principle.

We are interested in developing further enrichment exercises based on assessed family strengths and weaknesses, both in group-enrichment and self-help (book) formats. Based on *overall* ratings of competence and style, as well as a within-family profile of strengths and weaknesses, core activities and awareness exercises can be developed. For example, for a midrange CP family showing considerable strength in structure and coalition patterns, but difficulty in communication clarity and affective expression, certain family discussion tasks can be constructed; these would be more "advanced" than those a borderline family could handle, and intermediate to the complexity level that would be appropriate for an adequate family. Likewise, enrichment exercises and group activities can be designed for CF families, based upon our experience with clinical and nonclinical families. A common theme in CF families is a diminished value on words, so nonverbal trust-building exercises and cooperation-enhancing activities can facilitate relational clarity and growth. Such tailored assessment-based education models could be useful tools for identification and prevention of family-based child disorders.

But before we get too pie-in-the-sky, we must close off this chapter and volume with the realities. With many of our multifamily interventions and educational approaches, it is the rich who get richer. Our challenge is to promote systems thinking, tailoring appropriate interventions to the needs and strengths of all our clients/patients; these are beginning attempts at spreading the wealth.

APPENDICES

A BEAVERS INTERACTIONAL SCALES: FAMILY COMPETENCE

Family Name _____   Rater _____

Segment _____   Date _____

Instructions: The following scales were designed to assess the family functioning on continua representing interactional aspects of being a family. Therefore, it is important that you consider the entire range of each scale when you make your ratings. Please try to *respond on the basis of the videotape data alone*, scoring according to what you see and hear, rather than what you imagine might occur elsewhere.

I. Structure of the Family

A. Overt Power: Based on the entire tape, check the term that best describes your general impression of the overt power relationships of this family.

1	1.5	2	2.5	3	3.5	4	4.5	5
chaos		marked dominance		moderate dominance		led		egalitarian
Leaderless; no one has enough power to structure the interaction.		Control is close to absolute. No negotiation; dominance and submission are the rule.		Control is close to absolute. Some negotiation, but dominance and submission are the rule.		Tendency toward dominance and submission, but most of the interaction is through respectful negotiation.		Leadership is shared between parents, changing with the nature of the interaction.

B. Parental Coalitions: Check the terms that best describe the relationship structure in this family.

1	1.5	2	2.5	3	3.5	4	4.5	5
parent-child coalition				weak parental coalition				strong parental coalition

197

C. Closeness

1	1.5	2	2.5	3	3.5	4	4.5	5
amorphous, vague and indistinct boundaries among members				isolation, distancing				closeness, with distinct boundaries among members

Note any invasions (when family member clearly "speaks for" the thoughts or feelings of another, without invitation):
—invasion(s) observed
—invasion(s) not observed

II. Mythology: Every member has a mythology; that is, a concept of how it functions as a group. Rate the degree to which this family's mythology seems congruent with reality.

1	1.5	2	2.5	3	3.5	4	4.5	5
very congruent	mostly congruent					somewhat incongruent		very incongruent

III. Goal-Directed Negotiation: Rate this family's overall efficiency in negotiating problem solutions.

1	1.5	2	2.5	3	3.5	4	4.5	5
extremely efficient	good					poor		extremely inefficient

IV. Autonomy

A. Clarity of Expression: Rate this family as to the clarity of disclosure of feelings and thoughts. This is not a rating of the intensity or variety of feelings, but rather of clarity of individual thoughts and feelings.

1	1.5	2	2.5	3	3.5	4	4.5	5
very clear				somewhat vague and hidden				hardly anyone is ever clear

B. Responsibility: Rate the degree to which the family members take responsibility for their own past, present, and future actions.

1	1.5	2	2.5	3	3.5	4	4.5	5
members regularly are able to voice responsibility for individual actions				members sometimes voice responsibility for individual actions, but tactics also include sometimes blaming others, speaking in 3rd person or plural				members rarely if ever, voice responsibility for individual actions

C. Permeability: Rate the degree to which members are open, receptive and permeable to the statements of other family members.

1	1.5	2	2.5	3	3.5	4	4.5	5
very open	moderately open					members frequently unreceptive		members unreceptive

V. Family Affect

A. Range of Feelings: Rate the degree to which this family system is characterized by a wide range expression of feelings.

1	1.5	2	2.5	3	3.5	4	4.5	5
direct expression of a wide range of feelings	direct expression of many feelings despite some difficulty			obvious restriction in the expressions of some feelings		although some feelings are expressed, there is masking of most feelings		little or no expression of feelings

B. Mood and Tone: Rate the feeling tone of this family's interaction.

1	1.5	2	2.5	3	3.5	4	4.5	5
usually warm, affectionate, humorous and optimistic	polite, without impressive warmth or affection; or frequently hostile with times of pleasure		overly hostile		depressed			cynical, hopeless and pessimistic

C. Unresolvable Conflict: Rate the degree of seemingly unresolvable conflict.

1	1.5	2	2.5	3	3.5	4	4.5	5
severe conflict, with severe impairment of group functioning		definite conflict, with moderate impairment of group functioning		definite conflict, with slight impairment of group functioning		some evidence of unresolvable conflict, without impairment of group functioning		little, or no unresolvable conflict

D. Empathy: Rate the degree of sensitivity to, and understanding of, each other's feelings within this family.

1	1.5	2	2.5	3	3.5	4	4.5	5
consistent empathic responsiveness		for the most part, an empathic responsiveness with one another, despite obvious resistance		attempted empathic involvement, but failed to maintain it		absence of any empathic responsiveness		grossly inappropriate responses to feelings

VI. Global Health-Pathology Scale: Circle the number of the point on the following scale that best describes this family's health or pathology.

10	9	8	7	6	5	4	3	2	1
most pathological									healthiest

Table 1
DESCRIPTIVE STATISTICS ON THE BEAVERS INTERACTIONAL COMPETENCE SCALE FOR NORMATIVE AND CLINICAL SAMPLES

Competence Subscale	Normative Sample (N = 149)		Clinic Sample (N = 61)	
	X	S.D.	X	S.D.
Overt Power	1.83	1.01	3.41	.88
Parental Coalition	1.40	.68	3.37	.93
Closeness	1.43	.78	3.26	.77
Mythology	1.61	.94	3.22	.90
Goal-Directed Negotiation	1.69	.78	3.73	.81
Clarity of Expression	1.68	.80	3.35	.97
Responsibility	1.53	.79	3.58	.75
Permeability	1.66	.82	3.48	.84
Range of Feelings	1.81	.94	3.67	.67
Mood and Tone	1.28	.77	3.34	1.02
Unresolvable Conflict	1.65	1.05	3.56	.88
Empathy	1.55	.73	3.34	.73
Global	3.14	1.88	6.19	1.50
Average of Subscales	3.22	1.38	6.00	1.00

Table 2
INTERRATER RELIABILITY FOR THE BEAVERS INTERACTIONAL COMPETENCE SCALE

Competence Subscale	r	N
Overt Power	.83	111
Parental Coalition	.85	111
Closeness	.74	111
Mythology	.86	111
Goal-Directed Negotiation	.73	111
Clarity of Expression	.82	111
Responsibility	.86	111
Permeability	.86	111
Rank of Feelings	.79	111
Mood and Tone	.75	111
Unresolvable Conflict	.89	111
Empathy	.85	111
Global	.89	111
Average of Subscales	.94	111

Note: Invasiveness has historically shown low interrater reliabilities (e.g., $r = .49$) and thus has been dropped as a Likert-rated scale.

B BEAVERS INTERACTIONAL SCALES: FAMILY STYLE

Family Name _____ Date _____

Rater _____

I. All families must deal with the dependency needs of members. In this family, the dependency needs of members are:

1	2	3	4	5
discouraged, ignored		sometimes discouraged, sometimes attended		encouraged, alertly attended

II. Adults in all families have conflicts. In this family, adult conflicts are:

1	2	3	4	5
quite open	usually open		sometimes hidden, covert	indirect, covert, hidden

III. All families, when together, space themselves physically in some way. In this family:

1	2	3	4	5
all members give and expect lots of room between members		some members touch, others stay apart		all members stay physically close, and there is much touching

IV. All families have some attitude about how they look to outsiders. In this family, members:

1	2	3	4	5
try hard to appear well behaved and to make a good impression on others		sometimes appear concerned with making a good impression		seem unconcerned with appearances and social approval

V. This scale does not address family closeness, but rather how much family members profess that they are close. In this family, members:

1	2	3	4	5
consistently emphasize that they are close		don't make an issue of closeness		deny being close

Note whether internal scapegoating (one member bearing the burden of blame for family problems) is observed:
—internal scapegoating observed
—internal scapegoating not observed

VI. All families must deal with the assertive and aggressive qualities of members. In this family, members:

1	2	3	4	5
discourage aggressive or disruptive behavior and expression				solicit or encourage assertive, even aggressive behavior and expression

VII. All people have both positive and negative feelings. Rate this family in terms of the relative ease with which one or the other is expressed.

1	2	3	4	5
positive feelings are easier to express than negative		about the same		negative feelings are easier to express than positive

VIII. Global Centripetal/Centrifugal Family Style Scale.

1	1.5	2	2.5	3	3.5	4	4.5	5
Family has a strong, inner orientation, an inward pull. The outside world is seen as relatively threatening. The family is seen as the main hope for gratification of crucial needs.						Family has a strong outer orientation, an outward push. The outside world is less threatening than close family relationships. Main hope for gratification of crucial needs is seen as existing outside the family.		

Table 3
DESCRIPTIVE STATISTICS ON THE BEAVERS
INTERACTIONAL STYLE SCALE

Subscales	Normal Families		Clinic Families	
	x	S.D.	x	S.D.
Dependency	1.69	.81	3.00	1.08
Adult Conflict	1.94	.88	2.94	1.26
Proximity	3.05	.94	3.32	.99
Social Presentation	2.44	.86	2.54	1.09
Expressed Closeness	2.28	.90	2.78	1.02
Aggressive/Assertive Behavior	2.04	.80	2.71	1.09
Expression of Positive/Negative Feelings	1.90	.82	3.31	1.16
Global	1.95	.75	2.82	.98
Average of Subscales	2.27	.41	2.88	.54

Table 4
INTERRATER RELIABILITY FOR THE BEAVERS
INTERACTIONAL STYLE SCALE

Subscale	r	N
Dependency	.73	111
Adult Conflict	.64	111
Proximity	.83	111
Social Presentation	.62	111
Expressed Closeness	.81	111
Aggressive/Assertive Behavior	.67	111
Expression of Positive/Negative Feelings	.83	111
Global	.75	111
Average of Subscales	.79	111

SELF-REPORT FAMILY INVENTORY (SFI) VERSION II

For each question, mark the answer that best fits how you see your family now. If you feel that your answer is between two of the labeled numbers (the odd numbers), then choose the even number that is between them.

	Yes: Fits our family very well		Some: Fits our family some		No: Does not fit our family
1. Family members pay attention to each other's feelings.	1	2	3	4	5
2. Our family would rather do things together than with other people.	1	2	3	4	5
3. We all have a say in family plans.	1	2	3	4	5
4. The grownups in this family understand and agree on family decisions.	1	2	3	4	5
5. Grownups in the family compete and fight with each other.	1	2	3	4	5
6. There is closeness in my family but each person is allowed to be special and different.	1	2	3	4	5
7. We accept each other's friends.	1	2	3	4	5
8. There is confusion in our family because there is no leader.	1	2	3	4	5
9. Our family members touch and hug each other.	1	2	3	4	5
10. Family members put each other down.	1	2	3	4	5
11. We speak our minds, no matter what.	1	2	3	4	5
12. In our home, we feel loved.	1	2	3	4	5
13. Even when we feel close, our family is embarrased to admit it.	1	2	3	4	5
14. We argue a lot and never solve problems.	1	2	3	4	5
15. Our happiest times are at home.	1	2	3	4	5
16. The grownups in this family are strong leaders.	1	2	3	4	5
17. The future looks good to our family.	1	2	3	4	5
18. We usually blame one person in our family when things aren't going right.	1	2	3	4	5
19. Family members go their own way most of the time.	1	2	3	4	5

20. Our family is proud of being close.	1	2	3	4	5
21. Our family is good at solving problems together.	1	2	3	4	5
22. Family members easily express warmth and caring towards each other.	1	2	3	4	5
23. It's okay to fight and yell in our family.	1	2	3	4	5
24. One of the adults in this family has a favorite child.	1	2	3	4	5
25. When things go wrong we blame each other.	1	2	3	4	5
26. We say what we think and feel.	1	2	3	4	5
27. Our family members would rather do things with other people than together.	1	2	3	4	5
28. Family members pay attention to each other and listen to what is said.	1	2	3	4	5
29. We worry about hurting each other's feelings.	1	2	3	4	5
30. The mood in my family is usually sad and blue.	1	2	3	4	5
31. We argue a lot.	1	2	3	4	5
32. One person controls and leads our family.	1	2	3	4	5
33. My family is happy most of the time.	1	2	3	4	5
34. Each person takes responsibility for his/her behavior.	1	2	3	4	5

35. On a scale of 1 to 5, I would rate my family as:

1	2	3	4	5
My family functions very well together			My family does not function well together at all. We really need help.	

36. On a scale of 1 to 5, I would rate the independence in my family as:

1	2	3	4	5
(No one is independent. There are no open arguments. Family members rely on each other for satisfaction rather than on outsiders.)		(Sometimes independent. There are some disgreements. Family members find satisfaction both within and outside of the family.)		(Family members usually go their own way. Disagreements are open. Family members look outside of the family for satisfaction.)

Table 5
FACTOR STABILITY OF THE SELF-REPORT FAMILY INVENTORY AT ONE AND THREE MONTH FOLLOW-UPS

SFI Factor	Test 1-2	Test 2-3	Test 1-3	Average
Family Health	.87*	.85*	.84*	.85*
Conflict	.59*	.50*	.52*	.54*
Cohesion	.70*	.59*	.50*	.60*
Directive Leadership	.41*	.41*	.49*	.44*
Expressiveness	.84*	.89*	.79*	.81*

Note: Correlations were based on a normal college sample (N = 189).
*$p < .01$

Table 6
CORRELATIONS OF THE SELF-REPORT FAMILY INVENTORY WITH THE LOCKE-WALLACE MARITAL SATISFACTION SCALE

SFI Factor	Parents Combined (N = 100)
Family Health	− .567*
Conflict	− .610*
Cohesion	− .424*
Directive Leadership	.092
Expressiveness	− .185

* = $p < .01$

Table 7
CORRELATIONS OF SFI FACTORS WITH FACES II AND FACES III DIMENSIONS

SFI Factor	FACES II		FACES III	
	Adaptability	Cohesion	Adaptability	Cohesion
Family Health	− .79*	− .93*	− .22**	− .78*
Conflict	− .55*	− .69*	.02	− .45*
Family Cohesion	− .59*	− .81*	− .17	− .67*
Directive Leadership	− .49*	− .62*	− .39*	− .37*
Expressiveness	− .35*	− .58*	− .18	− .73*

Note: All correlations were corrected for sampling error. Correlations between SFI and FACES II and FACES III were based on normal college populations (N = 279 and 71, respectively).
* = $p < .01$
** = $p < .05$

Table 8

CORRELATIONS OF SELF-REPORT FAMILY INVENTORY FACTORS AND FAMILY ENVIRONMENT SCALE FACTORS

	SFI Factors				
FES	Health	Conflict	Cohesion	Leadership	Expressiveness
Cohesion	−.733**	−.484**	−.648**	−.244*	−.708**
Expressiveness	−.496**	−.353**	−.371**	.102	−.388**
Conflict	.656**	.676**	.494**	.174	.594**
Independence	−.258*	−.193	−.238*	−.092	−.046
Achievement					
Orientation	.136	.292**	.139	−.192	.069
Intellectual-Cultural					
Orientation	−.395**	−.125	−.322**	−.249*	−.359**
Active-Recreational					
Orientaiton	−.375**	−.183	−.225*	−.006	−.217*
Moral-Religious					
Emphasis	−.209*	−.232*	−.086	−.313**	−.215*
Organization	−.179	−.246*	−.140	−.236*	−.164
Control	.276*	.168	.216*	−.376**	.211*

Note: Correlations based on a normal college sample (N=71).
* = p < .05
** = p < .01

Table 9

CORRELATIONS OF SELF-REPORT FAMILY INVENTORY FACTORS AND FAMILY ASSESSMENT DEVICE FACTORS

FAD	Health	Conflict	Cohesion	Leadership	Expressiveness
Problem Solving	.551**	.290**	.454**	.269*	.615**
Communication	.577**	.376**	.574**	.179	.626**
Roles	.474**	.328**	.288**	.341**	.481**
Affective					
Responsiveness	.640**	.411**	.607**	.132	.693**
Affective					
Involvement	.538**	.526**	.295**	.291**	.432**
Behavior					
Control	.080	.143	−.107	.360**	.118
General					
Functioning	.766**	.531**	.612**	.272*	.678**

Note: Correlations based on a normal college sample (N=71).
* = p < .05
** = p < .01

Table 10
**CORRELATIONS OF THE BEAVERS SYSTEMS MODEL CONSTRUCTS
ACROSS METHODS AND WITHIN METHOD WITH FACES II
CONSTRUCTS**

Clinic Sample (N = 44)

| | Observational | | Self-Report | |
| | Beavers | | Olson's FACES II | |
SFI	Competence	Style	Cohesion	Adaptability
Health	.77**	.58**	− .85**	− .75**
Conflict	− .65**	− .63**	.67**	.57**
Cohesion	.69**	.46**	− .61**	− .53**
Leadership	.56**	.57**	− .36	− .32
Expressiveness	− .20	.26	− .21	− .61**
FACES II				
Cohesion	− .50**	− .43*		
Adaptability	.34	− .42*		
Nonclinical Sample	(N = 62)		(N = 279)	
Health	.38*	.31*	− .93**	− .79**
Conflict	− .36*	− .26	.69**	.55**
Cohesion	.29	.35*	− .81**	− .30
Leadership	.22	.13	− .62**	− .49
Expressiveness	.40*	.32*	− .58**	− .35**

Note: Correlations corrected for sampling error
$* = p < .05$
$** = p < .01$

D SFI SCORING AND PROFILE GUIDE

For each numbered item, fill in the score from the SFI. For items marked (R), reverse the score using the following formula; 6 – SFI raw score = reversed score to enter on score sheet.

Health/Competence:	Conflict:	Cohesion:
2 ____	5(R) ____	2 ____
3 ____	6 ____	15 ____
4 ____	7 ____	19(R) ____
6 ____	8(R) ____	27(R) ____
12 ____	10(R) ____	36 ____
15 ____	14(R) ____	
16 ____	18(R) ____	Sum: ____
17 ____	24(R) ____	
18(R) ____	25(R) ____	Leadership:
19(R) ____	30(R) ____	
20 ____	31(R) ____	8(R) ____
21 ____	34 ____	16 ____
24(R) ____		32 ____
25(R) ____	Sum: ____	
27(R) ____		Sum: ____
28 ____		
33 ____		Expressiveness:
35 ____		
36 ____		1 ____
		9 ____
Sum: ____		13(R) ____
		20 ____
		22 ____
		Sum: ____

SFI Style = ((_____ × – .25) + (_____ × .30) + (_____ × .22) + 2.11)
(SFI Item #)   14   4   27

For interpretation, plot the competence score for the health/competence scale on the horizontal axis on Figure 1. Plot the SFI style factor on the vertical axis.

SFI Scale Average	H	CON	COH	LEAD	EXP	Observational Competence Score Equivalent
5	95	60	26	15	25	10
	90	57			24	
4.5	86	54			23	9
	81	51			21	
4	76	48	20	12	20	8
	71	45			19	
3.5	67	42			18	7
	62	39			16	
3	57	36	15	9	15	6
	52	33			14	
2.5	48	30			13	5
	43	27			11	
2	38	24	10	6	10	4
	33	21			9	
1.5	29	18			8	3
	24	15			6	
1	19	12	5	3	5	2
$\overline{X}$	H	CON	COH	LEAD	EXP	BT

E INDIVIDUAL FAMILY STYLE SCALE

For each item, please choose the sentence which best describes your perceptions of your family, then rate whether the sentence describes your family "very much" or "somewhat." If your family falls in between the two descriptions, you would rate in the "middle" (3).

1. My parents have usually been the ones to make most decisions for me. [or] I've always been given a lot of freedom to make my own decisions.

very much	somewhat	middle	somewhat	very much
1	2	3	4	5

2. My parents have a lot of arguments and fights. [or] I've never seen my parents argue or fight.

very much	somewhat	middle	somewhat	very much
1	2	3	4	5

3. My parents have had a lot of control over me. [or] My parents have tried to control me, but it hasn't really worked.

very much	somewhat	middle	somewhat	very much
1	2	3	4	5

4. My family isn't concerned about apeearing close-knit and happy. [or] My family always tries to show other people that we are close-knit and happy.

very much	somewhat	middle	somewhat	very much
1	2	3	4	5

5. There's a lot of arguing and yelling in my family. [or] Family members keep their disagreements well-covered and under control.

very much	somewhat	middle	somewhat	very much
1	2	3	4	5

6. Most of our best times are at home. [or] Each family member does best outside the home.

very much	somewhat	middle	somewhat	very much
1	2	3	4	5

7. When family members get angry, they usually come right out and say what's wrong.

[or]

When family members get angry, they usually hide it by disappointment or distancing.

| very much 1 | somewhat 2 | middle 3 | somewhat 4 | very much 5 |

8. It's easy to talk about love and closeness in our family.

[or]

We usually don't talk about love and closeness in our family.

| very much 1 | somewhat 2 | middle 3 | somewhat 4 | very much 5 |

9. My parents have told me that they try to control me because they love me.

[or]

My parents have tried to control me but it has never really worked.

| very much 1 | somewhat 2 | middle 3 | somewhat 4 | very much 5 |

10. When in public, our family members keep our distance from each other.

[or]

When in public, our family members remain pretty close together.

| very much 1 | somewhat 2 | middle 3 | somewhat 4 | very much 5 |

11. I think that my parents have always treated me like a child younger than my age.

[or]

I think my parents have expected me to be on my own a lot.

| very much 1 | somewhat 2 | middle 3 | somewhat 4 | very much 5 |

12. My parents usually let me know when I've done something good.

[or]

My parents usually let me know when I've done something wrong.

| very much 1 | somewhat 2 | middle 3 | somewhat 4 | very much 5 |

13. My parents spend pretty much time together.

[or]

My parents hardly ever spend time together.

| very much 1 | somewhat 2 | middle 3 | somewhat 4 | very much 5 |

14. When I have been distant from my parents, I am (or have been) very angry with them.

[or]

When I have been distant from my parents, I have been more upset and sad with them.

| very much 1 | somewhat 2 | middle 3 | somewhat 4 | very much 5 |

15. When things go wrong at home, there is one family member who gets blamed.

[or]

When things go wrong at home, it varies on who is blamed or considered responsible.

| very much 1 | somewhat 2 | middle 3 | somewhat 4 | very much 5 |

REFERENCES

1. Abidin, R. R. (1976). *Parenting skills*. New York: Human Sciences Press.
2. Adler, G. (1985). *Borderline psychopathology and its treatment*. Northdale, NJ: Aronson.
3. Alanen, Y. O. (1971). The families of schizophrenic patients. In R. Cancro (Ed.), *The schizophrenic syndrome: An annual review* Vol. 1. New York: Brunner/Mazel.
4. Alanen, Y. O., & Laine, A. (1973). Development of a hospital centered community psychotherapy service for schizophrenic patients. In J. K. Wing & H. Hafner (Eds.), *Roots of evolution: An epidemiological basis for planning psychiatric services*. London: Oxford University Press.
5. Alexander, J. F., & Parsons, B. V. (1982). *Functional family therapy*. Monterey, CA: Brooks/Cole.
6. Anderson, C., Hogarty, G., & Reiss, D. (1980). Family treatment of adult schizophrenic patients: A psychoeducational approach. *Schizophrenia Bulletin, 6*, 490–505.
7. Arieti, S. (1955). *Interpretation of schizophrenia*. New York: Brunner.
8. Auerbach, A. E. (1968). *Parents learn through discussion*. New York: Wiley.
9. Beavers, J. S., Hampson, R. B., Hulgus, Y. F., & Beavers, W. R. (1986). Coping in families with a retarded child. *Family Process, 25*, 365–378.
10. Beavers, W. R. (1977). *Psychotherapy and growth: A family systems perspective*. New York: Brunner/Mazel.
11. Beavers, W. R. (1981). A systems model of family for family therapy. *Journal of Marital and Family Therapy, 7*, 299–307.
12. Beavers, W. R. (1982). Healthy, midrange, and severely dysfunctional families. In F. Walsh (Ed.), *Normal family processes*. New York: Guilford.
13. Beavers, W. R. (1983). Hierarchical issues in a systems approach to illness and health. *Family Systems Medicine, 1*, 47–55.
14. Beavers, W. R. (1984). Response to Dr. Waterman's address, "The human element of enterprise." *Perkins Journal, 38*, 43–46.
15. Beavers, W. R. (1985). Marital therapy with a couple plagued with physical illness. In A. Gurman (Ed.), *Casebook of marital therapy*. New York: Guilford.
16. Beavers, W. R. (1985). *Successful marriage: A family systems approach to marital therapy*. New York: W. W. Norton.
17. Beavers, W. R. (1985). Therapy of a family with a schizophrenic member. In S. Coleman (Ed.), *Failures in family therapy*. New York: Guilford.
18. Beavers, W. R. (1988). A clinically useful model of family assessment. In C. Ramsay (Ed.), *Family systems in medicine*. New York: Guilford.

19. Beavers, W. R., & Blumberg, S. (1968). A follow-up study of adolescents treated in an inpatient setting. *Journal of Diseases of the Nervous System, 29,* 606–612.
20. Beavers, W. R., Blumberg, S., Timken, K. R., & Weiner, M. D. (1965). Communication patterns of mothers of schizophrenics. *Family Process, 4,* 95–104.
21. Beavers, W. R., Hampson, R. B., & Hulgus, Y. F. (1985). The Beavers systems approach to family assessment: A reply to Green, Kolevzon and Vosler. *Family Process, 24,* 398–405.
22. Beavers, W. R. & Voeller, M. N. (1983). Family models: Comparing the Olson Circumplex Model with the Beavers Systems Model. *Family Process, 22,* 85–98.
23. Becker, W. C. (1971). *Parents are teachers: A child management program.* Champaign, IL: Research Press.
24. Becvar, D. S., & Becvar, R. J. (1988). *Family therapy: A systemic integration.* Boston: Allyn and Bacon.
25. Bergin, A. E. (1967). Further comments on psychotherapy research and therapeutic practice. *International Journal of Psychiatry, 3,* 317–323.
26. Bergin, A. E., & Lambert, M. J. (1978). The evaluation of therapeutic outcomes. In S. L. Garfield & A. E. Bergin (Eds.), *Handbook of psychotherapy and behavior change: An empirical analysis.* New York: Wiley.
27. Bloom, B. L. (1985). A factor analysis of self-report measures of family functioning. *Family Process, 24,* 225–239.
28. Bloom, B., & Lipetz, M. E. (1987). *The Colorado family checkup: An automated procedure for multilevel family assessment.* University of Colorado.
29. Boszormenyi-Nagy, I., & Ulrich, D. N. (1981). Contextual family therapy. In A. S. Gurman & D. P. Kniskern (Eds.), *Handbook of family therapy.* New York: Brunner/Mazel.
30. Bowen, M. (1978). Theory in the practice of psychotherapy. In *Family therapy in clinical practice.* New York: Aronson.
31. Boyd-Franklin, N. (1989). *Black families in therapy: A multisystems approach.* New York: Guilford.
32. Brown, G. W., Birley, J. L. T., & Wing, J. K. (1972). Influence of family on the course of schizophrenic disorders: A replication. *British Journal of Psychiatry, 121,* 241–258.
33. Brown, G. W., Monck, E. J., Carstairs, G. M., & Wing, J. K. (1962). The influence of family life on the course of the schizophrenic illness. *British Journal Prev. Soc. Med., 16,* 55–68.
34. Burgers, J. M. (1975). Causality and anticipation. *Science, 189,* 194–198.
35. Carkhuff, R. R. (1972). The development of systematic human development models. *Counseling Psychologist, 3,* 4–10.
36. Coleman, S. B., Kaplan, J. D., & Downing, R. W. (1986). Life cycle and loss—The spiritual vacuum of heroin addiction. *Family Process, 25,* 5–23.
37. Crowne, D. P., & Marlowe, D. (1960). A new scale of social desirability independent of psychopathology. *Journal of Consulting Psychology, 24,* 349–354.
38. Curran, D. (1983). *Traits of a healthy family: Fifteen traits commonly found in healthy families by those who work with them.* New York: Harper & Row.
39. Davenport, Y. B. (1981). Treatment of the married bipolar patient in conjoin-

ing couples psychotherapy groups. In M. R. Lansky (Ed.), *Family therapy and major psychopathology*. New York: Grune & Stratton.

40. Dinkmeyer, D., & McKay, G. D. (1982). *Systematic training for effective parenting (STEP)*. Circle Pines, MN: American Guidance Service.

41. Engel, G. L. (1977, April 8). The need for a new medical model: A challenge for biomedicine. *Science*, 129–136.

42. Epstein, N. B., Bishop, D. S., & Baldwin, L. M. (1982). McMaster Model of Family Functioning: A view of the normal family. In F. Walsh (Ed.), *Normal family processes*. New York: Guilford.

43. Erikson, E. H. (1963). *Childhood and society* (2nd Ed.). New York: W. W. Norton.

44. Eysenck, H. J. (1961). The effects of psychotherapy. In H. J. Eysenck (Ed.), *Handbook of abnormal psychology*. New York: Basic Books.

45. Fairweather, G. W., Sanders, D. H., Maynard, H., & Cressler, D. L. (1969). *Community life for the mentally ill: An alternative to institutional care*. New York: Aldine.

46. Falloon, I. R. H. (1981). Communication and problem-solving skills: Training with relapsing schizophrenics and their families. In M. R. Lansky (Ed.), *Family therapy and major psychotherapy*. New York: Grune & Stratton.

47. Falloon, I. R. H., Boyd, J. L., & McGill, C. W. (1984). *Family care of schizophrenia*. New York: Guilford.

48. Farber, L. (1958). The therapeutic despair. *Psychiatry, 21*, 7–20.

49. Fenton, F. R., Tessier, L., & Struening, E. L. (1979). A comparative trial of home and hospital psychiatric care: One year follow-up. *Archives of General Psychiatry, 36*, 1073–1079.

50. Fisch, R., Weakland, J. H., & Segal, L. (1982). *The tactics of change: Doing therapy briefly*. San Francisco: Jossey-Bass.

51. Foote, M. S. (1984). *Psychological health and chronic illness in the family system*. Doctoral dissertation, Texas Woman's University.

52. Ford, F. (1975). Personal communication to W. R. Beavers.

53. Freud, S. (1927). *The future of an illusion*. In J. Strachey (Ed.), *The standard edition of the complete psychological works of Sigmund Freud*. Volume 21, 1–56. New York: W. W. Norton.

54. Friedman, T. T., Becker, A., & Weiner, L. (1964). The psychiatric home treatment service: Preliminary report of five years of clinical experience. *American Journal of Psychiatry, 120*, 782–788.

55. Friedman, A. S., Utada, A., & Morrissey, M. R. (1987). Families of adolescent drug abusers are "rigid": Are these families either "disengaged" or "enmeshed" or both? *Family Process, 26*, 131–148.

56. Garfield, S. L. (1978). Research on client variables in psychotherapy. In S. L. Garfield & A. E. Bergin (Eds.), *Handbook of psychotherapy and behavior change: An empirical analysis*. New York: Wiley.

57. Glick, I. D., & Clarkin, J. F. (1982). The effects of family presence and brief family intervention for hospitalized schizophrenic patients: A review. In H. T. Harbin (Ed.), *The psychiatric hospital and the family*. New York: Spectrum.

58. Goldstein, M. J., Rodnick, E. H., Evans, J. R., May, R. A., & Steinberg, M. R. (1978). Drug and family therapy in the aftercare of acute schizophrenics. *Archives of General Psychiatry, 35*, 1169–1177.

59. Green, R. G., Kolevzon, M. S., & Vosler, N. R. (1985). The Beavers-Timberlawn Model of Family Competence and the Circumplex Model of Family Adaptability and Cohesion: Separate, but equal? *Family Process, 24*, 385–398.

60. Greenson, R. R. (1967). *The technique and practice of psychoanalysis (Vol. 1).* New York: International Universities Press.

61. Group for the Advancement of Psychiatry (GAP), Committee on Psychiatry in Industry. (1982). *Job loss—A psychiatric perspective* Vol. 11, No. 109. New York: Mental Health Materials Center.

62. Group for the Advancement of Psychiatry (GAP), Committee on the Family (1985). *The family, the patient, and the psychiatric hospital: Toward a new model.* Report No. 117. New York: Brunner/Mazel.

63. Grunebaum, H. (1984). Personal communication to W. R. Beavers.

64. Gurman, A. S., & Kniskern, D. P. (1981). Family theory outcome research: Knowns and unknowns. In A. S. Gurman & D. P. Kniskern (Eds.), *Handbook of family therapy.* New York: Brunner/Mazel.

65. Gurman, A. S., Kniskern, D. P., & Pinsof, W. M. (1986). Research on marital and family therapy: Progress, perspective, and prospect. In S. L. Garfield & A. E. Bergin (Eds.), *Handbook of psychotherapy and behavior change* (3rd Ed.). New York: Wiley.

66. Guttman, H. (1989). The GAP committee on the family: The consideration of family factors in *DSM-IV. American Journal of Psychiatry, 146*(6).

67. Haley, J. (1970). Approaches to family therapy. *International Journal of Psychiatry, 9*, 233–242.

68. Haley, J. (1971). Family therapy. *International Journal of Psychiatry, 9*, 233–242.

69. Haley, J. (1963). Marriage therapy. *Archives of General Psychiatry, 8*, 213–234.

70. Hampson, R. B. (1985). Foster parent training: Assessing its role in upgrading foster home care. In M. P. Cox & R. D. Cox, (Eds.), *Foster care: Current issues and practices.* Norwood, NJ: Ablex Press.

71. Hampson, R. B. (1988). Special foster care for exceptional children: A review of programs and policies. *Children and Youth Services Review, 10*, 19–41.

72. Hampson, R. B., & Beavers, W. R. (1988). Comparing males' and females' perspectives through family self-report. *Psychiatry, 50*, 24–30.

73. Hampson, R. B., Beavers, W. R., & Hulgus, Y. F. (1988). Comparing the Beavers and Circumplex models of family functioning. *Family Process, 27*, 85–92.

74. Hampson, R. B., Beavers, W. R., & Hulgus, Y. F. (in press). Cross-ethnic family differences: Interactional assessment of white, black and Mexican-American families. *Journal of Marital and Family Therapy.*

75. Hampson, R. B., Beavers, W. R., & Hulgus, Y. F. (1989). Insiders' and outsiders' views of family: The assessment of family competence and style. *Journal of Family Psychology, 3*, 118–136.

76. Hampson, R. B., Hulgus, Y. F., Beavers, W. R., & Beavers, J. (1988). The assessment of competence in families with a retarded child. *Journal of Family Psychology, 2*, 32–53.

77. Hampson, R. B., Schulte, M. A., & Ricks, C. C. (1983). Individual vs. group training for foster parents: Efficiency/effectiveness evaluations. *Family Relations, 32*, 191–201.

78. Hampson, R. B., & Tavormina, J. B. (1980). Relative effectiveness of behavioral and reflective group training with foster mothers. *Journal of Consulting and Clinical Psychology, 48*, 294–295.

79. Hansen, J. C., & L'Abate, L. (1982). *Approaches to family therapy*. New York: Macmillan.
80. Hawking, S. W., & Israel, W. (Eds.), (1987). *Three hundred years of gravitation*. Cambridge: Cambridge University Press.
81. Hines, P. M., & Boyd-Franklin, N. (1985). Black families. In M. McGoldrick, J. K. Pearce, & J. Giordano (Eds.), *Ethnicity and family therapy*. New York: Guilford.
82. Jencks, C. (1972). *Inequality: A reassessment of the effect of family and schooling in America*. New York: Basic Books.
83. Jensen, B., & Haynes, S. (1986). Self-report questionnaires and inventories. In A. Ciminero, K. Calhoun, & H. Adams (Eds.), *Handbook of behavioral assessment*. New York: Wiley.
84. Justice, B., & Justice, R. (1976). *The abusing family*. New York: Human Sciences Press.
85. Kabacoff, R. I., Miller, I. W., Epstein, N. B., Bishop, D. S., Keitner, G. I., & Fristad, M. A. (1989). *The development of a clinical rating scale for the McMaster Model of Family Functioning*. Manuscript under editorial review.
86. Keeney, B. F. (1983). *Aesthetics of change*. New York: Guilford.
87. Kelsey-Smith, M., & Beavers, W. R. (1981). Family assessment: Centripetal and centrifugal family systems. *American Journal of Family Therapy, 9*, 3–21.
88. Killorin, E., & Olson, D. H. (1984). The chaotic flippers in treatment. In E. Kaufman (Ed.), *Power to change: Family case studies in the treatment of alcoholism*. New York: Gardner.
89. Klerman, G. L., & Weissman, M. (1984). *Interpersonal psychotherapy of depression*. New York: Basic Books.
90. Koch, S. (1981). The nature and limits of psychological knowledge. *American Psychologist, 36*, 257–269.
91. Kolevzon, M. S., Green, R. G., Fortune, A. E., & Vosler, N. R. (1988). Evaluating family therapy: Divergent methods, divergent findings. *Journal of Marital and Family Therapy, 14*, 277–286.
92. Korzybski, A. (1933). *Science and sanity*. Lancaster, PA: The International Non-Aristotelian Library Publishing Co.
93. Kuhn, T. S. (1970). *The structure of scientific revolutions*. (2nd ed.). Chicago: University of Chicago Press.
94. Langsley, D. G., Machotka, P., & Flomenhaft, K. (1971). Avoiding mental hospital admission: A follow-up study. *American Journal of Psychiatry, 127*, 1391–1394.
95. Leff, J., Kuipers, L., Berkowitz, R., Eberlein-Vries, R., & Sturgeon, D. (1982). A controlled trial of social intervention in the families of schizophrenic patients. *British Journal of Psychiatry, 141*, 121–134.
96. Levant, R. F. (1984). *Family therapy: A comprehensive overview*. Englewood Cliffs, NJ: Prentice-Hall.
97. Lewis, J. M., Beavers, W. R., Gossett, J. T., & Phillips, V. A. (1976). *No single thread: Psychological health in family systems*. New York: Brunner/Mazel.
98. Lidz, T., Fleck, S., & Cornelison, A. (1965). *Schizophrenia and the family*. New York: International Universities Press.
99. Luepnitz, D. A. (1982). *Child custody: A study of families after divorce*. Lexington, MA: Lexington Press.
100. May, P. R. A., Tuma, A. H., & Dixon, W. J. (1981). Schizophrenia: A follow-

up study of the results of five forms of treatment. *Archives of General Psychiatry, 38,* 776–784.

101. McGoldrick, M., Anderson, C. M., & Walsh, F. (1989). *Women in families: A framework for family therapy.* New York: W. W. Norton.
102. McGoldrick, M., & Gerson, R. (1985). *Genograms in family assessment.* New York: W. W. Norton.
103. McGoldrick, M., Pearce, J. K., & Giordano, J. (1985). *Ethnicity and family therapy.* New York: Guilford.
104. Minuchin, S. (1974). *Families and family therapy.* Cambridge: Harvard University Press.
105. Minuchin, S., Montalvo, B., Guerney, B. G., Rosman, B. L., & Schumer, F. (1967). *Families of the Slums.* New York: Basic Books.
106. Minuchin, S., & Fishman, H. C. (1981). *Family therapy techniques.* Cambridge: Harvard University Press.
107. Minuchin, S., Rosman, B. L., & Baker, L. (1978). *Psychosomatic families: Anorexia nervosa in context.* Cambridge: Harvard University Press.
108. Morgan, C. T. (1961). *Introduction to psychology* (2nd Ed.). New York: McGraw-Hill.
109. Murray, E. J., & Jacobson, L. I. (1978). Cognition and learning in traditional and behavioral psychotherapy. In S. L. Garfield & A. E. Bergin (Eds.), *Handbook of psychotherapy and behavior change: An empirical analysis.* New York: Wiley.
110. Olson, D. H. (1985). Commentary: Struggling with congruence across theoretical models and methods. *Family Process, 24,* 203–207.
111. Olson, D. H., Russell, C. H., & Sprenkle, D. H. (1983). Circumplex Model of Marital and Family Systems, VI: Theoretical update. *Family Process, 22,* 69–83.
112. Olson, D. H., Portner, J., & Lavee, Y. (1985). *FACES III.* St. Paul: University of Minnesota.
113. Olson, D. H., & Killorin, E. (1985). *Clinical rating scale for the Circumplex Model.* St. Paul: University of Minnesota.
114. Pattison, E. M. (1975). A psychosocial kinship model for family therapy. *Scientific Proceedings,* 128th Annual Meeting, American Psychiatric Association.
115. Paul, N. L., & Paul, B. B. (1982). Death and changes in sexual behavior. In F. Walsh (Ed.), *Normal Family Processes.* New York: Guilford.
116. Paul, N. L., & Grosser, G. H. (1965). Operational mourning and its role in conjoint family therapy. *Community Mental Health Journal, 1,* 339–345.
117. Piercy, F. P., Laird, R. A., & Mohammed, Z. (1983). A family therapist rating scale. *Journal of Marital and Family Therapy, 9,* 49–59.
118. Piercy, F. P., & Sprenkle, D. H. (1986). *Family therapy sourcebook.* New York: Guilford.
119. Popper, K. R. (1963). *Science: Problems, aims, responsibilities.* Proceedings of Meeting of the Federation of American Societies for Experimental Biology. Atlantic City.
120. Popper, K. R. (1959). *The logic of scientific discovery.* New York: Basic Books.
121. Quay, H. C. (1964). Dimensions of personality in delinquent boys as inferred from the factor analysis of case history data. *Child Development, 35,* 479–484.

122. Riessman, F. (1965). The "helper" therapy principle. *Social Work, 10*, 27–32.
123. Rogers, C. R. (1957). The necessary and sufficient conditions of therapeutic personality change. *Journal of Consulting Psychology, 21*, 95–103.
124. Sager, C. J., Brown, H. S., Crohn, H., Engel, T., Rodstein, E. & Walker, L. (1983). *Treating the remarried family*. New York: Brunner/Mazel.
125. Satir, V. (1972). Family systems and approaches to family therapy. In G. D. Erickson & T. P. Hogan (Eds.), *Family therapy: An introduction to theory and technique*. Monterey, CA: Brooks/Cole.
126. Schneider, J. (1984). *Stress, loss and grief*. Rockville, MD: Aspen.
127. Scovern, A. W., Bukstel, L. H., Kilmann, P. R., Laval, R. A., Busemeyer, J., & Smith, V. (1980). Effects of parent counseling on the family system. *Journal of Counseling Psychology, 27*, 268–275.
128. Selvini Palazzoli, M. (1986). Towards a general model of psychotic family games. *Journal of Marital and Family Therapy, 12*, 339–349.
129. Selvini Palazzoli, M., Cirillo, S., Selvini, M., & Sorrentino, A. M. (1989). *Family games*. New York: Norton.
130. Sigafoos, A., & Reiss, D. (1985). Rejoinder. Counterperspectives on family measurement: Clarifying the pragmatic interpretation of research methods. *Family Process, 24*, 207–211.
131. Skinner, B. F. (1972). Humanism and behaviorism. *Humanist, 32*, 18–20.
132. Skinner, B. F. (1971). *Beyond freedom and dignity*. New York: Knopf.
133. Sluzki, C. (1979). Migration and family conflict. *Family Process, 18*, 379–380.
134. Stanton, M. D. (1981). Strategic approaches to family therapy. In A. S. Gurman & D. P. Kniskern (Eds.), *Handbook of family therapy*. New York: Brunner/Mazel.
135. Stanton, M. D., & Todd, T. C. (1979). Structural family therapy with drug addicts. In E. Kaufman & P. Kaufman (Eds.), *The family therapy of drug and alcohol abuse*. New York: Gardner.
136. Steele, B. F., & Pollock, C. B. (1968). A psychiatric study of parents who abuse infants and small children. In R. E. Helfer & C. H. Kempe (Eds.), *The battered child*. Chicago: University of Chicago Press.
137. Steidl, J. H., Finkelstein, F. O., Wexler, J. P., Feigenbaum, H., Kitsen, D., Kliger, A. S., & Quinlan, D. M. (1980). Medical condition, adherence to treatment regimens, and family functioning. *Archives of General Psychiatry, 37*, 1025–1027.
138. Steidl, J. H. (1984). Personal communication to W. R. Beavers.
139. Stent, G. (1975). Limits to the scientific understanding of man. *Science, 187*, 1052–1057.
140. Stierlin, H. (1972). *Separating parents and adolescents*. New York: Quadrangle Press.
141. Stolorow, R. D., & Lachman, F. M. (1980). *Psychoanalysis of developmental arrests: Theory and treatment*. Madison, CT: International Universities Press.
142. Strachan, A. M., Feingold, D., Goldstein, M. J., Miklowitz, D. J., & Neuchterlein, K. H. (1989). Is expressed emotion an index of transactional process? II. Patient's coping style. *Family Process, 28*, 169–182.
143. Straus, M. A., & Tallman, I. (1971). SIMFAM: A technique for observational measurement and experimental studies of families. In J. Aldous (Ed.), *Family problem solving*. Hinsdale, IL: Dryden Press.
144. Sullivan, H. S. (1956). *Clinical studies in psychiatry*. New York: W. W. Norton.

145. Sullivan, H. S. (1972). *Personal psychopathology: Early formulations*. New York: W. W. Norton.
146. Sullivan, H. S. (1953). *The interpersonal theory of psychiatry*. New York: W. W. Norton.
147. Tavormina, J. B. (1977). Relative effectiveness of behavioral and reflective group counseling with parents of mentally retarded children. *Journal of Consulting and Clinical Psychology, 43,* 22–31.
148. Tomm, K. (1986). On incorporating the therapist in a scientific theory of family therapy. *Journal of Marital and Family Therapy, 12,* 373–378.
149. Turner, R. H. (1970). *Family interaction*. New York: Wiley.
150. Vaughn, C. E., & Leff, J. P. (1976). The influence of family and social factors in the course of psychiatric illness: A comparison of schizophrenic and depressed neurotic patients. *British Journal of Psychiatry, 129,* 125–137.
151. Visher, E. B., & Visher, J. S. (1980). *Stepfamilies: Myths and realities*. Secaucus, NJ: Citadel Press.
152. Von Bertalanffy, L. (1971). System, symbol and the image of man. In I. Galdston (Ed.), *The interface between psychiatry and anthropology*. New York: Brunner/Mazel.
153. Von Bertalanffy, L. (1969). General systems theory—An overview. In W. Gray, F. J. Duhl, & N. D. Rizzo (Eds.), *General systems theory and psychiatry*. Boston: Little, Brown.
154. Walters, M., Carter, B., Papp, P., & Silverstein, O. (1988). *The invisible web: Gender patterns in family relationships*. New York: Guilford.
155. Watson, J. D. (1968). *The double helix*. Patterson, NJ: Atheneum Press.
156. Watzlawick, P. (1966). A structured family interview. *Family Process, 5,* 256–271.
157. Watzlawick, P. (1987). If you desire to see, learn how to act. In J. K. Zeig (Ed.), *The evolution of psychotherapy*. New York: Brunner/Mazel.
158. Watzlawick, P., Weakland, J. N., & Fisch, R. (1974). *Change: Principles of problem formation and problem resolution*. New York: W. W. Norton.
159. Wentzel, L. (1988). Personal communication to W. R. Beavers.
160. Whitaker, C. A., & Keith, D. V. (1981). Symbolic-experiential family therapy. In A. S. Gurman & D. P. Kniskern (Eds.), *Handbook of family therapy*. New York: Brunner/Mazel.
161. Wynne, L. (1987, May). *Panel discussion: The families of the mentally ill*. Presented at American Psychiatric Association Annual Meeting, Chicago.
162. Wynne, L. C., McDaniel, S. H., & Weber, T. T. (1986). *Systems consultation: A new perspective for family therapy*. New York: Guilford.
163. Wynne, L. C., Jones, J. E., & Al-Khayyal, M. (1982). Healthy family communication patterns: Observations in families "at risk" for psychopathology. In F. Walsh (Ed.), *Normal family processes*. New York: Guilford.
164. Yalom, I. (1975). *The theory and practice of group psychotherapy*. New York: Basic Books.
165. Young, F. D. (1981). Front door, side door, back door approaches. *Journal of Strategic and Systemic Therapies, 1,* 16–27.
166. Zuk, G. H. (1975). *Process and practice in family therapy*. Haverford, PA: Psychiatry and Behavior Science Books.

NAME INDEX

SUBJECT INDEX